T'ang
Poems

**A text in the reading
and understanding of
T'ang Poetry**

Hugh M. Stimson

Far Eastern Publications
Yale University

Library of Congress Catalog
Card Number: 76-19687
Stimson, Hugh M.
Fifty-five T'ang Poems

ISBN-13: 978-0-88710-026-0

Preface

This book is a collection of fifty-five Chinese poems, with anno-
tations and a general glossary which together provide enough material
for an English-speaking reader to understand them. The poems were
written during the eighth and ninth centuries, a period of outstanding
literary production in China. Most of the poems are by major literary
figures; some are by less well-known poets. I have tried to choose
poems that show promise of being interesting and accessible, not only
to students who know some modern Chinese, but also to those who have
no experience whatever in Chinese language or literature.

The book is a study text. It is cumulatively arranged, by which
I mean that I have prepared later parts assuming that the student can
remember some of the material presented earlier. A Chinese-English
glossary of the words in the poems appears at the end of the book.
As the student works through the text, he learns some of the grammar
and vocabulary of the poetic language and the basic prosodic rules for
the various kinds of poems of the general type known as shi. By using
the glossary, he learns the basic principles of how the characters of
traditional Chinese orthography are written and how they are organized
in standard dictionaries. Finally, he learns something of the sound
system underlying the pronunciation of standard Chinese as spoken
during the eighth and ninth centuries.

The first poems in the book are presented without reference to
the glossary. Later, increasing reference is made to it; the last
poems of the book are annotated under the assumption that now the
student can begin to find characters in the glossary on his own.

ACKNOWLEDGEMENTS

The author wishes to express his sincere gratitude to Mr. John Montanaro and the staff of Far Eastern Publications for their patience and ingenuity in producing this book.

Thanks are also due to Dr. John M. Ortinau, who helped prepare the manuscript and who brought to the author's attention some of the poems by Wáng Jiàn and Dù Mù; and to Mr. R. Drake Pike, who helped prepare the glossary.

The author is especially grateful to Mrs. Hwei Li Chang, whose calligraphy graces this volume, and who pointed out some important inconsistencies.

New Haven, Connecticut   Hugh M. Stimson

September, 1976

Table of contents

Preface

Titles of poems (with first lines in parentheses)   iii

General background   vii

    Table 1: Eleven Chinese dynasties viii

Instructions to the student   x

Chapter 1: The Middle Chinese spellings   1

    Table 2: Symbols for Middle Chinese initials   3

    Table 3: How finals are spelled when they have no
             nuclear vowel   5

    Table 4: Finals in the order of the traditional
             rhyming dictionaries   6

Chapter 2: Grammatical sketch   7

Chapter 3: Iuɑng Ui (Wáng Wéi, 699-759)   22

    Selections 1-12

    Prosodic note 1: Line length, caesura, and rhyme   23

    Prosodic note 2: Seven-syllable shi   37

    Prosodic note 3: Poem length, parallelism, and
                the regulated poem   40

    Prosodic note 4: Tonal regulation   44

    Prosodic note 5: Old-style poems   49

    Prosodic note 6: Music Bureau poetry   51

Chapter 4: Lǐ Bhæk (Lǐ Bái, 701-762)   52

    Selections 13-21

    Prosodic note 7: The quatrain   54

Chapter 5: Dhǒ Biǒ (Dù Fǔ, 712-770) 91

    Selections 22-26

Chapter 6: Poets of the Mid and Late Dhang (Táng) 120

    A. Mæng Gau (Mèng Jiāo, 751-814) 121

        Selections 27-35

    B. Iuang Giæn (Wǎng Jiàn, 768?-830?) 143

        Selections 36-38

    C. Bhæk Giu-ì (Bái Jū-yì, 772-846). 148

        Selections 39-48

    D. Lǐ Huà (Lǐ Hè, 791-817). 165

        Selections 49-50

    E. Dhǒ Miuk (Dù Mù, 803-852) 169

        Selections 51-53

    F. Lǐ Shiang-qiǒn (Lǐ Shāng-yǐn, 812?-858) 172

        Selections 54-55

Glossary 177

    Introduction 177

    Table 5: Radicals 180

    Table 6: Order of strokes of the 214 radicals 183

    Table 7: Obvious radicals 189

    Glossary 191

Bibliography 239

Titles of poems with first line in parentheses

Page

Wáng Wéi (selections 1 through 12)

1. Parting 送別 (山中相送罷)   23

2. Unclassified poem 雜詩 (君自故鄉來)   28

(3-7 From the Wáng River Collection) 輞川集

3. No. 5: Deer Park 鹿柴 (空山不見人)   30

4. No. 11: Yī Lake 欹湖 (吹簫凌極浦)   32

5. No. 13: Luán Family Rapids 欒家瀨 (颯颯秋雨中)   34

6. No. 17: Hut in bamboos 竹里館 (獨坐幽篁裏)   35

7. No. 18: Magnolia Wall 辛夷塢 (木末芙蓉花)   36

8. Seeing Yuán Number Two off; he is being sent on a mission to An-xi 送元二使安西 (渭城朝雨裛輕塵)   37

9. Composed in reply to Secretary Sū of the Board of Concern who passed by the villa at Indigo Field but did not stay   39
酬虞部蘇員外過藍田別業不見留之作 (貧居依谷口)

10. In reply to County Police Chief Zhāng   42
酬張少府 (晚年唯好靜)

11. Suffering from heat   47
苦熱 (赤日滿天地)

12. First of two Hymns of the Goddess of Fish Mountain: Verse welcoming the divinity   50

魚山神女祠歌：迎神曲 (坎坎擊鼓)

Lǐ Bái (selections 13 through 21)

13. Feelings of grief 怨情 (美人卷珠簾)   53

14. Thoughts on a quiet night 靜夜思 (牀前明月光)   57

15. Misery Pavilion 勞勞亭 (天下傷心處)   58

(16-17 From Old airs) 古風

16. No. 1: (大雅久不作)   59

17. No. 47: (桃花開東園)   66

18. First of four poems entitled: Pouring a drink alone under the moon 月下獨酌 (花間一壺酒)   69

iii

19. With some wine in my hand, I put a question to the moon 72
把酒問月 (青天有月來幾時)

20. First of two poems entitled Long Gully song 長干行 76
(妾髮初覆額)

21. The road to Shǔ is difficult 蜀道難 (噫吁嚱危乎 81
高哉)

Dù Fǔ (selections 22 through 26)

22. Northward journey 北征 (皇帝二載秋) 92

23. The officer at Stone Moat 石壕吏(暮投石壕村) 112

24. Grieving about Green Slope 悲青坂(我軍青坂在東門) 115

25. Spring view 春望 (國破山河在) 117

26. I hear that government troops have recovered Hé-nán
and Hé-běi 聞官軍收河南河北 (劍外忽傳收薊北) 118

Poets of the Mid and Late Táng

Mèng Jiāo (selections 27 through 35 from Cold stream) 寒溪

27. No. 1: (霜洗水色盡) 122

28. No. 2: (洛陽岸邊道) 124

29. No. 3: (晚飲一盃酒) 127

30. No. 4: (篙工破玉星) 129

31. No. 5: (一曲一直水) 131

32. No. 6: (因凍死得食) 135

33. No. 7: (尖雪入魚心) 137

34. No. 8: (溪老哭甚寒) 139

35. No. 9: (溪風擺餘凍) 141

Wáng Jiàn (selections 36 through 38)

36. Song of the newly-wed bride 新嫁娘詞 (三日入廚內)143

37. I sent away my son's wife 去婦 (新婦去年胼手足) 144

38. Seeing the moon while traveling 行見月 (月初生) 146

Bái Jū-yì (selections 39 through 48)

39. Simplicity's song　簡簡吟　(蘇家小女名簡簡)　148

40. Lady True's tomb　真娘墓　(真娘墓)　151

41. (New music bureau poem, No. 4 of fifty) The sea is vast 153
　　新樂府　海漫漫　(海漫漫)

42. The parrot　157
　　鸚鵡　(隴西鸚鵡到江東)

43. Some years ago, a white horse of mine died at Dense
　　Mulberry Trees, and I wrote a poem on the wall of the
　　government building there. I come here now, and it is
　　still there. I am moved again and write another
　　quatrain.　往年桐柔曾喪白馬題詩廳望今來尚存又 159
　　復感懷更題絕句　(路旁埋骨蓬蒿合)

44. I ask myself a question　自問　(黑花滿眼絲滿頭)　160

45. Coffin-pullers' song for Minister Yuán　161
　　元相公輓歌　(墓門已閉笳簫去)

46. Sighing about my hair falling out　歎落髮　(多病多 162
　　愁心自知)

47. Shining Lady Wáng　王昭君　(滿面胡沙滿鬢風)　163

48. The red parrot　紅鸚鵡 (安南遠進紅鸚鵡)　164

Lǐ Hè (selections 49 and 50)

49. I am moved to make an indirect criticism　感諷　165
　　(南山何其悲)

50. The tomb of Sū the Tiny　蘇小小墓　(幽蘭露)　167

Dù Mù (selections 51 through 53)

51. Returning home　歸家　(稚子牽衣問)　169

52. Quatrain on passing the Palace of Flowery Purity　170
　　過華清宮絕句　(長安迴望繡成堆)

53. The Hàn River　171
　　漢江　(溶溶漾漾白鷗飛)

Lǐ Shāng-yǐn (selections 54 and 55)

54. Untitled　無題　(相見時難別亦難)　172

55. The patterned zither　錦瑟　(錦瑟無端五十絃)　174

v

General background

Chinese history stretches back for more than three thousand years.
Until the beginning of the Republic in 1912, and except for periods of
disunion totalling about five hundred years, the Chinese people have
been at least nominally united in allegiance to one or another ruling
family. The authority by which these dynasties ruled was said to em-
anate from Heaven; when the rule passed from one family to another,
the dynastic change was rationalized as a shift in the mandate of
Heaven.

Eleven major dynasties ruled China before the Republic (Table 1,
see page viii). Some held sway for only a few decades, others for two
or three centuries, and one early dynasty held the allegiance of the
people (which in the last centuries was only nominal) for an unequalled
nine hundred years.

The seventh of these major dynasties is known as the Dhang 唐
(Táng)[1] Dynasty, whose emperors all bore the surname Lǐ 李 . The Lǐ's
ruled China for 289 years, from 618 to 907. The Dhang Empire extended
several thousand kilometers along the eastern coast of Asia, from the
Yellow Sea in the north to about halfway down the coast of modern Viet-
nam. To the west it included most of the present Sì-chuān (or Sze-
chuan) 四 川 Province[2] and followed the arm of what is now Gān-sū
(or Kansu) 甘肅 Province in an enormous extension far into what is
now Russian Turkestan, between Uighur territory which lay to the north
and Tibetan territory in the west.

This vast area was governed by an elaborate civil and military
bureaucracy, which was essentially a continuation of the governmental
system established some eight hundred years earlier. Civil service
examinations, which were highly competitive, demanded a familiarity
with the works of the Confucian canon, compiled over a thousand years
earlier, and with subsequent historical and exegetical works. The
system brought forth a bureaucratic elite, and it was from this elite
that most of the literary figures of China emerged.

Among the works which Dhang civil servants had to study were col-
lections of poetry. The earliest of these anthologies is the Confucian
classic called the Shi geng 詩經 (Shī jīng or Shih ching, the Poetry
classic or Book of songs), compiled around the fifth century B.C.,
supposedly by Confucius. Like the philosophical and historical texts
compiled in subsequent centuries, the Book of songs is largely con-
cerned with events occurring in the area of the Yellow River. Later
than this northern-style poetry is a small collection of poetry in a

---

1. Chinese words are regularly presented as follows: first the
Middle Chinese transcription, then the characters of the traditional
orthography, and then the Modern Mandarin transcription according to
the pīn-yīn 拼音 system used in mainland China.

2. Purely modern terms in Chinese are given only Modern Mandarin
spellings (with spellings familiar to western readers given in paren-
theses, if these are different enough to be confusing).

Table 1

Eleven Chinese dynasties

Shiang 商 (Shāng)		B.C. 1766 (?) - 1122 (?)
Jiou 周 (Zhōu, or Chou)		B.C. 1122 (?) - 221
Dzhin 秦 (Qín, or Ch'in)		B.C. 221 - 207
Xàn 漢 (Hàn)		B.C. 206 - 220 A.D.
Western Tzìn 晋 (Jìn, or Chin)		265 - 316
Zui 隋 (Suí)		589 - 618
Dhang 唐 (Táng)		618 - 907
Northern Sòng 宋 (or Sung)		960 - 1126
Yuán 元		1280 - 1368
Míng 明		1368 - 1644
Qīng 清 (or Ch'ing)		1644 - 1912

different style associated with writers who date from around the fourth century B.C. and who lived in the south, around the Yangtse River. This collection of southern-style poetry is called the Chriǔ zi 楚辭 (Chǔ cí or Ch'u tz'u, the Songs of the state of Chǔ). These two early collections had considerable influence on the development of later Chinese poetry. A third body of poems important in the history of Chinese poetry consists of folk songs collected by the government in the first century B.C. and of later imitations of these songs composed by literati. These poems, more than the Book of songs or the Songs of the state of Chǔ are directly associated with the rise of the type of poem that became the chief poetic medium of the Dhang, seven hundred years later, and which is the subject of this book.

This type of poem is called shi 詩 (shī, shih[3]). A typical shi has lines that all contain the same number of syllables, either five or seven, arranged around one or two fixed caesuras so that there are four metrical beats to the line. The last syllables of the even-numbered lines rhyme.

3. When Middle Chinese and Modern Mandarin transcriptions are both given, and when there is a transcription that western readers are likely to be familiar with and that is different enough from the standard modern spelling to be confusing, this second transcription follows the standard spelling. Following the usual (and deplorable) western practice, this second spelling, when it occurs, lacks any indication of modern tone.

Four masters of the shi, who are generally considered to be giants
in the entire history of Chinese literature, are represented in this
book: three from the eighth century, and one from the ninth. A few
works by other less well-known poets are also included.

The poems are presented after brief instructions to the student,
a description of the Middle Chinese phonological system and the spel-
ling system used here, and a general sketch of the grammar of Dhang
shi, insofar as it is known.

It is hoped that by reading the poems in the original language
the reader can appreciate the beauty of their sound and meaning
directly, without the inevitable distortions of translation. The
transcriptions into standard Dhang Chinese, the grammatical and seman-
tic annotations, and the expansion of the allusions are all designed
to contribute to this end.

Instructions to the student

If you are interested in reading the Dhɑng shi collected here and
in appreciating their style and diction, you should go through the
poems and the appended notes with something of the attitude of a lan-
guage student. In fact, you will be learning a language, Middle Chi-
nese, the standard language of the Dhɑng Dynasty. You should proceed
systematically from the first poem to the last, making your own notes
on grammar and building up your own vocabulary file.
    Before reading the poems themselves, you should familiarize your-
self with the transcription of Middle Chinese used here. It is pre-
sented in the next chapter. Read through it and learn how to find your
way around in it so that you can refer to it easily.
    Next, learn the basic principles of Middle Chinese grammar. These
appear in Chapter 2 and will be referred to continually throughout the
book, especially in the first part.
    In the first poems, comprising Chapter 3, complete vocabulary and
grammatical notes are provided, with some reference to the outline of
grammar in Chapter 2, but with no reference to a general glossary,
because the focus here is on grammar rather than on vocabulary or
orthography.
    Beginning with Chapter 4, you should familiarize yourself with
traditional Chinese lexicographical habits by learning to look up
Chinese characters in a glossary arranged in the traditional Chinese
way known as the "radical-remainder" system. Such a glossary appears
at the end of this book. Read its introduction, which explains the
structure of Chinese characters; learn to identify radicals, to count
strokes, and to write Chinese characters accurately.
    Start a vocabulary file. On each file card, put the character,
its radical-remainder code, the line of the poem it occurs in, and its
meaning there in English, all in some arrangement on the card that you
keep to consistently. Add new but related meanings onto the cards as
they appear in the poems.
    From this chapter on, you will be encouraged to a greater and
greater degree to remember words that have already appeared. All mean-
ings appear in the glossary, and you will also be expected to be able
to make simple look-ups there.
    Beginning with Chapter 5, words that have already been given
English glosses will not be glossed again when they reappear with the
same meaning.
    Beginning with Chapter 5, Poem 22, you will be referred to the
glossary for new glosses; radical-remainder codes will be given for
all new characters and for new meanings of old characters.
    From Poem 23 on, you will be expected to familiarize yourself
with the common radicals in their most obvious positions in the char-
acters, so that you yourself can develop reliable radical-remainder
codes for new characters as they appear. Codes will be given in the
notes to the poems only where the character is itself a radical, or
where the radical is obscure.
    It is hoped that by learning to use a Chinese dictionary in this
way you can begin to read Dhɑng shi outside this collection.

Chapter 1

The Middle Chinese spellings

The Middle Chinese (MC) spellings used here are based on those of the Swedish sinologist Bernhard Karlgren, as found in Karlgren 1957[1]. Successive revisions of these spellings appear in Martin 1953[2] and Stimson 1966[3]: I have taken the spellings of the latter work and made them simpler and more practical for use in this book. These revisions are presented in Stimson 1976[4].

In what follows, letters and combinations of letters used to spell MC syllables are described in terms of articulatory phonetics and compared with sounds in English or German. These descriptions and comparisons are presented as a matter of convenience, without any claim to phonetic accuracy. The structure of MC phonology is well understood-- we know which sounds contrast with which other sounds. But it is true in the reconstruction of MC phonology, as in the reconstruction of the sound system of any dead language, that how the contrasts were realized phonetically and how the skeleton of the phonological structure was given phonetic flesh are entirely matters of conjecture, and the likelihood that our guesses about the phonetic realities are accurate varies with different parts of the phonological structure.

The MC syllable is conveniently and traditionally thought of as consisting of a final plus any preceding initial. A syllable with no initial is said to have zero (∅) initial.

According to the traditional analysis, every MC syllable is said to belong to one of four tonal categories, and the resulting four-way distinction is assigned to the MC final. This means that MC is a language in which tones play a part in making semantic distinctions between words. In modern Chinese languages, where tones play a similar role, they are pitches and pitch changes, having such contours as "level" (having a steady pitch), "rising" (going from a lower to a higher pitch), and "falling" (going from a higher to a lower pitch). Tones on MC syllables must have had similar contours, but we cannot be certain exactly how the four tonal categories were realized in terms of pitch or duration.

The traditional names for the four tonal categories in MC are "level" 平 bhiæng (píng), "raised" or "rising" 上 zhiǎng (shǎng), "departing" 去 kiù (qù, ch'ü), and "entering" 入 njip (rù, ju). These names are themselves examples of the respective tone categories, and they may also have descriptive value. In practice, I have found it convenient to pronounce "level" syllables with a level tone, "raised" or "rising" syllables with a rising tone, "departing" syllables with a falling tone, and "entering" syllables with a level tone and short, that is, with a syllable length that is shorter than that of a "level" syllable.

In the present transcription, "level" syllables are unmarked; that is, the spelling of a "level" syllable includes neither any diacritic mark nor a -p, -t, -k ending. "Raised" or "rising" syllables have a wedge (ˇ) over the main vowel. "Departing" syllables have a grave accent (`) over the main vowel. "Entering" syllables have no diacritic mark but are distinguished from "level" syllables in that they end in -p, -t, or -k.

Initials (see Table 2, page 3) are described in terms of manner and place of articulation. An articulation is a movement of some organ, usually on the lower part of the vocal tract, such as the lower lip or the tongue, toward another part of the vocal tract, such as the upper lip or the roof of the mouth, which has the effect of constricting or otherwise altering the flow of air from the lungs produced during speech. A manner of articulation describes how the air flow is altered at the place of articulation. A place of articulation identifies the vocal organ that is moving to alter the air flow and the place on the vocal tract toward which it is moving.

Initials in MC are conveniently grouped first by manner of articulation, according to whether they are stops, spirants, or affricates. A stop is a sound made by completely blocking the air flow (at least along its median axis) at the place of articulation--the initial sounds of English (E) bat, pat, mat, dot, tot, not, lot, etc., are stops, in this sense. A spirant (sometimes called a fricative) is a sound made by blocking the air flow incompletely, but enough so that constriction at the place of articulation creates a hissing turbulence of the air flow--the initials of E fat, vat, that, thaw, see, she, zebra, etc., are spirants. An affricate is a stop followed by a spirant that is made at the same place of articulation--the initials of E cheese and Jesus are affricates, and, at least in the speech of some, so are the initials of train and drain.

MC initials are next grouped according to whether they are plain, aspirated, voiced, or resonant. In the case of stops, aspiration means a build-up of air pressure behind the place of articulation followed by the sudden release of this pressure when the articulation is relaxed--the initials of E pat, tot, and cat are aspirated. In the case of affricates, aspiration involves a lengthening of the spirant portion --the initials of E cheese and train are aspirates. An initial is voiced if during its production the vocal cords are buzzing--the initials of E mat, not, lot, vat, that, bat, dot, etc. are all voiced, but in MC it is convenient to segregate voiced initials that are also resonant. A resonant initial in MC, in addition to being voiced, involves a diversion of the air stream, through the nasal passages (in the cases of m-, n-, nj-, and ng-), or to the side of the tongue tip (in the case of l-)--the initials of E mat, not, and lot are resonant in this sense. Otherwise, MC initials are plain.

In the case of MC stops and affricates there is a four-way contrast of voicing and aspiration, whereas in E the contrast is only three-way. Thus, at the same place of articulation, MC has a four-way stop contrast: b-/p-/bh-/m-; the corresponding three-way contrast in E, p-/b-/m-, is illustrated by the initials of E pat, bat, and mat. In this example, it is convenient to think of MC p- and m- as being like their E counterparts in pat and mat, and of MC bh- as being like the initial in E bat, or, if the outcomes of MC voiced initials in certain modern Chinese dialects are any indication, something like the -b h- combination in E Nob Hill. The plain initials of MC have nothing quite like them in E in absolute initial position. Closest to the MC plain initials are the stops that occur after initial s- in E words like span, Stan, and scan, where the sounds spelled with -p-, -t-, and -c- roughly correspond to the MC initials spelled b-, d-, and g-.

As in E, in MC a two-way contrast obtains for spirants: voiced and voiceless. In Table 2, voiceless spirants are grouped with aspi-

Table 2

Symbols for MC initials

	Plain	Aspirated	Voiced	Resonant
Labial stops	b	p	bh	m
Apical stops	d	t	dh	n l
Apical affricates	tz	ts	dzh	
Apical spirants		s	z	
Retracted affricates	jr	chr	jrh	
Retracted spirants		shr	zhr	
Frontal stops	dj	tj	djh	nj
Frontal affricates	j	ch	jh	
Frontal spirants		sh	zh	
Dorsal stops	g	k	gh	ng
Dorsal spirants		x	h	
Glottal stop (and zero initial)	q		(ϕ)	

rated stops and affricates because they share certain features of development into their modern outcomes.

Finally, MC initials are grouped according to place of articulation. An initial is labial if the lower lip articulates against the upper lip, like E p-, b-, and m-. It is apical if the tip of the tongue articulates against the front part of the roof of the mouth, like E t-, d-, n-, and l-. It is retracted if the tip of the tongue articulates at the point where the roof of the mouth arches up in a dome, something like the E initial combination tr- in tree, dr- in dress, and shr- in shrimp. It is frontal if the front part of the tongue, that is, the part just behind the tip, articulates against the front part of the roof of the mouth, something like E ch- in cheese, j- in Jesus, and sh- in she. It is dorsal if the back of the tongue articulates against the soft palate, like E k- and "hard" g- as in gull. A glottal stop is made by drawing the vocal cords together; it occurs in the speech of some E speakers for the -tt- in written and before the u's in the grunted unh-unh meaning "no".

Other initials difficult to relate to E sounds include the apical affricates. These initials are something like the -ts in E hats and the -dds in E adds, but in MC they only occur initially, whereas in E they never do (except perhaps in tsetse).

What are labelled "frontal stops" in Table 2 represent a neutralization, in the case of stops, of the retracted/frontal position dis-

tinction, which obtains with affricates and spirants. I follow Karl-
gren in calling these stops "frontals", but evidence from Chinese
transcriptions of Sanskrit words indicates that the stops were pro-
nounced at the same place of articulation as the retracted affricates,
that is, like the initials of E tree and dress, but with no spirant
following the initial stop.

zhr- is like the initial of E shrimp, but voiced.

The voiced frontal spirant zh- does not occur initially in E; it
is voiced counterpart of MC sh- (like the initial of E she) and is like
the -s- in E pleasure.

The frontal resonant nj- occurs initially in E new, as pronounced
by some speakers; it is also like the -ni- in E onion.

The dorsal resonant does not occur initially in E; it is like
-ng of long.

The dorsal spirant x- is like the German -ch in Bach; h- is x-
with voicing.

In addition to a tone category, the MC final consists of one or
two medials, a nucleus, or an ending, or various combinations of these
elements.

Medials are -i-, like the glide after the initial sound in E cute,
and -u-, like the glide after the initial sound in E quit. The com-
bination -iu- occurs and resembles the ü- of German über. Structur-
ally, it is likely that when the two medials both occur in the same
syllable, the -u- follows the -i-, but to give a visual reminder of the
rhyme, this structurally proper order is reversed in the two finals -ui
and -uin.

Nuclear vowels are -α-, -ə-, -a-, -æ-, -ϵ- and -e-. Our uncer-
tainties about MC pronunciation are greatest with respect to these
vowels. MC -α- and -ə- are probably something like the vowels in E
cot and cut, respectively. MC -a-, -æ-, and -ϵ- are all somewhere in
the neighborhood of the vowel in E man, but, though it is clear that
they are distinct, it is not clear how they are distinguished. Purely
as a matter of convenience, I read -a- as in German Mann, -æ- as in E
man, and -ϵ- as in E met. MC -e- is probably like the vowel in German
See.

Absence of nuclear vowel (-∅-) is represented in a variety of ways,
given in Table 3 (see page 5). Again, the pronunciation of MC finals
without nuclei is speculative, and I offer my own realizations of these
finals for the convenience of the student. The -u- in -ung I read like
the -oo- in E cool. The -o- of -ong, -io, and -o I read like the -o
of German so. The -i- in -i, -ui, -in, -uin, and -im I read like the
-i- in E machine. The -u- in -ui and -uin is like the ü- in German
über, as is the combination -iu and the -i- in -io. The -o- in -iou,
-ou, and -om is like the -u- in E cut.

MC endings are -i, like the last sound of E coy; -u, like the
last sound of E cow; -m, -p, -n, -t, -ng, and -k, all like the E
sounds usually represented by these letters.

Syllables of the "entering" tone category comprise all MC sylla-
bles that end in -p, -t, or -k. Syllables ending in -p are the "en-
tering" correlates of syllables ending in -m from the other tone cat-
egories; those ending in -t correlate to those ending in -n, those in
-k to those in -ng. Thus it is possible when listing finals to sub-
sume -p under -m, -t under -n, and -k under -ng, as in Tables 3 and 4.

Table 4 (see page 6) is a list of MC finals, in the order of the

Table 3

How finals are spelled when they have no nuclear vowel

Structural spelling	Present spelling
-Øng	-ung
-uØng	-ong
-iØi	-i
-iuØi	-ui
-iØ	-iu
-iuØ	-io
-uØ	-o
-iØn	-in
-iuØn	-uin
-iØu	-iou
-Øu	-ou
-iØm	-im
-Øm	-om

Note: -m represents also -p; -n, -t; and -ng, -k.

---

traditional rhyming dictionaries. It is made according to simplifica-
tions suggested in Stimson 1976. Only finals in the "level" tone cat-
egory are entered, except if a final only occurs in the "departing"
tone. The 31 rhyme groups are arranged in larger groups, separated by
periods (.), according to whether they have roughly the same endings.
Different finals considered to be mutually rhyming according to the
strictest rhyming conventions, even though they are in different rhyme
groups in the dictionaries, are separated by semi-colons.
    Most important in reading the transcriptions is not that the pro-
nunciations be according to the suggestions made above, but that ini-
tials spelled in the same way in different words be pronounced in the
same way, and similarly with finals. For in this way the structural
identities and differences, which are all we really know about MC
phonology, will be preserved.

Table 4

Finals in the order

of the traditional rhyming dictionaries

(1) -ung, -iung; (2) -ong; -iong; (3) -ang.

(4) -i, -ui; (5) -iəi, -iuəi; (6) -iu; (7) -io; -o; (8) -ei, -uei;

-iɛi, -iuɛi; (9) -ɑi, -uɑi; (10) -ai, -uai; (11) -uəi; -əi;

-iæi.

(12) -in, -uin; (13) -iuən; -iən; (14) -iæn, -iuæn; -uən; -ən;

(15) -ɑn; -uɑn; (16) -an, uan; (17) -en, -uen; -iɛn, -iuɛn.

(18) -eu; -iɛu; (19) -au; (20) -ɑu; (21) -ɑ; -uɑ; (22) -a, -ua,

-ia.

(23) -ɑng, -uɑng, -iɑng, -iuɑng; (24) -æng, -uæng, -iæng, -iuæng;

(25) -eng, -ueng; (26) -iəng, -iuəng; -əng, -uəng.

(27) -iou; -ou.

(28) -im; (29) -om; (30) -iɛm; -em; (31) -am; -iæm.

---

1. Bernhard Karlgren, "Grammata Serica recensa," Bulletin of the Museum of Far Eastern Antiquities, no. 29 (1957), pp. 1-332.

2. Samuel Martin, "The phonemes of Ancient Chinese," Supplement to Journal of the American Oriental Society, no. 16 (1953).

3. Hugh M. Stimson, The Jongyuan in yunn: A guide to Old Mandarin pronunciation, Sinological Series no. 12 (New Haven: Far Eastern Publications, 1966).

4. Hugh M. Stimson, A T'ang poetic vocabulary, (New Haven: Far Eastern Publications, 1976).

Chapter 2

Grammatical sketch

Words

1. Most MC words are one syllable long:

n<u>jin</u> "man, men, people"

<u>giuəi</u> "return home"

The preponderance of one-syllable words has given Chinese the reputa-
tion of being a monosyllabic language. That label is not perfectly
accurate, however, as there are some words of two or more syllables
which cannot be further analyzed:

<u>sin-i</u> "(magnolia)"*

<u>bhio-iong</u> "lotus"

Other polysyllabic words can be analyzed as being built according to
certain rules.

2. One such rule is that a word may be optionally marked as
plural in number by the addition of another word, which precedes it
and acts like a pluralizing prefix:

<u>ghiuən</u> "flock"; <u>dzhəi</u> "talented man"; <u>ghiuən</u> <u>dzhəi</u> "talented

men"

<u>jiŭng</u> "multitude"; <u>seng</u> "star"; <u>jiŭng</u> <u>seng</u> "stars"

3. Another rule is that a word may be marked as intensive by
being repeated.

<u>tsiĕn</u> "shallow"; <u>tsiĕn</u> <u>tsiĕn</u> "very shallow"

<u>piən</u> "scattered"; <u>piən</u> <u>piən</u> "very scattered"

<u>miət</u> "thing"; <u>miət</u> <u>miət</u> "all things"

<u>nen</u> "year"; <u>nen</u> <u>nen</u> "year after year"

In <u>miət</u> <u>miət</u> the basic intensive meaning of the reduplication is ex-
tended to a universal sense; in <u>nen</u> <u>nen</u> the extension is to an itera-
tive sense.

4. An important word-building process that operated productively
in the earliest period in the history of the Chinese language is the

_____

*"(X)" has two meanings. Here, it is "(a kind of X)".

complete or partial reduplication of a syllable chosen for its onomato-
poeic value.   The resulting word is called a descriptive. Partially
reduplicating descriptives are alliterative or rhyming.

> sop-sop "(wind, rain)"*
>
> ngai-nguəi "(rockiness)"
>
> jrhæng-huæng "(loftiness)"

Typically, the syllable that is reduplicated in a descriptive is
chosen only for its sound and its sound-associative value, and the
meaning of the descriptive has no relation to the meaning of any word
represented by the syllable when it stands alone, at least at the time
of its formation. However, sometimes a descriptive is built on a syl-
lable that retains its original meaning after an otherwise meaningless
rhyming or alliterating syllable is added:

> djiuĕn "turn"; qiuĕn-djiuĕn "(turning)"
>
> huəi "go back"; bhəi-huəi "(going back and forth)"

5. Another way of building a new word is to attach a manner
suffix:

> kuɑ̀ng "expansive"; kuɑ̀ng-njiɛn "in an expansive manner,
>
>   (expansiveness)"
>
> xuɑ̌ng-xuət "(muddled, unable to make precise plans)";
>
>   xuɑ̌ng-njiu "(vague)"

Words with a manner suffix often occur as descriptives.

6. Finally, a compound word may be formed of two words that are
synonyms; the meaning of such a compound is usually more general than
that of either of the components. Or the two words making up the com-
pound may be two members of the same set, and the meaning of the com-
pound is the meaning of the whole set.

> leu "void"; kuɑk "void"; leu kuɑk "vast, empty spaces"
>
> djhi "fine linen"; kiæk "coarse linen"; djhi kiæk "linen
>
>   cloth"
>
> shran "hill, mountain"; ngak "one or all of five specific
>
>   sacred mountains"; shran ngak "all the various mountains"

---

*Here, "(X)" means "(descriptive of X)" or "(descriptive of being
X)".

7. To the Western student, what is most interesting about Chinese word formation is not so much what there is of it, since there is so little, but instead what is not there. For example, unlike nouns in English and other European languages, a Chinese noun is not required to carry an overt mark to show whether it is singular or plural, or whether it is the subject or object of a verb. Nor does a Chinese verb indicate person, tense, mood, etc. The meanings expressed by oblig-atory endings on nouns and verbs in the extraordinarily complicated morphological systems of such languages as Latin and Greek are in Chi-nese optionally, indeed rarely, expressed by an occasional pronoun, adjective, or adverb. When it is said that Chinese has no grammar, what is meant is that Chinese lacks this sort of noun or verb morphol-ogy.   This lack of a developed morphology is one of the reasons why the definition of parts of speech is difficult in Chinese and will not be attempted in the present grammatical description. Instead, Chinese grammar is easier to describe in terms of the meanings of words and in terms of their syntax.

Syntax

8. Elements of a Chinese text--the words, phrases and sentences that make up the text--stand in grammatical relationship one to an-other. Definition of the kinds of elements--parts of speech--that occur in Chinese is beyond the scope of this sketch, but throughout this book I shall refer to such parts of speech as noun, verb, and adverb without rigorously defining them.

9. It is useful to name the elements that have a semantic rela-tionship to the verb. The actor is the performer of the action of the verb. The subject is the person or thing that possesses the quality expressed by the verb. The direct object is the recipient of the action of the verb. A verb is transitive if it normally has a direct object; otherwise it is intransitive. Included in Chinese intransi-tive verbs are what correspond to English adjectives. Thus:

qiĕm biəi "I close my door": qiĕm "close" is a transitive

verb with biəi "door" as its object

njin giuəi "people return home": njin "man, men, people"

is the actor performing the action expressed by the

intransitive verb giuəi

tsău liok "grasses will be green": tsău "grass, grasses"

is the subject of the intransitive verb liok "be green"

cf. liok tsău "green grass"

10. In Chinese, elements that stand in grammatical relationship to each other are always adjacent. The kind of syntactic freedom possible without confusion in languages with complicated morphologies is not

possible in Chinese. These relationships number five: coordinate,
subordinate, verb-object, topic-comment, and the rare appositive. For
the subordinate, verb-object, and topic-comment relationships, the
order of the elements is crucial to the meaning.

11. The coordinate relationship. Most commonly, this relation-
ship is expressed in English as "and", but if the elements are whole
sentences, "and" is usually best left out:

> tsău muk "grass and trees": tsău "grass", coordinate with
>
> muk "tree"
>
> qiěm biəi, njin giuəi "I close my door; people return
>
> home": qiěm biəi "close door", coordinate with njin
>
> giuəi "people return home"

12. Sometimes "or" is implied, as when a pair of elements that
have opposite meanings are coordinated in a question that asks for
a choice between the two opposites:

> giuən giuəi biət giuəi "will you return home or not?"
>
> giuən "you, Sir", giuəi "return home", biət giuəi
>
> "not return home"

13. Sometimes "but" seems to be intended:

> tsău liok, giuən giuəi biət giuəi "the grasses will be
>
> green, but will you return home or not?": tsău liok
>
> "the grasses are green" is coordinate with giuən giuəi
>
> biət giuəi "will you return home or not?"

14. The coordinate relationship is sometimes overtly specified
by one of the conjunctions, such as iǔ "together with, and", tsiă
"furthermore, and", and nji "and", placed between the coordinated
elements. Use of conjunctions is rare in poetry.

15. When the coordinate elements are verbs or verb phrases,
sometimes there is an additional meaning to the relationship: "in
order to" or "with the result that":

> ngiuæt ləi jiɛu "the moon comes to shine": ngiuæt "moon";
>
> ləi "come" and jiɛu "shine" are verbs in a coordinate
>
> relationship, with the additional meaning of "in order

to" implied in the coordination

qen <u>miɛt</u> <u>dzhĭn</u> "the mist is dissipated away": <u>qen</u> "mist";

<u>miɛt</u> "be dissipated" and <u>dzhĭn</u> "be gone" are also verbs

in a coordinate relationship, but here the additional

meaning implied in the coordination is "with the result

that"

When the second of the coordinate verbs is <u>ləi</u> "come", it is often
merely added to indicate direction and should be translated "here,
toward (the speaker)":

<u>lɑng</u> ghi djiuk mǎ ləi "You would ride over on a bamboo

horse": <u>lɑng</u> "young man, you"; <u>ghi</u> "straddle, ride";

<u>djiuk</u> "bamboo"; <u>mǎ</u> "horse"; <u>ləi</u> "come": ghi mǎ and <u>ləi</u>

are in a coordinate relationship, but "ride a horse and

come" is better rendered in English as "ride a horse here"

or "ride a horse over"

16. The <u>subordinate</u> relationship. When this relationship obtains,
the first element <u>always</u> modifies the second. In Chinese the order is
crucial: modifier always precedes modified. The English order is the
same only when the modifier is simple:

liok tsǎu "green grasses": <u>liok</u> "green" modifies <u>tsǎu</u>

"grass"

hæng njin "traveling person, travelers": <u>hæng</u> "travel"

modifies <u>njin</u> "person"

In the second example above, notice that a logically equivalent English
version where <u>hæng</u> is translated as a clause, "who travel", has a word
order that is <u>the</u> reverse of the Chinese: "people who travel".

17. An important subclass of subordinate expressions comprises
those where the modified element is one of a small number of common
<u>place</u> nouns:

shran djiung "center of the mountain, midst of the mountains":

shran "mountain" modifies the place noun djiung "center,

midst"

dhî zhiàng "surface ·of the ground": dhî "ground" modifies

another place noun zhiàng "top, surface"

njin gan "people's intervals, intervals between people":

njin "people" modifies gan "interval"

Such expressions are place expressions.

18. Similarly, time expressions consist of two elements in a sub-ordinate relationship where the second element is a time noun:

ləi njit "the day you came": ləi "come" modifies the time

noun njit "day"

sěng zhi "the time of being sober, when sober": sěng

"sober" modifies zhi "time"

tzuî hòu "the aftermath of getting drunk, after getting

drunk": tzuî "get drunk" modifies the time noun hòu

"time afterward"

19. An adverb is an element that modifies a verb:

biət giuəi "will not return home": biət "not" is an

adverb modifying the verb giuəi "return home"

siang sùng "mutually·see off, see each other off":

siang "mutually, each other" is an adverb modifying

the verb sùng "see off, send (a friend) off (on a

journey)"

Just as nouns and adjectives always precede the elements that they modify, so too with adverbs: first the adverb, then the verb. Whereas in English adverbs sometimes precede, sometimes follow, the verb, in Chinese the order is fixed.

20. The subordinate relationship is sometimes overtly marked with the subordinate particle ji, so that A ji B means that "A modifies B":

shran ji hă "bottom of the mountain": shran "mountain"

modifies the place noun hă "bottom", and the relation-

ship of subordination that obtains between the two words

is overtly marked by ji

jhin ji ləi "coming of the divinity": jhin "divinity, god"

modifies ləi "coming", and the subordinate relationship

is overtly marked by ji

ji is the most common particle in the prose that is written in the
same language as Dhɑng shi, but it is rare in the poetry.

21. The verb-object relationship. The order is first the verb,
then the object. When a place or a time expression occurs at object
position and specifies the place or time at which, from which, or to
which the action of the verb takes place, that expression is a place
object or a time object:

njip lim "enters into the forest, enters the forest":

njip "enter into, enter" has lim "forest" as place

object

dzhì dzhiong giæn gɑn "proceed from (the time of the

reign period called) Establish Peace": dzhì dzhiong

is a synonym compound (see 6, above) verb meaning

"proceed from", and it has the name of a reign period,

giæn "establish", gɑn "peace", as its time object

22. When the meaning of the time or place object is "at" or "to"
the object, sometimes a locative particle, such as qiu, precedes the
object, but this use of the locative particle is rare in poetry.

23. An object that is not a place or time object is direct. Of-
ten the direct object names the recipient or beneficiary of the action
of the verb:

qiěm biəi "I close my door": qiěm "close" has a direct

object, biəi "door"

iǒu shriɑng "has frost, there is frost": iǒu "have, there

is" has a direct object, shriɑng "frost"

24. When a direct object and a place or time object both occur
after a verb, the word order is fixed: first the direct object, then
the place or time object:

gek gǒ shran ji hǎ "beat drums at the bottom of a mountain":

gek "beat" has both a direct object, gŏ "drum", and a

place object shran ji hǎ "bottom of the mountain"

25. When a direct object of a verb consists of another verb (plus any object that this second verb might have), the first verb is often most conveniently translated by an English auxiliary verb. The first verb in the Chinese construction is therefore also called an auxiliary verb:

qiəng dji X "ought to know about X": qiəng "should, ought"

has its object dji "know about" (which is in turn fol-

lowed by its own object, here represented by X); qiəng

is therefore auxiliary to dji

26. When a verb-object construction modifies another verb (plus any object that this second verb might have), the first verb is called a co-verb:

dzhì xiɑng ləi "come proceeding from my home town, come

from my home town": dzhì "proceed from" has xiɑng "home

town" as its place object, and this verb-object construc-

tion modifies ləi "come", so dzhì is a co-verb

biət iǔ dzhin sèi tung njin qen "did not have human com-

munication with the frontier lands of Dzhin": biət "not"

is adverb to the co-verb iǔ "accompany, be together with",

which, with its object expression dzhin sèi "frontier

lands of Dzhin", modifies tung "let through, exchange"

and its object expression njin qen "human smoke, smoke

of human (habitation)", this expression being a metonym

for the simple njin "people"

Often the English for a co-verb is most conveniently a preposition, such as "from" and "with" in the above examples.

27. The object is often omitted after certain co-verbs, especially when it has just been mentioned:

iǒu dèu dhǎu, kǎ ǐ tziuɛt den "there is a path suitable

only for birds, and one can by means of it cut across to

a certain mountain peak": i̯ŏu "there is" has a direct

object dĕu dhău "bird path, path suitable only for birds";

kă is an auxiliary verb "can"; Ḭ is usually a co-verb

"using...as an instrument, with, by means of" but here

it stands for Ḭ dhău "by means of a road", the dhău

being omitted because it has just been mentioned, so

Ḭ here is best translated with a pronoun replacing "path":

"by means of it"; the Ḭ is adverbial to tziuєt "cut

across" and its place object den "mountain peak"

28. When a transitive verb is negated sometimes the expected
object is lacking:

njin biət dji "no one will know about it": njin "person"

is the actor to the transitive verb dji "know about"

preceded by the negative adverb biət "not"

29. The topic-comment relationship. Every Chinese sentence con-
sists of at least a comment. The comment is the point of the sentence.
Sometimes there is also a topic; if so, it always precedes the comment,
except under certain conditions.

30. The topic, if present, specifies the circumstances under
which what is expressed in the comment applies. Often it identifies
the actor performing the action in the comment or the subject which
has the quality mentioned in the comment. But Chinese sentences often
lack any mention of either actor or subject. Again, the topic some-
times tells the time or place in which whatever is expressed in the
comment occurs. Often the topic is more vaguely related to the com-
ment, so that a first try at an English translation might begin "About
..." In any case the information in the topic is less interesting,
more likely to be common knowledge, or at least presumed by the speak-
er to be familiar to his audience. Such a presumption is often sig-
nalled in English by the definite article "the".

31. The comment, on the other hand, contains new, more interesting
material. If a sentence has a comment in which the main word is a
verb, it is a verbal sentence with a verbal comment. There are also
nominal sentences, with nominal comments whose main word is a noun,
but these seem to occur far less often than verbal sentences in Dhang
shi.

32. Usually the meaning of a nominal sentence is identification-
al: what is mentioned in the comment is identified as equivalent to

what is mentioned in the topic, or as a member of the set mentioned in
the topic:

> ten hǎ shiɑng sim chiù, lɑu-lɑu sùng kæk dheng "The most
>
> heart-wounding place in the world is Misery Pavilion,
>
> where people are sent off on journeys": chiù "place"
>
> is the main word of the topic, and dheng "pavilion",
>
> a noun, is the main word of the comment, and the meaning
>
> of the topic-comment relationship here is identification-
>
> al (see 15.1-2 for further analysis of these lines)

33. When a nominal comment identifies the place where what is
mentioned in the topic is located, it is a place comment:

> som nom ngiæp zhiæng shiò "My three sons are at Ngiæp
>
> City Garrison": nom "son", modified by som "three", is
>
> the main word of the topic, and shiò "garrison", mod-
>
> ified by ngiæp zhiæng "Ngiæp City", is the head of a
>
> nominal place comment

34. In verbal sentences, the topic is sometimes an actor topic:

> giuən giuəi "you will return home": giuən "you, Sir"
>
> is the actor topic, specifying the one who performs
>
> the action mentioned in the comment: giuəi "return
>
> home": "About you, Sir, I make the comment that you
>
> will return home."

35. Sometimes it is the subject:

> tsǎu liok "The grasses will be green": tsǎu "grass" is
>
> the topic, specifying the subject commented on, and
>
> liok "be green" is an intransitive verb acting as
>
> comment: "About the grasses I make the comment that
>
> they will be green."

36. Often the topic of a verbal sentence identifies the place where the action mentioned in the comment occurs, a place topic, or the time when it occurs, a time topic:

> mò qiěm biəi "In the evening, I close my door": mò
> "evening" is a time topic, telling when the verb-
> object comment qiěm biəi "close door" takes place:
> "About the evening I make the comment that I close
> my door then."

> kung shran biət gěn njin "On the empty mountain, no one
> else is seen": kung "empty" modifies shran "mountain",
> the main word of a place topic, telling where the
> comment (biət "not", adverb to gěn "see", and njin
> "person", object to gěn) takes place: "About the
> empty mountain I comment that we see no one else
> there."

37. Frequently place expressions (see 17, above) occur as place topics:

> shran djiung qiěm biəi "Amid the mountains I close my
> door": shran djiung "midst of the mountains" is a
> place expression, topic to qiěm biəi "close door",
> the verb-object comment: "About the midst of the
> mountains I make the comment that I close my door
> there."

38. Usually English prepositional phrases afford the most convenient means of translating place expressions when they occur at topic or object position. Usually such a translation shows that what in English is expressed in a single preposition (or preposition-like expression) corresponds in Chinese to three things: the meaning of the place noun, the meaning of the modifier-modified relationship obtaining between the preceding noun and the place noun (expressed in English by "of"), and the meaning the place-topic- comment relationship or the verb- place-object relationship obtaining between the place topic and the comment or between the verb and the place object (in either case expressed in English by "at"). Thus in the example at 37

above, "midst", translating the place noun djiung, plus "of", translat-
ing the modifier-modified relationship obtaining between shran and
djiung, plus "at", translating the relationship obtaining between the
place topic shran djiung and the rest of the sentence, which is its
comment, combine to give the preposition "in": "at the midst of the
mountains" becomes "in the mountains".

39. The difference in meaning between a place expression at topic
position and the same place expression at object position is largely a
difference in presumption as to what is familiar to the hearer (see 30,
above). Changing the example in 37 above to qiĕm biəi shran djiung
puts the place expression into the comment, where the interest is fo-
cussed. One way to reflect this difference in focus in the English
version is to change "amid the mountains" as a translation for the
place topic (with the important word "the" signalling the fact that
the speaker presumes that the hearer is familiar with the mountains
mentioned) to "amid mountains" or "amid some mountains" for the place
object.

40. Sometimes a word which names the recipient of the action of
a verb, and is therefore the semantic object of the verb, appears in
topic position. In such cases it is helpful to think of an original
verb-object arrangement of the words which has been disturbed so that
the object now appears in topic position. We may call such a process
topicalization:

> dhài ngă giŏu biət tzɑk "The Greater Odes--no one has
>
> written (a poem like them) in a long time": here the
>
> topic, dhài ngă "great odes" has been shifted from
>
> its original position of object after tzɑk "compose,
>
> write" (modified by two adverbs, giŏu "in a long
>
> time" and biət "not")

The effect of this process is what we might expect: the topicalized
element is moved from a position of focus of interest where something
new is said to one where the universe of discourse first begins to be
narrowed and where something that the hearer is presumed to know
about is mentioned.   The effect is to change "For a long time no one
has written (a poem like) the Greater Odes" to something like the
English version given above, or, to make the topicalization painfully
explicit: "Of course you are familiar with the Greater Odes; well,
what I want to say about them is that no one has written anything like
them in a long time."

41. Certain auxiliaries (see 25, above) are regularly associated
with the topicalization of the object of the following verb.
Such an auxiliary is kă "can, be able to". A frequent expedient in
the English translation is to put the second verb in the passive voice:

guan dhěm biət kǎ ghiən "(No matter which of the various)

mats: (I) cannot approach (them)": guan "mat made of

rushes" and dhěm "bamboo mat" form a synonym compound

(see 6, above), the topicalized object of ghiən "approach";

the negative adverb biət "not" precedes the auxiliary in

Chinese, but follows it in English; using the English

passive: "The mats cannot be approached."

42. When the subordinate particle ji (see 20, above) appears be-
tween the topic and the comment of a sentence, the sentence becomes a
clause or a phrase. Thus:

jhin ləi "The divinity is coming": jhin "divinity", topic

to ləi "come"; jhin ji ləi "Whether the divinity comes..."

or "The coming of the divinity..."

43. Sometimes two sentences overlap so that the object of the
first sentence is also the topic of the second. In such a sentence,
the word that functions as both object and topic is called a pivot.

kiuən giuən dzhǐn tziǒu "I urge you to finish the wine":

kiuən "urge" has giuən "you, Sir" as its direct object,

but giuən is in turn actor topic to the comment dzhǐn

"finish" and tziǒu "alcoholic beverage", a verb-object

construction

44. Place topics and time topics are often followed by comments
whose main word is the verb iǒu, a transitive verb which basically
means "have", but which in such sentences is better translated with
the appropriate form of "there is":

dhǐ zhiàng iǒu shriang "There is frost on the ground":

dhǐ zhiàng "surface of the ground" is a place topic

consisting of a noun modifying a place noun; iǒu shriang

"have frost, there is frost" is a verb-object comment

njin gan iǒu siɛn "There are immortals among people":

njin gan "intervals of people, intervals between people"

(and notice how "at" plus "intervals" plus "of/between"

combine to become the English preposition "among"--see

38, above), place topic to iŏu siɛn "have immortals,

there are immortals"

In the above examples, notice how the English word order changes when
instead of "have", "there is" is used to translate iŏu.

45. The usual order, first topic, then comment, is sometimes dis-
turbed when the comment is a descriptive (see 4, above). Here are
examples that follow the usual order:

biung sop-sop "The wind is so sad": biung "wind" is the

topic, and sop-sop "(wind, rain)"--usually with sad

connotations--is a descriptive and the comment

ngiuæt bhəi-huəi "The moon is so unstable": ngiuæt "moon"

is the topic, and bhəi-huəi "(going back and forth)"

is another descriptive functioning as a comment

Because descriptives are forceful, vivid words, they inherently attract
grammatical focus, so that when they precede words they describe, they
still function as comment in a rhetorical inversion:

huɑn-huɑn djhin tziɑ̀ng-giuən "How martial General Djhin

is!": huɑn-huɑn "(martial)" is the comment, even though

it precedes the topic, djhin tziɑ̀ng-giuən "General

Djhin"

huɑng-huɑng ngiæp "How resplendent the mission was!":

huɑng-huɑng "(resplendent)" is the comment, preceding

the topic, ngiæp "mission"

46. The appositive relationship. Apposition is rare in Dhɑng
shi. As in English, we say that what follows is in apposition to
what precedes, so that in "Karlgren, the Swedish sinologist", the
term "the Swedish sinologist" is said to be in apposition to "Karl-
gren". The terms in apposition are nouns or nominal expressions, the
second of the terms is an explanatory equivalent of the first, and
the two terms function together as a unit that has a single grammati-
cal relationship to other terms in the sentence. Thus:

njĭ iuăn dhŏu ji njin "you, a person of a distant road"

njĭ "you" and iuăn dhŏu ji njin "person of a distant

road" are in apposition, and together function as topic

to the rest of the sentence (see below, 21.32)

47. The brief grammatical sketch above will be referred to fre-
quently during the presentation of the poems, especially the first
twenty poems or so. The paragraph will be referred to by the number
assigned to it here, preceded by the letters GS (for "Grammatical
sketch"). This sketch is not intended to be complete; further details
will be filled in during the presentation of the poems.

Chapter 3

Iuang Ui 王維(Wáng Wéi, 699-759)

Literary historians have divided the Dhang Dynasty into four periods: the Early Dhang, lasting from the beginning of the dynasty in 618 until about 720; the High Dhang, culminating in the middle decades of the eighth century, when the greatest and best-known Dhang shi were written; the Mid Dhang, lasting until about 830; and the Late Dhang, lasting until the dynasty ended in 907.

The poems presented in this and the next two chapters are by the three greatest poets of the High Dhang: Iuang Ui, Lǐ Bhæk, and Dhǒ Biǒ, all close contemporaries.

Iuang Ui is the oldest of these three poets. He attained a high position in the government and spent most of his life near the newer of the two chief capital cities of the Dhang empire: Djhiang-qan 長安 (Cháng-ān, literally, "Eternal Peace"; the modern Xī-ān [or Sian] in southern Shǎn-xī [or Shensi] Province), also known as the Western Capital. In the mountains south of this huge metropolis, he acquired a villa in a beautiful natural setting of parks, groves, lakes, and streams, which is the subject of some of his most famous poems.

During a devastating upheaval that rocked the Dhang government in the 750's, rebel forces occupied the other chief capital city: Lak-iang 洛陽 (Luò-yáng, literally "Sunny Side of the Lak"--so named because it is situated on the north bank of the Lak River; the modern city has the same name and is in Hé-nán [or Honan] Province, in the north central region, just south of the Yellow River), also called the Eastern Capital, and then moved on to capture the Western Capital. The rebels captured Iuang Ui when he was in the Eastern Capital, and they tried to get him to serve in their government. Iuang Ui managed to avoid cooperating with them, and when loyal forces eventually recaptured the two capitals he was cleared of charges of treason.

In spite of the terrible distress caused by the rebellion, Iuang Ui avoids the subject in his poetry. A serious student of Zen Buddhism, and a famous painter renowned for his pioneering work in monochrome landscapes, he brings to his poetry a Buddhist detachment and a special perception of the beauty of nature.

1. Parting 送 別 Sùng bhiɛt (Sòng bié)

山 中 相 送 罷

shran djiung siɑng sùng bhǎi

      mountain midst   each-other
      send-off finish

日 暮 掩 柴 扉

njit mò qiěm jrhai biəi

      sun/day evening   shut brushwood
      door

春 草 明 年 綠

chuin tsǎu miæng nen liok

      springtime grass   next year green

王 孫 歸 不 歸

iuɑng suən giuəi biət giuəi

      prince grandson   return not return

          (Five-syllable regulated quatrain)

Note: Poems in this anthology are numbered consecutively from 1
to 55. Reference to a particular line is made by giving the poem num-
ber, then the line number, with a decimal point between them: "1.1"
means "Poem 1, Line 1". The title of every poem is given an English
translation. This is followed by the Chinese title, first in the stan-
dard orthography, next in MC transcription, and last, in parentheses,
in pīn yīn, the official romanization used in the People's Republic of
China to transcribe the national language, Modern Standard Mandarin.

In this chapter, poems are presented line by line: first, the
line in the traditional orthography; next, below the Chinese charac-
ters, the MC transcription of the line; last, to the right of the line,
word-by-word glosses in English of the Chinese. Each English gloss
appears in the same position in the line as the Chinese word that it
translates. English words connected by a hyphen translate a single
Chinese word at the corresponding position in the line; Chinese syl-
lables connected by a hyphen are glossed by a single English word (or
by two words connected by a hyphen) at the corresponding position in
the English line. A slash " / " between two words indicates that they
are alternate translations of the same Chinese word. A double space
in both the MC and English, indicates the position of the chief cae-
suras. After a poem has been transcribed and glossed in this way, its
prosodic form is identified. The main features of the prosody of Dhɑng
shi will be presented gradually below in "Prosodic notes", the first of
which follows.

Prosodic note 1: Line length,

caesura, and rhyme

Except for an important sub-group, to be discussed in a later
prosodic note, a shi regularly has lines all consisting of the same
number of syllables, usually five or seven.

A five-syllable line has a fixed caesura after the second syl-
lable. There is also a caesura in the last three syllables of the

line, optionally placed after the third or fourth syllable. The posi-
tion of the first caesura is fixed, and it usually, though not always,
corresponds to a natural break in the grammatical structure of the
line. However, the second caesura is not fixed, and its position is
determined by a grammatical break.

It is impossible to determine exactly how Dhɑng shi were read. An
extrapolation from the way they are read nowadays suggests that a five-
syllable line has pauses that are placed so that a four-beat rhythmical
unit results:

1	2	3	4
shran djiung,	siɑng sùng,	bhǎi	(pause)
njit mò,	qiɛ̌m,	jrhai biəi	(pause)
chuin tsǎu	miæng nen,	liok	(pause)
iuɑng suən,	giuəi,	biuət giuəi	(pause)

The four beats are evenly spaced in the modern reading, and if two
syllables occupy one measure between beats, they are in turn spaced so
that they occupy approximately the first two-thirds of the measure.
In place of the fourth beat, there is a pause of about one measure in
duration at the end of the line. The correlation between caesuras and
natural breaks in the grammatical structure should become apparent as
the poem is analyzed, line by line, below.

Shi always rhyme. In quatrains, such as Poem 1, there is one
rhyme to the poem; even lines rhyme; the first line rhymes optionally
(see Poem 8, below). The qualifications for rhyming are about the
same in Chinese as in English. To rhyme, two syllables must have the
same consonant or vowel sounds at the end of the syllable, and the pre-
ceding vowel sounds must be the same or at least similar. See Poems 2
and 6 below for certain permitted imperfect rhymes.

What is peculiar about the rhyming conventions of shi is the role
of tones in determining rhyme. Up to the Mid Dhɑng period, syllables
had to belong to the same tone category in order to rhyme. Thus, dung,
dǔng, and dùng do not rhyme, even though they have the same -ng ending
and -u- vowel quality, because they belong to different tone catego-
ries. In the Mid Dhɑng and after, syllables in the "raised" or "rising"
category could rhyme with those in the "departing" category, but syl-
lables in these two categories never rhymed with those in the "level"
category: dǔng and dùng could rhyme, but neither syllable rhymed with
dung. At no time did duk rhyme with any of the other three syllables:
syllables of the "entering" tone category were always kept separate.

Tones also play a part in the tone patterns of regulated poems;
see "Prosodic note 7", below.

Title. sùng "send (a friend) off (on a journey)" and bhiɛt "part,
leave" are verbs in a co-ordinate relationship (GS 11)*: "I send some-
one off and we part", but the words appear together often enough to be

---

*See Chapter 2, Paragraph 11.

considered a compound: sɨng bhiɛt "parting", that is, "all the activities associated with taking leave of a friend, including sending him off and actually parting from him" (GS 6). Taking leave of friends is a common occasion for the composition of a poem.

1.1 Notice that shran is glossed in the singular, and see GS 7. In general, nouns will be given in the singular, verbs in the infinitive, and the student will be expected to determine from context the number, person, tense, mood, etc. of the word. shran modifies djiung, which is a place noun (GS 17), and the two words are in a subordinate relationship (GS 16) and constitute a place expression (GS 17) which is place topic (GS 36-38) to the rest of the line. siang is an adverb (GS 19). A basic meaning of siang is "mutually, each other", but frequently this meaning is weakened to something like "transitively", merely calling attention to the fact that the following verb is transitive (GS 9). In either case, when siang precedes a transitive verb, the direct object is regularly lacking. For sɨng, see GS 7 again, and the gloss to shran, above. siang sɨng means simply "someone sees someone else off". Nothing in the Chinese says who is sending whom off here, but the total context makes it clear that the persona (i.e. the person saying the poem) is seeing a friend off, rather than the other way around.

Notice the semantic effect of having the place expression at the topic position. It is not likely that "in some mountains or other" is intended; more likely is "in the mountains (that you, my audience, join me in seeing before us and which constitute no surprise to either of us)...", with the important "the" before "mountains" (see also GS 30). The intransitive verb (GS 9) bhǎi "finish, be finished, be done" is a comment to the first four words, which constitute the topic (GS 30-31): "About my seeing someone off in the mountains, my comment is that it is finished."

1.2 The first two words, njit "sun, day" and mὸ "evening, become evening", are plausibly either in a topic-comment relationship (GS 29-31) or in a subordinate relationship (GS 16). If they are considered topic and comment, two further possibilities arise. First, the resulting complete sentence could be considered to be in a coordinate relationship to the rest of the line (GS 11): "The day has become evening, and...." A second possibility is that the two words constitute a time topic (GS 36): "While the day becomes evening,..." or "When the day is at evening,..." If the two words are considered to be in a subordinate relationship, where njit modifies mὸ: "day's evening, evening of the day", it is most likely that they constitute a phrase that functions as a time topic to the rest of the line: "At day's evening,..." or "At the evening of the day,..." qiɛm is a transitive verb (GS 9), and biəi is its direct object (GS 9, 21, 23); jrhai modifies biəi (GS 16); and the three words, qiɛm jrhai biəi, constitute a comment, topicless (GS 29), or having the first two words of the line as topic, depending on how those two words are treated. The entire line may be in a coordinate relationship with the preceding line; this is the usual relationship between lines, and from now on no further mention will be made

of it when it obtains. But another possibility is that the first line
is a time topic to the second line as comment: "After finishing...,
when the day is at evening, I close my brushwood door." Notice that
the actor (GS 9, 34), lacking in the Chinese, is expected in English.
It seems most appropriate to assign the action of the verb to the per-
sona, and to assume that the door he is shutting is his own, hence the
"I" and the "my" in the translation.

　　　　1.3 chuin tsău: GS 16. miæng is literally "bright, become
bright". When miæng modifies nen it means "next", probably by analogy
to another common time expression, miæng njit "bright day, at bright
day" or, in smoother English, "when the day is bright", extended to
mean "when another day becomes bright", and finally "on the next day,
tomorrow". chuin tsău is subject (GS 9, 35) to the rest of the line.
Because miæng nen obviously implies future time, the translation of
the intransitive verb liok (GS 9) will have appropriate English auxil-
iaries: "About the spring grasses I make the following comment: next
year they will be green."

　　　　1.4 iuang "prince" modifies suən "grandson, descendent" to form
a poetic cliché used as an honorific term of address: "You, noble
sir,..." Its use here is probably meant to recall its occurrence in
"Summons for a gentleman who became a recluse 招 隱 士   Jièu qiăn
jrhĭ (Zhào yĭn shì)", one of the Songs of the state of Chŭ (see above,
"General background", p.viii). In the "Summons", the poet tries to per-
suade the recluse to come out of retirement. After enumerating the
hardships of life alone in the wilds, the poet ends with this couplet:

　　　　　　　　You, noble sir, oh,

　　　　　　　　　　come back here;

　　　　　　　　in the mountains, oh,

　　　　　　　　　　you cannot stay long.

　　　　　　　　　　　　　(Cf. Hawkes 1959, p. 120)

In the present poem, iuang suən is an actor topic to a two-part com-
ment that follows. These two parts are in a coordinate "or" relation-
ship (GS 12). The whole line is in a coordinate relationship to the
preceding line, but more than just "and" seems implied (GS 13), because
it is certain that grass will be green again next year, but it is not
certain whether the persona's friend will similarly return.
　　　　Many possible translations emerge from the above. Let me suggest
a few extremes. First, avoiding the addition of clarifying articles,
pronouns, and conjunctions as far as possible:

　　　　　　amid mountains parting done

　　　　　　day at dusk shut a brushwood door

　　　　　　spring grass next year green

　　　　　　noble sir return? not return?

Adding more words, but keeping the relationships as   coordinate as
possible:

>   amid the mountains   our parting is done
>
>   the day is at dusk   I shut my brushwood door
>
>   spring grasses   next year will be green
>
>   noble sir   will you return?

Finally, forcing subordination:

>   amid the mountains   after we have parted
>
>   when the day is at dusk   I shut my brushwood door
>
>   though spring grasses   will be green again next year
>
>   noble sir   will you likewise return?

2. Unclassified poem 雜 詩 Dzhop shi (Zá shī)

君 自 故 鄉 來
giuən dzhī gò xiɑng ləi   lord from   old home-town come

應 知 故 鄉 事
qiəng dji gò xiɑng jrhī   should know-about   old home-town
                                             matter

來 日 綺 牕 前
ləi njit kǐ chrang dzhen   come day (silk) window front

寒 梅 著 花 未
hɑn məi djiù xua miəi   winter plum-tree   produce flower
                                             not-yet

                                             (Five-syllable regulated quatrain)

     Title. dzhop basically means "varied, miscellaneous" and modifies
shi "poem". dzhop shi is a frequently occurring title originally in-
dicating that the subject matter of the poem so titled was such that
none of the usual classifications applied. Later, compilers of poetic
anthologies gave this title to poems that were otherwise untitled.

     2.1 giuən "lord, (honorific form of address)" is an actor topic
to two comments (GS 29-31, 34) which are in a coordinate relationship
(GS 11): the first comment consists of the rest of this line; the sec-
ond consists of the whole next line. dzhī is a common transitive verb
(GS 9), here in its usual function of co-verb (GS 26). Notice that
when an English preposition translates a Chinese co-verb, the preposi-
tional phrase regularly comes after the verb, whereas the corresponding
Chinese words precede the verb. gò "old, from an earlier time in one's
life" modifies xiɑng, the object of dzhī; the whole phrase, dzhī gò
xiɑng modifies ləi, the main word of the first comment to giuən.

     2.2 qiəng "should, ought to" is an auxiliary verb (GS 25). Its
object is the rest of the line. The following verb dji is transitive,
and its object is jrhī, which is modified by gò xiɑng (which has the
same grammatical structure as in the preceding line). This line, which
is the second comment to giuən, is in a coordinate relationship to the
last four words of the preceding line, which constitute the first com-
ment to giuən. "About you, Sir, I make the following two comments:
first, that you have come from my old home town, and second, that you
ought to know about things that happen in my old home town." Here
again, "my" is supplied on the basis of context.

2.3 ləi njit is a time expression (GS 18) and should be turned
into a clause, with "you" as subject in English: "the day that you
(left my home town to) come (here)". The phrase is a time topic (GS
30, 36) to the rest of the poem as comment: "On the day...." The rest
of the poem, comment to ləi njit, consists itself of a topic and a
comment. dzhen is a place noun (GS 17) modified by kǐ chrang, and the
three-word phrase functions as a place topic (GS 36) to the following
line. kǐ is a kind of patterned silk cloth used to make windows; the
word modifies chrang. Here "at" plus "front" plus "of" could be trans-
lated by the simple preposition "before", but the quasi-prepositional
expression "in front of" seems clearer. The persona is referring to a
window in his own house, or in a house that he used to occupy.

2.4 This line is a comment to the preceding line, and once again
this comment consists of a topic and two comments. Here the topic is
an actor topic, hɑn məi, where hɑn modifies məi. The first of the two
comments consists of a verb djiù "set out, produce (flowers)" and xua
"flower", its object. The second comment, coordinate to the first in
an "or" relationship, is the word miəi, a common adverb (GS 19). Here
it stands for miəi djiù "has not yet bloomed" and forms with djiù xua
a question involving choice (GS 12).

Paraphrase: "Sir you come from my home town and should know what
is going on there. On the day you left, had the winter plum in front
of my silked window bloomed yet?"

3-7. <u>From the Miɑ̌ng River collection</u> 輞川集 Miɑ̌ng Chiuen
dzhip (Wɑ̌ng Chuān jí)

3. <u>No. 5</u>: Deer Park 鹿柴 Luk Jrhai (Lù Chái)

空山不見人
kung shran biət gèn njin   empty mountain not see person

但聞人語響
dhɑ̌n miən njin ngiǔ xiɑ̌ng   only hear person talk echo

返景入深林
biɑ̌n qiɑ̌ng njip shim lim   return shadow/light enter deep
                                           forest

復照青苔上
bhiuk jiɛu tseng dhəi zhiɑ̌ng   again illuminate green moss rise

                                    (Five-syllable unregulated quatrain)

        Title: Iuɑng Ui's villa was situated near the Miɑ̌ng River, south
of Djhiɑng-qɑn. The collection consists of twenty pairs of five-
syllable quatrains, each on a particular scenic spot on the grounds of
his estate. In each pair of quatrains, the first poem is by Iuɑng Ui
and the second is by a friend. Seven of Iuɑng Ui's poems are recorded
here, of which the first is from the fifth pair. The meaning "park"
for <u>jrhai</u> is an extension of the meaning found at 1.2: from "brush-
wood" to "something made of brushwood, fence" to "fenced-in enclosure,
stockade, park".

        3.1 See GS 36. <u>kung</u> "empty" here must mean "devoid of other
visible persons". Notice the lack of an actor and compare <u>siɑng sùng</u>
in 1.1. <u>biət</u> and <u>njin</u> should be combined in English: "no one, no-
body".

        3.2 The verb <u>miən</u> has <u>xiɑ̌ng</u> as its object; notice again that no
actor is mentioned. <u>dhɑ̌n</u> is an adverb modifying <u>miən</u>, and the phrase
<u>njin ngiǔ</u> (where <u>njin</u> modifies <u>ngiǔ</u>, and that phrase modifies <u>xiɑ̌ng</u>).
The entire line is a comment, either standing alone, with no topic, or
else in a coordinate relationship with the preceding comment, <u>biət gèn</u>
<u>njin</u>, in which case <u>kung shran</u> would be the place topic to both comments.

3.3 biən modifies qiæng (GS 16), and the phrase is actor topic
(GS 34) to three comments, the first of which consists of the three
words that make up the rest of this line. The usual meaning of qiæng
is "shadow", but sometimes it means "shadow-maker, light"; because it
is actor topic to jiɛu "illuminate" in the next line, the latter mean-
ing is more appropriate. njip has lim "collection of trees, grove,
woods, forest" as its place object (GS 21). For the difference between
a place topic and a place object, see GS 39. shim lim biən qiæng njip
would mean "About the deep forest, my comment is that the returning
light enters it", whereas the present line is more "About the returning
light, my comment is that it enters a deep forest." The emphasis in
the present line is on the whole comment: "entering a deep forest",
which is what is new and interesting.
     One interpretation of this line is that the light is returning at
evening, when the sun is lower in the sky, as it was in the morning,
unblocked by the heavy foliage of the trees so that it can penetrate
into the forest once again on the same day.

     3.4 bhiuk modifies jiɛu, which has dhəi (modified by tseng) as
its object. These four words constitute the second comment to biən
qiæng in the preceding line. zhiǎng is the third comment. The three
comments are in a coordinate relationship.

     Paraphrase: On the empty mountain, no one else is seen; I just
hear the echoes of someone talking. Returning light enters a deep
forest, shines again on green moss, and rises.

4. <u>No. 11</u> Qi Lake 歙湖 Qi Ho (YĪ Hú)

吹簫凌極浦
chui seu liəng ghiək pǒ   blow flute   cross far beach

日暮送夫君
njit mò sùng bio giuən   sun/day evening   send-off man lord

湖上一回首
ho zhiàng qit huəi shiǒu   lake top   one return head

山青卷白雲
shran tseng giuěn bhæk iuən   mountain green/blue/gray   curl
                                           white cloud

                                    (Five-syllable regulated quatrain)

    4.1 The verb-object expression <u>chui seu</u> either stands alone as a
(topicless) comment in a co-ordinate relationship with the rest of the
line, or it is a topic to the rest of the line as a comment (cf. 1.1-2).
In the latter case, it is a time topic: "While playing a flute,..."
or "After playing a flute,...."; or it is an actor topic: "(The sound
of your) playing a flute...." <u>liəng...pǒ</u> is a verb place-object con-
struction (3.3), and <u>ghiək</u> modifies <u>pǒ</u>. The basic meaning of <u>ghiək</u> is
"end, extreme"; here it is extended to mean "far".

    4.2 <u>njit mò</u>: 1.2. <u>sùng</u> (1.1) has a direct object here: <u>bio
giuən</u>, a modifier-modified phrase, used as an honorific term of address
to a friend. The four main parts of these two lines may be all in co-
ordinate relationships, or various topic-comment relationships may ob-
tain, with <u>sùng bio giuən</u> as the final comment, or some combination of
these two relationships may obtain.

    4.3 <u>ho zhiàng</u> is a place topic (2.3). <u>qit</u> as an adverb means
"once". <u>huəi</u> is often intransitive: "return"; when it is transitive,
as here, it means "make...turn around", so <u>huəi shiǒu</u> means "make the
head turn around, turn back the head (to look)".

    4.4 <u>shran</u> is a topic to the following two comments. It is the
subject (1.3) to the first comment, <u>tseng</u>, an intransitive verb that
translates as an English adjective (GS 9): "green, blue, gray".
Usually it is possible to tell which color is meant (see its occur-
rence at 3.4, for example); here it is ambiguous. <u>shran</u> is the actor
topic to the second comment, the verb-object phrase <u>giuěn iuən</u>. <u>giuěn</u>
is usually an intransitive verb: "be curling", but here, with a direct
object, it is transitive: "make...curl, set...curling".

A translation emphasizing coordination:

    you play a flute   cross to a distant beach

    the day is at evening   I have sent off my lord

    on the lake   turn the head back once

    the mountain is gray   and sets a white cloud curling

Another translation emphasizing subordination:

    while playing a flute   after crossing to a distant beach

    when the day is at dusk   I have sent off my lord

    on the lake   upon turning the head back once

    where the mountain is gray   it sets a white cloud curling

5. No. 13:   Luan Family Rapids   欒家瀨 Luɑn Gɑ Lài
(Luǎn Jiā Lài)

颯 颯 秋 雨 中
sop-sop tsiou iǒ djiung   (blowing wind) autumn rain midst

淺 淺 石 溜 瀉
tsiěn tsiěn zhiæk liǒu siǎ   shallow shallow stone slip slide

跳 波 自 相 濺
dheu bɑ   dzhì siɑng tziɛn   jump wave of-themselves each-other
                                  splash

白 鷺 驚 復 下
bhæk lò   giæng bhiuk hǎ   white egret startle and descend

                                  (Five-syllable unregulated quatrain)

        Title: luɑn, in addition to being a surname, is also the name of
a kind of tree, so the title could also read: "Rapids by Luɑn-tree
House".

        5.1 sop-sop is a descriptive (GS 4) modifying the phrase tsiou
iǒ; then all four words modify djiung (GS 17), and the resulting phrase
is a place topic (GS 37) to the next line as comment.

        5.2 tsiěn tsiěn is intensive (GS 3). zhiæk is a place topic
to liǒu "(water) slip": "on stone the water slips"--the phrase is a
compound meaning "waterfall". siǎ is virtually synonymous to liǒu
"(water) slide"; it is an (actorless) comment to the first four words
as another place topic, the whole line being a topic-comment comment
on the first line: "Amid autumn rain in whooshing (wind), over the
waterfall, so shallow, (water) slides."

        5.3 dheu modifies bɑ (cf. biǎn qiǎng at 3.3), and the phrase is
an actor topic to the rest of the line. siɑng modifies tziɛn, and both
words are in turn modified by dzhì (GS 19).

        5.4 Another actor topic, followed by two intransitive verbs, the
first meaning "start up, take flight", in a coordinate relationship
overtly marked by the conjunction bhiuk (GS 14).

6. <u>No. 17</u>: Hut in bamboos 竹里館 Djiuk lǐ guàn
(Zhú lǐ guǎn)

獨坐幽篁裏
dhuk dzhuǎ qiou huɑng lǐ

弾琴復長嘯
dhɑn ghim bhiuk djhiɑng sèu

深林人不知
shim lim njin biət dji

明月來相照
miæng ngiuæt ləi siɑng jièu

alone sit   secluded bamboo-thicket
            inside

pluck (zither) again long whistle

deep forest   person not know

bright moon   come mutually illumi-
              nate

(Five-syllable unregulated (?) quatrain)

Title: <u>lǐ</u> "inside" (usually written 裏 , as in Line 1, below)
forms a place expression (GS 17) with <u>djiuk</u> "bamboo", and this expres-
sion modifies <u>guàn</u>, usually "inn, hostel", here "outbuilding, hut".
This is one of the best known Dhɑng poems. The question of whether or
not this poem is regulated is discussed in Prosodic note 7, p. 54.

6.1 <u>dhuk</u> is an adverb modifying <u>dzhuǎ</u>. <u>qiou huɑng lǐ</u> is the
place object (GS 21, 39; 3.3). The whole line is a topicless comment.

6.2 This line consists of two more topicless comments. <u>bhiuk</u>:
5.4 <u>ghim</u> "(zither)": GS 1, footnote. A <u>ghim</u> is a plucked, stringed
musical instrument. It has five or seven strings on a long, shallow,
oblong body that is placed crosswise in front of the performer. <u>sèu</u>
"engage in whistling" is an intransitive verb, modified by the adverb
<u>djhiɑng</u> "at length, protractedly".

6.3 <u>shim lim</u>: 3.3. Combine <u>njin</u> and <u>biət</u>: 3.1. <u>biət dji</u>:
GS 28.

6.4 <u>miæng ngiuæt</u>: actor topic to two comments, <u>ləi</u> and <u>siɑng</u>
<u>jièu</u>, in a coordinate relationship, but see GS 15. <u>siɑng</u>: 1.1.

7. __No. 18__: Magnolia Wall 辛夷塢 Sin-i Qǒ (Xīn-yí Wù)

木末芙蓉花

muk mɑt bhio-iong xua   tree end   lotus flower

山 中 發 紅 萼

shran djiung biæt hung ngɑk   mountain midst   produce red calyx

澗 戶 寂 無 人

gàn hǒ dzhek mio njin   stream gate   quiet not-have person

紛 紛 開 且 落

piən piən kəi tsiǎ lɑk   scattered scattered open and fall

                                         (Five-syllable regulated quatrain)

Title: __sin-i__: GS 1.

7.1 __muk__ "tree" stands for "branch"--an example of synecdoche: here, the name of the whole stands for the name of the part. __muk mɑt__ is a place topic (GS 36) to a comment that extends through the second line. This comment consists in turn of another topic-comment construction, with the topic here, __bhio-iong xua__, naming the actor of the verb __biæt__ in the next line. __bhio-iong__ "lotus" is another two-syllable word; this water plant with large, lush blossoms is used as a metaphor for the magnolia blossoms.

7.2 This line, comment to the first line, is again in turn a topic-comment construction. Here the topic, __shran djiung__, is another place topic. The comment consists of a transitive verb __biæt__ "let loose, produce (flowers)" and a direct object __ngɑk__ (modified by __hung__). Extracting the actor, the verb, and the direct object from these two lines, we get "flowers produce calyces", which does not make much sense unless we take "flower" to be general, not fixed in time or place, and "calyx" to be the particular manifestation of "flowers" here and now. "Calyx" is therefore another synecdoche, but this time a word for a part stands for a word for the whole.
    For another long string of comments successively analyzed as themselves consisting of topic-comment constructions, see 2.3-4.

7.3 __gàn__ is more precisely "stream in a mountain ravine". It modifies __hǒ__ "one-leafed door, door" here standing for "dwelling"-- another synecdoche. The phrase is a topic to two comments. First, it is the subject (GS 9, 35) of __dzhek__. Then it is a place topic to __mio njin__, where __mio__ "not have, there is not" is the negative correlate to __iǒu__ (GS 44). For __njin__ with a negative, see 3.1 and 6.3.

7.4 __piən piən__ is intensive (GS 3, 5.2). The two intransitive verbs __kəi__ and __lɑk__ are in a coordinate construction that is overtly expressed by __tsiǎ__, a frequent "and" between verbs (GS 14, 6.2). Two possible analyses of the line are: (1) __piən piən__ constitutes a separate comment, coordinate to the rest of the line: "They are so scattered, opening and falling"; (2) __piən piən__ is adverbial to the two verbs that follow: "They very scatteredly open and fall."

8. Seeing Ngiuæn Number Two off; he is being sent on a mission to Qan-sei   送元二便安西   Sùng Ngiuæn Njì; shrì Qan-sei (Sòng Yuán Èr; shì An-xi)

渭城朝雨裛輕塵

iuɜi zhiæng djiɛu iǒ

  qip kiæng djhin

客舍青青柳色新

kæk shià tseng tseng

  liǒu shriɜk sin

勸君更盡一杯酒

kiuæn giuən gæng dzhǐn

  qit bɜi tziǒu

西出陽關無故人

sei chuit iɑng guan

  mio gò njin

Iuɜi City   morning rain
  moisten light dust

traveler shelter green green
  willow color new

urge lord more finish
  one cup wine

west go-out Iɑng Pass
  have-not old-time person

(Seven-syllable regulated quatrain)

Prosodic note 2: Seven-syllable <u>shi</u>

The seven <u>shi</u> introduced so far have had five-syllable lines. The other important category of Dhɑng <u>shi</u> is the seven-syllable <u>shi</u>, composed of seven-syllable lines. A seven-syllable line is essentially a five-syllable line with two syllables added at the beginning. There are two fixed caesuras, one after the second syllable, another after the fourth; a third caesura comes after the fifth or sixth syllable, depending on the natural break in the grammatical structure of the line. Extrapolating from modern reading practice, we may guess that in spite of the addition of an extra beat to the line, a seven-syllable line occupies the same four-beat space as a five-syllable line: the fourth beat, which in the case of the five-syllable line is silent, falls on the last foot of the seven-syllable line. Thus:

1	2	3	4
iuɜi zhiæng,	djiɛu iǒ,	qip,	kiæng djhin
kæk shià,	tseng tseng,	liǒu shriɜk,	sin

kiuæn giuən,   gæng dzhǐn,   qit bəi,   tziǒu

sei chuit,   iang guan,   mio   gò njin

Title: Ngiuæn is a surname. Chinese surnames regularly precede
given names, titles, and informal names. One way to address a person
is to give his surname and follow it with a number representing his
rank according to age held among the male members of his generation in
the family--brothers and cousins. Beyond what can be inferred from the
title of this poem, we know nothing of Mr. Ngiuæn. Qan-sei is the name
of a Chinese outpost in the far west, near the modern Turfan. This
poem has another title: "Song of Iuòi City 渭城曲 Iuòi Zhiæng kiok
(Wèi Chéng qǔ)".

8.1 The Iuòi River flows just north of the Western Capital,
Djhiang Qan. Iuòi City is on the north bank, about 20 km. northwest of
the capital; it is thus a natural place to send off a friend who is go-
ing to a western outpost. The four main constituents of the line are:
place topic, actor topic, verb, object.

8.2 The main division of the line is at the second caesura. The
first part, consisting of the first four syllables, divides at the first
caesura, and the constituents are: topic, comment. In the second
part, the main constituents are in topic-comment relationship. The two
main parts of the whole line may be treated as though they were in a
coordinate "and" relationship; treating them as though they were in a
topic-comment relationship, however, and interpreting this relation-
ship as indicating that the cause for the condition described in the
topic is given in the comment, results in the following translation:
"The hostel is so green because the willow color is new(ly arrived)."

8.3 giuən: GS 43. gæng is an adverb to dzhǐn. tziǒu, strictly
speaking, is "alcoholic beverage", not just wine. Notice how the ad-
verb travels in English: "more finish wine" must be reordered to
"finish more wine". qit bəi is a number-measure expression and modi-
fies tziǒu: "wine in the amount of one cup"; a more fluent English
version reverses the modification: "one cup of wine".

8.4 For another place object, see 3.3; njip "enter (into)" and
chuit "emerge (from), go beyond" are semantic opposites. sei is an
adverb to chuit, and the whole clause "westwardly go beyond Iang Pass"
ought to be reordered: "go west beyond Iang Pass". Iang Pass is
the name of one of two passes that provide access to the territory west
of the Dhang heartland. Since it is even farther west than Qan-sei,
it is an example of hyperbole. These four words constitute a time
topic (GS 36) to the rest of the line. The time relationship is either
"when" or "after" the action of the topic occurs, the condition de-
scribed in the comment will obtain. gò: 2.1.

9. Composed in reply to Secretary So of the Board of Concern,
who passed by the villa at Indigo Field but did not stay

酬州虞部蘇員外過藍田別業不見留之作

Zhiou Ngio Bhǒ So Iuɛn-nguǎi guà Lom Dhen bhiɛt-ngiæp, biət gèn liou
ji tzɑk (Chóu Yú Bù Sū Yuán-wài guò Lán Tián bié-yè, bú jiàn liú zhī zuò)

貧居依谷口

bhin giu qiəi guk kǒu   poor dwelling set-in valley mouth

喬木帶荒村

ghiɛu muk dài xuɑng tsuən   tall tree belt ruined village

石路枉迴駕

zhiæk lò qiuǎng huəi gà   stone road purposeless return ride

山家誰候門

shran ga zhui hòu mən   mountain home who? attend gate

5 漁舟膠凍浦

ngiu jiou gau dùng pǒ   fish boat get-stuck freeze shore

獵火燒寒原

liɛp xuǎ shiɛu hɑn ngiuæn   hunt fire burn cold plain

惟有白雲外

ui iǒu bhæk iuən nguài   only have white cloud outside

疎鐘聞夜猿

shriu jiong miən ià iuæn   sparse bell hear night gibbon

(Five-syllable regulated poem)

Title: The civil government of Dhɑng China had six Boards 部
Bhǒ (Bù). One of these, the Board of Works, had a subdivision called
the Board of Concern 虞部 Ngio Bhǒ (Yú Bù), whose head was a Secre-
tary 員外 Iuɛn-nguài (Yuán-wài). This board concerned itself with
parks and forests. We know nothing about the man surnamed So mentioned
here, other than his official position and the incident referred to in
this poem. Indigo Field 藍田 Lom Dhen (Lán Tián) is the name of the
district south of Djhiɑng-qɑn where Iuɑng Ui's bhiɛt-ngiæp "other resi-
dence, villa" and surrounding parks were located (see Poems 3-7). A
grammatical analysis of the title is roughly as follows: zhiou "to

reply" has ngio bhǒ so iuɛn-nguǎi as a pivot (GS 43) to two comments:
the first consists of a verb guà "pass by, visit" and a place object
lom dhen bhiɛt-ngiæp; the second consists of an adverb biət "not", an
auxiliary verb (GS 25) gèn "see", extended here to "experience", and a
verb liou "stay, detain". The effect of gèn is to turn a following
transitive verb into a verb with passive meaning: "did not experience
being detained", or, more smoothly expressed, "did not stay". tzɑk
"compose" is the main word of the entire title, the preceding words
comprising a modifying clause where the modifier-modified relationship
is overtly expressed by the particle ji (GS 20).

9.1 qiəi "depend on, be set in" takes a place object. The main
word of the place expression here, kǒu, basically means "mouth", but as
a place noun it means "beginning, opening".

9.2 dài is here a transitive verb: "form a belt around". It is
conventional in writing shi to characterize one's own home as poor and
in barren, wasted surroundings; Iuɑng Ui's villa was surely in beauti-
ful surroundings and appropriately staffed with servants.

9.3 zhiæk lò: place topic. qiuǎng "under conditions of not
having achieved (your) purpose, to no purpose" is an adverb modifying
the following verb-object phrase. huəi "return, cause to return" is
transitive here, with gà "ride (in a carriage)", originally a verb,
here a noun and the direct object of huəi. (Note that huəi also ap-
pears in 4.3, but written differently.)

9.4 zhui "who?" appearing pre-verbally, as here, is counted as an
adverb for purposes of parallelism (see below, "Prosodic note 3").

9.5 ngiu "to fish (as an occupation)" modifies jiou. dùng mod-
ifies pǒ; the phrase is the place object of gau.

9.6 liɛp "hunt (game)" modifies xuǎ. hɑn modifies ngiuæn, and
again the phrase is place object to shiɛu.

9.7 iǒu "have, there is", with no topic, is modified by ui:
"There was only..., all that there was....". The object of iǒu is a
sentence consisting of the rest of this line and all of the next. The
first main element of this sentence is a place topic (the first of two)
consisting of the last three words in this line.

9.8 shriu jiong is the second place topic: "(amid) sparse (tol-
ling of) bells". The actor of miən has to be supplied; it is probably
the persona: "(I) hear...", or, nominalizing the English so that the
sentence will fit properly after the translation of iǒu: "(my) hear-
ing....". Thus: "All that there was...was my hearing a nighttime
gibbon." The gibbon was once widespread over China. Its loud singing
cries are often mentioned in poems and are associated with sadness.

Prosodic note 3: Poem length, parallelism,

and the regulated poem

Poems of the type shi are generally no shorter than four lines
nor longer than two or three hundred. Two favorite lengths are four

lines, as in the quatrains presented above, Poem 1-8, and eight lines,
as in this poem.

It is true of shi, and indeed of Chinese formal writing in general,
that there is parallelism of grammar and meaning obtaining between two
(or more, especially in the case of prose) phrases, clauses, or sen-
tences. In shi, parallelism, when it occurs, obtains between adjacent
feet or half-lines within a line, or between the two lines of a couplet.
Such pairs of units are parallel if the words that occupy the same po-
sition in them have meanings that are of the same general semantic area,
and have the same grammatical relationships to the other words in the
unit. In Poem 9, Line 1 is parallel to Line 2: "poor" and "tall", the
first words in each line, modify the second words: "dwelling" and
"tree", and in each line, the first two words comprise the actor topic,
with the rest of the line as comment. The third words are both verbs:
"set in" and "to belt", and the fourth and fifth words, in both cases
comprising a noun phrase where the fourth word modifies the fifth, make
up place objects: "valley's mouth" and "ruined village".

Parallelism between the two lines of a couplet is an important
feature of regulated poetry. In general, shi are divided into two
classes: regulated (or new-style) and unregulated (or old-style).
Regulation has to do primarily with the arrangement of the tones of
syllables within the line and between lines; the details will be dis-
cussed in "Prosodic note 4", after the next poem. The majority of
regulated poems are four or eight lines long, but longer ones do exist.
The three defining characteristics of the regulated poem, stated in
terms of the eight-line variant, are: (1) the lines are tonally regu-
lated, (2) there is one rhyme throughout the poem placed on the even
lines (with the first line rhyming optionally), and (3) the lines of
the two middle couplets are parallel. (The first and last couplets are
optionally parallel.)

10. In reply to County Police Chief Djiang 酬張少府 Zhiou
Djiang Shiłu-biǒ (Chóu Zhāng Shào-fǔ)

晚年唯好静
miǎn nen ui xòu dzhiǎng   late year   only like quiet

萬事不關心
miǎn jrhì biət guan sim   ten-thousand affair   not concern
                                              heart

自顧無長策
dzhì gò mio djhiang chræk   self take-care   have-not long
                                              strategy

空知返舊林
kung dji biǎn ghiòu lim   vain know   return old-time grove

松風吹解帶
5 ziong biung chui gǎi dài   pine wind   blow loosen belt

山月照彈琴
shran ngiuæt jiłu dhən ghim   mountain moon   illuminate pluck
                                              (zither)

君問窮通理
giuən miən ghiung tung lǐ   lord ask   exhaust pervade principle

漁歌入浦深
ngiu ga   njip pǒ shim   fish song   enter shore deep

                                 (Five-syllable regulated poem)

     Title: It is not known who County Police Chief Djiang was. The
official title that the poet gives him was used many centuries earlier,
not in Dhang times. This sort of archaizing is common in Dhang shi.

     10.1 miǎn nen "years of my old age" is a time topic (GS 36). The
rest of the line is the comment: adverb, verb, object.

     10.2 miǎn is a cardinal number, often used in a general sense:
"all the various". jrhì is somewhat pejorative: "mundane affairs".

     10.1-2 are parallel (see above, "Prosodic note 3", pp. 40-41).

     10.3 dzhì "self, by oneself, of one's own accord" is regularly
an adverb, and must come before the verb. English "self" would be a
direct object and follow the English verb. gò "turn the head to look
back at, look after, care for, take care of". The phrase dzhì gò is
topic to the rest of the line: "About taking care of myself...."
djhiang "long, long-range".

10.4 kung "empty, void" (cf. 3.1); as an adverb: "in vain, to no
purpose, pointlessly"--the word as Iuang Ui uses it has Buddhist over-
tones signifying a locality or a state of mind which is detached from
material, worldly considerations. dji "know, know about, know how to,
know enough to" is an auxiliary verb (GS 25).

10.3-4 are roughly parallel: adverb, verb, modifier, noun in both
lines. But in 10.3, the last three words constitute a comment to the
first two, whereas in 10.4 they constitute a direct object.

Perhaps an expansion of the couplet would be helpful: "I am at
the age now when making long-range plans about personal activities
would be pointless. In a manner devoid of the career expectations
usual among others of my class, I know enough to return to the parks
and groves of my villa at Indigo Fields. It is best for me to do this,
because continued government service would very likely subject me to
compromise and shame. However, the mere consideration of the possibil-
ity of such a retirement would be a waste of time for others of my
class, since for them to do so would mean their denying one of their
main goals as members of the literary elite: to devote their talents
to the proper governing of the nation." The couplet summarizes with
great compression an ambiguity of feeling that is often encountered in
Chinese poetry: mixed with the desire to help mankind through govern-
ment service is a competing desire to avoid the moral compromises which
often mar a government career and to retire from sullying influences of
worldly involvement. Iuang Ui's poetic life is dominated by this idea
of kung; here he says that now, at the end of his life, he can realize
his dream of retiring.

10.5-6: The major constituents of both lines are: actor topic,
verb, object. In both lines the object is modified by a verb: "which
I have loosened" and "which I am plucking", respectively.

10.7 The direct object of the transitive verb miən is the matter
asked about. The main word of the object here is lǐ; the two preceding
words are in coordinate relationship and together modify lǐ: "the lǐ
of ghiung and tung". ghiung and tung occur in a passage from a collec-
tion of Taoist writings, the Jriang-tzǐ 莊子 (Zhuāng-zǐ or Chuang-
tzu), stemming from about the fourth century B.C. and associated with
the philosopher of the same name, ch. 28, "Abdicating princely author-
ity 讓王 Njiàng iuang, (Ràng wáng)":

> Those of ancient times who attained the Way were happy
> when (their resources were) exhausted (ghiung) and when
> (their goals were) pushed through to (tung), but what
> made them happy was neither the exhausting nor the push-
> ing through.

10.8 ngiu (see 9.5) modifies ga; njip pǒ are verb and place ob-
ject; ngiu ga and njip pǒ are actor topic and comment. All four words
constitute a topic to which the last word, shim, is comment. A trans-
lation of the line that preserves the major topic-comment break in the
Chinese line is awkward: "The fishing song's penetration of the shore
is deep."

Prosodic note 4: Tonal regulation

Early in the history of shi, poets began to pay attention to tonal
balance within the line and between the lines of a couplet, and to ton-
al variety from couplet to couplet. By Dhang times, the subgenre
called "regulated shi 律詩 luit shi (lü shī)" had evolved specific
and carefully observed rules about tonal distribution.

For the purposes of regulated shi, the four tonal categories (see
Chapter 2) are regrouped into two: one called "level 平 bhiæng
(píng)", identical to the "level" tone category, and the other called
"oblique 仄 jriək (zé or tse)", comprising the other three tone cate-
gories: "raised", "departing", and "entering". In terms of the pres-
ent transcription these two groups are marked as follows: a syllable
is "level" if the spelling includes no diacritic and if it does not end
in -p, -t, or -k; a syllable· is "oblique" if the spelling includes a
diacritic or if it ends in -p, -t, or -k. In discussing tonal regula-
tion it is convenient to extract the tonal value of a syllable and
identify it alone according to this two-term system: o if the syllable
is "level", x if it is "oblique".

The tones of the syllables in 10.1 may now be extracted and writ-
ten out separately as follows:

x o o x x

This line is a perfect illustration of the principle of tonal balance
within the line, which may be roughly formulated thus: alternate syl-
lables alternate tones. The alternation of the tones of the two sets
of alternate syllables in this line can be shown as follows: one set
of alternate syllables comprises the first, third and fifth syllables.
Their tones alternate: x...o...x. The other set comprises the second
and fourth syllables, and their tones alternate, too: ...o...x....

The tones of 10.2 are:

x x x o o

The tones of the first, third, and fifth syllables do not alternate
properly. Which syllable (or syllables) has the wrong tone? Are the
tones on the third and fifth syllables wrong? No, because the fifth
syllable must rhyme, and in order to rhyme with the syllables at the
end of the even-numbered lines in this poem, it must have the same tone
as they have: it must have the "level" tone, and indeed it has. So
the tones of the fifth and the third syllables follow the alternation
rule. It is the first syllable that has the wrong tone. The line
should go:

o x x o o

The tones of the first and third syllables of a regulated five-
syllable line break the alternation rule often enough to merit a re-
vision of the rule:

The alternation rule: The alternate syllables in a line
alternate tones, with the occasional exception of the
first and third syllables in a five-syllable line.

The corrected tones of the couplet are:

x o o x x

o x x o o

The tone patterns of this couplet illustrate

The inversion rule: The tone patterns of the two lines
of a couplet are opposite.

The next rule is best observed in a display of the tone patterns
of all the lines of the poem. First the patterns of two more lines
should be "corrected" in order to show their underlying ideal forms.
10.5 is:

o o o x x

The fifth syllable has the correct tone, opposite to that of the rhyme;
the tone of the third syllable is also correct, opposite to that of the
fifth. The first syllable has a wrong tone: it should be opposite to
that of the third. The ideal line is therefore:

x o o x x

10.7 is:

o x o o x

and, following the same line of reasoning as in 10.5, we discover that
the first syllable has a wrong tone. The ideal line is:

x x o o x

Now the ideal version of the whole poem, couplet by couplet:

10.1-2:	x o o x x	o x x o o
10.3-4:	x x o o x	o o x x o
10.5-6:	x o o x x	o x x o o
10.7-8:	x x o o x	o o x x o

These patterns illustrate

The diversity rule: In any four adjacent lines, no tone
pattern appears more than once.

Some implications of these rules should be pointed out now. First, the alternation rule guarantees that there will be only four possible ideal (corrected) tonal patterns for the regulated line. Second, the diversity rule guarantees that alternate couplets will have identical ideal tonal patterns. Now, regulated eight-line poems almost always rhyme in the "level" tone. This fact leads to a third implication, namely, that there are for all intents and purposes only two ideal tonal patterns for an eight-line five-syllable regulated poem: one is the one in Poem 10, the other is one that would start with the tone pattern of the second couplet of Poem 10, continue through the poem, and end with the tone pattern of the first couplet of Poem 10 as that of its last couplet.

The actual and ideal tone patterns for Poem 9 are:

Actual:	Ideal:
o o o x x	x o o x x
o x x o o	o x x o o
x x x o x	x x o o x
o o o x o	o o x x o
o o o x x	x o o x x
x x o o o	o x x o o
o x x o x	x x o o x
o o o x o	o o x x o

Poem 9 has an ideal tone pattern that is identical with that of Poem 10. Notice, however, that in Poem 9 that poem takes more frequent advantage of the options provided for in the alternation rule: there are 9 wrong tones on the first and third syllables of the lines of Poem 9 as compared to only 3 in Poem 10. (There are, of course, a total of 16 options available.) Notice further that in all but one line (9.1) wrong tones are balanced, either within the line (as in 9.6 and 9.7) where the wrong tones on both the first and third syllables balance each other, or between corresponding syllables in the two lines of a couplet (as in the first syllables of 9.5-6 and the third syllables of 9.3-4 and 9.7-8).

The regulation of seven-syllable verse involves the same principles as that of five-syllable verse. Regulated quatrains have slightly different principles of tonal balance. Finally, there is the disturbance of the tonal pattern brought about when a poet takes the option of having the first line rhyme. These matters will be treated in detail later.

The rules for regulated poetry are based on Downer and Graham 1963; see also Stimson 1968.43.

11. Suffering from heat 苦熱 Kǒ njiɛt (Kǔ rè)

赤日滿天地
chiæk njit   mǎn ten dhì   red sun   fill sky earth

火雲成山嶽
xuǎ iuən   zhiæng shran ngak   fire cloud   complete hill
                                                   sacred-mountain

草木盡焦卷
tsǎu muk   dzhǐn tziɛu giuěn   grass tree   exhaust scorch curl

川澤皆竭涸
chiuɛn djhæk   gai ghiɛt hɑk   river pond   all dry-up dry-up

5 輕紈覺衣重
  kiæng huɑn   gak qiəi djhiòng   lightweight (white, unbleached silk)
                                                   feel clothes heavy

密樹苦陰薄
mit zhiò   kǒ qim bhɑk   dense tree   bitter shade thin

莞簟不可近
guɑn dhěm   biət kǎ ghiàn   rush-mat bamboo-mat   not can
                                                   approach

絺綌再三濯
djhi kiæk   tzòi som djhak   fine-linen coarse-linen   again
                                                   three wash

思出宇宙外
si chuit   iǒ djhiòu nguɑ̀i   think exit   space time beyond

10 曠然在寥廓
   kuàng-njiɛn   dzhěi leu kuɑk   expansive -ly   be-at void void

長風萬里來
djhiɑng biung   miæn lǐ ləi   long wind   ten-thousand (mile) come

江海蕩煩濁
gang xǒi   dhǎng bhiæn djhak   river sea   cleanse trouble dirt

却顧身爲患
kiɑk gò   shin ui huɑ̀n   but regard   body be misfortune

始 知 心 未 覺
shǐ dji sim miᵊi gak   begin know heart not-yet awake

忽 入 甘 露 門
15 xuᵊt njip gom lᵇ mᵊn   sudden enter sweet dew gate

宛 然 清 涼 樂
qiu�æn-njiεn tsiæng liang lɑk   winding -ly pure cool joy

                                        (Five-syllable old-style poem)

     Title: The basic meaning of kǒ "bitter" is extended in a putative
sense: "consider...bitter, consider...a cause for pain, suffer from".

     11.1-2 The lines of this couplet are parallel: actor topic,
verb, object. zhiæng is ambiguous: "become, be made into"--and the
clouds are described as piling up into firy mountains in the sky.
Another meaning: "completely fill"--and the clouds are described as
filling the entire space of a mountainous area on earth. For the co-
ordinate objects of the verbs, see GS 6.

     11.3-4 Again, parallel: subject (GS 9), adverb, and intransitive
verbs in a coordinate relationship (GS 9, GS 6). dzhǐn (cf. 8.3) ap-
pears with a common extension of its basic meaning "finish, exhaust":
"exhaustively, completely, in all cases"--an adverb. Parallel to it is
gai, which is only an adverb: "in all cases". In English, it is pos-
sible to use adjectives to translate these words: "All the grasses and
trees...; Every river and pond...." ghiεt and hɑk are synonyms, both
meaning "use up", here extended to "dry up".

     11.5-6 Parallel: topic, verb, sentence object. In both lines,
the topic and the actor are different, and the topic is quite vaguely
related to the comment (GS 30). In both lines, this topic merely spec-
ifies the circumstances under which the action of the verb takes place,
whereas the actor is the persona and is unexpressed. Thus, in 11.5:
"(Under the circumstances of wearing) lightweight huɑn(-silk clothing),
(I)...." Both gak and kǒ have transitive meanings and often have as
their objects whole sentences: "...that (my) clothing is (too) heavy;
...that (their) shade is (too) thin/inadequate."

     11.7-8 Roughly parallel: topic, verbal comment. In Line 7, the
transitive verb is preceded by an adverb and the auxiliary kɑ̌ (GS 25,
41). In Line 8, the transitive verb is preceded by two adverbs, which
form a compound: tzᵇi "a second time, again" plus som "three, a third
time": tzᵇi som "two or three times", extended to "again and again".

     11.9 si is an auxiliary, taking as its object all the rest of the
line, and possibly all of the next line, too (cf. dji in 10.4). iǒ
djhiᵇu "space and time" refers to the real universe. The phrase forms
a place expression with the place noun nguᵃi "outside" (GS 17) and
functions as the place object (GS 21) of chuit "proceed out". Here,
"at, to", translating the meaning of the place object position, plus
"outside", translating nguᵃi, plus "of", translating the subordinate
relationship that obtains between iǒ djhiᵇu and nguᵃi, collapse into
the single English word "beyond" (cf. GS 38, 39).

11.10 n̲j̲i̲ɛ̲n̲:   GS 5. d̲z̲h̲ə̲̌i̲ "be at, be located in" takes a place
object. l̲e̲u̲ k̲u̲ɑ̲k̲:   GS 6.

11.11 d̲j̲h̲i̲ɑ̲n̲g̲ here means "from a great distance". In Chinese,
m̲i̲ă̲n̲ "10,000" is the next counting unit higher than t̲s̲e̲n̲ "thousand"
(see below, 16.22). Thus "3,000" is s̲o̲m̲ t̲s̲e̲n̲, and "30,000" is s̲o̲m̲
m̲i̲ă̲n̲. But m̲i̲ă̲n̲ is also used for designating any unspecified large
number: "myriad". A Chinese l̲ǐ̲ is a linear measure roughly equivalent
to one-third of an English mile, or about one-half of a kilometer. The
phrase m̲i̲ă̲n̲ l̲ǐ̲ is adverbial to l̲ə̲i̲: "...from a myriad l̲ǐ̲ away".

11.12 d̲h̲ǎ̲n̲g̲ could also be translated "wash away".

11.13 k̲i̲ɑ̲k̲ is an adversitive adverb, usually best translated by
one of the English conjunctions "but, nevertheless". Here it seems to
mean "now (I see things differently, and)...." s̲h̲i̲n̲ is a pivot: GS 43.
The basic meaning of u̲i̲ is "make, do", but it frequently has an extend-
ed meaning: "take the role of, be".

11.14 s̲h̲ǐ̲ "begin", here either an auxiliary verb (GS 25), or an
adverb: "beginningly, only then". d̲j̲i̲: 10.4. In 2.4, m̲i̲ə̲i̲ made a
rare appearance as a full verb: this common negative is most often an
adverb, as here.

11.15 x̲u̲ə̲t̲ is an adverb modifying n̲j̲i̲p̲. g̲o̲m̲ l̲b̲ is a Buddhist
term referring to the teachings of Buddhism. g̲o̲m̲ l̲b̲ m̲ə̲n̲ is a name of
the gate to the Buddhist nirvana.

11.16 n̲j̲i̲ɛ̲n̲ (cf. Line 10, above) forms a descriptive with the
preceding syllable (GS 4, 5), and the phrase functions as a comment in
a rhetorical inversion (GS 45): "How windingly (pervasive) will the
pure, cool joy be!"

Prosodic note 5:   Old-style poems

Unregulated s̲h̲i̲ are called "old-style poems" 古詩 g̲ǒ̲ shi (gǔ shī).
Some old-style poems, especially those that imitate songs, have lines
of unequal number of syllables, but most have lines all consisting of
the same number of syllables, five per line (as here), or seven per
line.

There is no constraint on the number of lines in an old-style
poem, but they tend to be longer than eight lines. Even-numbered lines
generally rhyme; sometimes more than one rhyme is used in a single
poem. Rhyming is freer than in regulated poetry. In Poem 11, rhymes
are drawn from two rhyme groups: -ak and -ɑk: the pronunciation of
these finals was close enough for the rhymes to work. In regulated
poems, however, the two rhymes were generally kept apart.

The lines are not tonally regulated.

Caesura placement in five- or seven-syllable old-style poems is
the same as in regulated poems.

12. <u>First</u> <u>of</u> <u>two</u> Hymns of the Goddess of Fish Mountain 魚山
神女祠歌 Ngiu Shran Jhin-niǔ zi-gɑ (Yú-Shān Shén-niǔ cí-gē): Verse
welcoming the divinity 迎神曲 Ngiæng jhin kiok (Yíng shén qǔ)

坎 坎 擊 鼓
kǒm-kǒm gek gǒ   (drumbeat) hit drum

魚 山 之 下
ngiu shran ji hǎ   fish mountain -'s bottom

吹 洞 簫
chui dhùng seu   blow hole flute

望 極 浦
miàng ghiək pǒ   gaze far beach

女 巫 進
5 niǔ mio tzìn   woman shaman approach

紛 屢 舞
piən liǒ miǒ   scatter slipper dance

陳 瑤 席
djhin iɛu ziæk   spread (fine jade) mat

湛 清 酤
djham tsiæng hǒ   fill-to-brim pure day-old-liquor

風 淒 淒 兮 夜 雨
biung tsei-tsei hei   wind (cold, desolate) oh

ià iǒ   night rain

10 神 之 來 兮 不 來
jhin ji ləi hei   divinity -'s come oh

biət ləi   not come

便 我 心 兮 苦 復 苦
shrǐ ngǎ sim hei   cause my heart oh

kǒ bhiuk kǒ   bitter again bitter

                        (Music Bureau poem)

Title: There is a Fish Mountain in western Shān-dōng Province,
near the modern Dōng-è Xiàn 東阿縣 . This poem imitates shamanistic
god-summoning hymns of the third century B.C., associated with the
southern Chinese state of Chriǔ 楚 (Chǔ), which was not originally
part of the Chinese heartland and was still regarded as exotic, though
it actually had become quite thoroughly imbued with Chinese civiliza-
tion.

12.1 The descriptive here is genuinely onomatopoeic. It is
either an adverb modifying the following verb, or it is a comment to
the following topic, in a rhetorical inversion.

12.2 <u>ji</u>: GS 20. For the order of the objects of <u>gek</u>, see GS 24.

12.3 A <u>seu</u> is played vertically, like a recorder. A dhùng <u>seu</u>
is "holed", which means that it is unstopped: unblocked at the end.

12.6 <u>piən lið</u> modifies <u>mið</u>.

12.9 It is typical of the <u>Songs of the state of</u> Chǔ (see "General
background",p.viii) to use the rhetorical particle <u>hei</u> "oh" at the end
of the line, or before the caesura in the middle of the line (as here).
In this line, the first three syllables constitute a sentence: topic,
followed by a descriptive comment. The relationship to the last two
syllables of the line is either coordinate: "The wind is desolate,
oh; in the night: rain", or topic-comment: "(The reason why) the wind
is (so) desolate, oh, is (because of) rain in the night."

12.10 <u>ji</u>: GS 42. Here, "the divinity's coming" had better be
interpreted further: "whether the divinity will come", to go with the
second half of the choice-type question (GS 12): "...or not come".
This line constitutes a topic, to which the last line of the poem is
the comment.

12.11 <u>sim</u> is a pivot (GS 43). <u>bhiuk</u> here indicates progressive
increase in the intensity of the quality or action specified in the
words immediately preceding and following: "get bitterer and bitterer",
"suffer more and more".

Prosodic note 6: Music Bureau poetry

An important subgroup of old-style poetry is called Music Bureau
poetry 樂府詩 <u>Ngak Bið shi</u> (Yuè Fǔ shī, or Yüeh Fu shih). A Music
Bureau (<u>Ngak Bið</u>) was set up early in the Xàn Dynasty (see "General
background",p.viii, Table 1) to collect popular songs and ballads. The
purpose of doing this was to enable the Emperor and the governing of-
ficials to understand from the songs what the unspoken needs of the
people were and how they felt about the activities of the government.
Folk songs collected then and later, and poems written by literati in
the style of these songs came to be called Music Bureau poetry, an ex-
ample of which is Poem 12.

Typical of Music Bureau poetry is the use of lines of various
length in a given poem. As in all old-style poetry, there is no regu-
lation of tones. There is occasional use of archaic rhyme, as here,
when <u>hǎ</u> (from Old Chinese <u>grǎg</u>) in Line 2 rhymes with <u>-o</u> (from Old
Chinese -<u>ǎg</u> without the medial -<u>r-</u>).

Chapter 4

Note to the student: Beginning with this chapter, you will be en-
couraged to learn how to use a Chinese dictionary that is arranged in
the traditional way. Such a dictionary is the "Glossary" at the end of
this volume, beginning on page 191. You should now read the introduc-
tion to the "Glossary", where the elements of the structure of Chinese
characters are presented. In order to use the glossary, you will have
to know how to write Chinese characters accurately, at least to the ex-
tent that you can correctly count the number of strokes in a character
or in a part of a character, and you should be able to identify the
radical under which a character is classified in the traditional system,
at least when the radical is common and obvious.

You will be encouraged to use the glossary gradually. For the
time being, every character will be assigned a character-remainder code
(see p. 179), so that you can refer to the glossary entry easily. At
the same time, you should verify the radical--be sure that you can
identify it in the character--and the number of strokes in the remain-
der. You should also begin your own list of characters encountered so
far, for easy reference. Codes for characters will be given the first
time they appear beginning with Poem 13. Codes will not be repeated
for recurring characters, unless the character has a new meaning.

Lǐ Bhæk 李 白 (Lǐ Bái or Lǐ Bó, Li Po, 701-762)

The second of the three greatest High Dhang poets, Lǐ Bhæk, was
born two years after Iuang Ui and died three years after him. Lǐ Bhæk,
in his early forties, served the Dhang court briefly as a member of the
national scholarly organization known as the Hàn-lim 翰 林 (Hàn-
lín) Academy. After only about a year, he was dismissed. Except for
this period, he traveled for most of his life from his mid-twenties on.
He managed to avoid the difficulties of the main rebellion of the 750's
in the north, but in 757 he got involved with rebel forces in the south-
east, and when the rebellion there was put down in that year, he was
arrested as a collaborator and briefly incarcerated. He was released
through the intervention of a friend, and in the next year he was ex-
iled to an area in the southwest, but on the way there he was pardoned.
During the last few years of his life, he lived and traveled in the
area around the lower reaches of the Yangtze.

Like Iuang Ui, Lǐ Bhæk avoids the subjects of war, human suffer-
ing and the like in his poetry. Also like Iuang Ui, his style is sim-
ple and direct, but unlike the older poet his best poems draw from a
wide range of themes commonly occurring in the Chinese literary tradi-
tion--the sadness of lonely ladies, the joy of viewing scenery while
drinking, the awe of travel in difficult mountain country--without
Buddhist overtones. For Iuang Ui, an experience leading to the com-
position of a poem seems also to lead to Buddhist enlightenment; for
Lǐ Bhæk, such an experience seems to be appreciated for its own sake
only.

13. Feelings of grief 怨情 Qiuăn dzhiæng (Yuàn qíng)

mĭ njin giuĕn jio liєm	美 人 卷 珠 簾
shim dzhuă bhin ngɑ mi	深 坐 嚬 蛾 眉
dhăn gèn luì hən ship	但 見 淚 痕 濕
biət dji sim hən zhui	不 知 心 恨 誰

(Five-syllable unregulated (?) quatrain)

Title: qiuăn 61/5 modifies dzhiæng 61/8.

13.1 mĭ 123/3 "beautiful". njin 9/0 in a specialized meaning:
"woman". giuĕn 26/6 in a transitive meaning: "roll up". jio 96/6
"pearl", here "decorated with pearls" or possibly "having a pearl-like
appearance". liєm 118/13 "screen"--used as a window blind.

13.2 shim 85/8, extended to "(set) far·back (from the window)".
dzhuă 32/4. bhin 30/16 "draw...into a frown". ngɑ 142/7 "moth (es-
pecially Bombyx mori, the larva of which is the silkworm)". mi 109/4
"eyebrow". ngɑ mi "moth eyebrows", "eyebrows slender and curved like
the antennae of a silkworm moth"--a phrase of great antiquity. Its
earliest occurrence is in a poem praising the beauty of a lady who is
about to be married. The second stanza reads:

> hands like soft sprouts
>
> skin like jelled fat
>
> neck like a tree grub
>
> teeth like melon seeds
>
> cicada head moth eyebrows
>
> artful smile how madder-red!
>
> beautiful eyes how black-and-white!

> (Book of songs, No. 57: "Great person 碩人
> Zhiæk njin [Shí rén]")

Of the rather startling images in this stanza, only "hands like soft
sprouts" and "moth eyebrows" seem to have gained any currency in later
literature, independent of direct reference to the song itself.

In 13.1-2, mĭ njin, the actor topic, is followed by three comments:

verb object, adverb, verb, and verb object again.

13.3 The actor in this and the following line shifts to the persona, but is not overtly expressed. dhǎn gèn (9/5, 147/0): 3.2. luì 85/8 "tear, teardrop"; hən 104/8 "trace"; ship 85/14 "wetness". The structure of this line happens to be identical with that of 3.2.

13.4 biət 1/3; dji 111/3, and see 10.4. sim 61/0 is a place topic (GS 36). hə̀n 61/6 "grieve about" is a transitive verb, with mǐ njin as actor and zhui 149/8 as direct object, a question word in an indirect question. Notice that Chinese question words stay in the position of the content words they replace, unlike English, where corresponding interrogatives move to the beginning of the sentence or clause.

Prosodic note 7: The quatrain

The quatrain--or, more literally, the form with "cut-off lines": dzhiuɛt giɔ 絕句 (jué jù or chüeh chü)--is a four-line shi with lines of uniform length and usually five or seven syllables per line; the second and fourth lines rhyme, and sometimes also the first line; optional are tonal regulation and parallelism between the lines of a couplet.

Poems 1-8 and 13 are all quatrains. Of these nine poems, two are definitely unregulated: Poems 3 and 5. In both couplets of Poem 3, the second and fourth syllables of both lines belong to the same tonal categories. Such irregularity is permitted in the case of the first and third syllables of a line (and the fifth syllable of a seven-syllable line), but not in the case of the second and fourth syllables (and the sixth syllable of a seven-syllable line). As for Poem 5, the last syllable of the third line irregularly belongs to the same tonal category as the rhyme syllables in the second and fourth lines.

Poems 6 and 13 are perhaps unregulated; they will be discussed at the end of this note.

The other five poems are all definitely regulated, if we adjust the tonal rules for quatrains to account for the fact that often in otherwise well-regulated poems, the diversity rule does not apply. In other words, in many poems the ideal underlying tonal patterns of both couplets are identical. Poems 1 and 4 observe the diversity rule. Their actual and ideal tonal patterns are as follows:

Actual, Poem 1	Actual, Poem 4	Ideal, both poems
o o o x x	o o o x x	x o o x x
x x x o o	x x x o o	o x x o o
o x o o x	o x x o x	x x o o x
o o o x o	o o x x o	o o x x o

Poems 2, 7, and 8 do not observe the diversity rule. The second
and fourth lines of Poem 2 and the second line of Poem 7 have tone pat-
terns that are irregular in identical ways. In all three lines, "wrong"
tones appear on the first, third, and fourth syllables. This combina-
tion of "wrong" tones occurs frequently in poetry that is otherwise
well-regulated. (In seven-syllable regulated verse, the "wrong" tones
occur on the first, third, fifth, and sixth syllables.) The combina-
tion is nearly always associated with a line that ends with a syllable
carrying an "oblique" tone, i.e. an x syllable. Therefore, it is best
to include in the listing of tonal rules for regulated poetry a variant
applying to lines that end in an x syllable: a tone opposite to the
one expected according to the tonal rules is permitted on the penulti-
mate syllable of a line that ends in an x syllable, only if opposite
tones also occur on the preceding odd-numbered syllables in the line.
Here are the tone patterns, actual and ideal, for Poems 2 and 7:

Actual, Poem 2	Actual, Poem 7	Ideal, both poems
o x x o o	x x o o o	o x x o o
o o x o x	o o x o x	x o o x x
o x x o o	x x x o o	o x x o o
o o x o x	o o o x x	x o o x x

Poem 8 has seven-syllable, regulated lines. The rules for tones
in seven-syllable regulated poetry are the same as those for five-
syllable regulated poetry, extended to include two syllables added to
the beginning of the five-syllable line. We should now change the al-
ternation rule so that it applies to both the five- and the seven-
syllable line:

The alternation rule: The alternate syllables in a line
alternate tones, with the occasional exception of the
odd-numbered syllables other than the last syllable.

Poem 8 also illustrates what is likely to happen when a poet takes
the option of having the first line rhyme. A rhyme on the last sylla-
ble of the first line of a regulated poem upsets the tonal balance that
otherwise obtains between two lines of a couplet: the inversion rule
is broken at a crucial point, the last syllable of a line, here, the
first line of the poem. When the inversion rule is thus broken by
rhyming the first line, the "wrong" tone on the last syllable of the
first line is often supported by an application of the alternation rule
to the other members of the set of alternate syllables to which the
last syllable belongs. Thus in a five-syllable rhyming first line,
"wrong" tones on the first and third syllables support the "wrong" tone
on the fifth; in a seven-syllable rhyming first line, as here, "wrong"
tones on the first, third, and fifth syllables support the "wrong" tone
on the seventh. Here then is the tone pattern, actual and ideal, for
Poem 8:

Actual: Ideal:

x o o x x o o   o o x x o o x

x x o o x x o   x x o o x x o

x o x x x o x   o o x x o o x

o x o o o x o   x x o o x x o

Poems 6 and 13 share the irregularity of having first lines that
end in syllables of the same tone category as the rhyme, but which do
not rhyme. Poem 6 also has the permitted combination of "wrong" tones
in its second line:

Actual: Ideal:

x x o o x (lǐ)   o x x o o .

o o x o x (sèu)   x o o x x

o o o x o   o o x x o

o x o o x   x x o o x

Poem 13:

Actual: Ideal:

x o x o o (liɛm)   x o o x x

o x o o o (mi)   o x x o o

x x x o x   x x o o x

x o o x o   o o x x o

In both poems, the tone pattern of the first line is upset, presumably
to support the "wrong" tone of the last syllable. In Poem 6, the al-
ternation rule is applied to the first and third syllables, as so often
happens in regulated poetry when the first line rhymes. In Poem 13,
support for the "wrong" tone takes the unusual form of putting "wrong"-
toned syllables in the rest of the second half-line. Otherwise the two
poems are well-regulated. But the fact that in both poems the first
lines end in unrhyming syllables that nevertheless belong to the same
tone category as the rhyming syllables in the second and fourth lines,
and the fact that in Poem 13 there is an unusual cluster of "wrong"
tones in the first line, lead me to the opinion that neither poem is
regulated.

Finally, it should be noted that in regulated quatrains, "oblique"
rhymes are much more frequent than in eight-line regulated poetry.

14. Thoughts on a quiet night   静夜思   Dzhiăng ià si (Jìng
yè si)

jrhiang dzhen   miæng ngiuæt guang   床 前 明 月 光

ngi zhǐ   dhǐ zhiàng shriang   疑 是 地 上 霜

giǔ dhou   miàng miæng ngiuæt   舉 頭 望 明 月

dei dhou   si gò xiang   低 頭 思 故 鄉

(Five-syllable unregulated quatrain)

Title: dzhiăng 174/8 modifies ià 36/5, and that phrase modifies
si 61/5.

14.1 jrhiang 90/4 "bed" and dzhen 18/7 form a place expression
(GS 17) functioning as a place topic (GS 37) to the rest of the line
as comment--cf. 2.3. miæng 72/4 "bright" modifies ngiuæt 74/0 "moon",
and these two words in turn modify guang 10/4 "light, radiance".

14.2 ngi 103/9 "think, suspect" is like dji in 13.4 and 10.4.
zhǐ 72/5 "be" is a transitive verb in sentences where the term pre-
ceding it is equated to or identified with the term following it, the
grammatical object. Contrast sentences with zhǐ, which are verbal,
with nominal sentences (GS 31-2), which also may have identificational
meaning. Here, the first term of the sentence is missing; presumably
it is guang of the preceding line. dhǐ 32/3, here "ground", forms a
place expression with zhiàng 1/2 (cf. 4.3), which modifies shriang
173/9 "frost", the main word of the second term of the sentence.

14.3 giǔ 134/10 "raise" and dhou 181/7 "head" constitute the
first of four comments that make up the rest of the poem. miàng 74/7,
miæng 46/0, and ngiuæt constitute another comment. The first comment
may be in either a coordinate or a subordinate relationship to the
second.

14.4 dei 9/5 "lower"; gò 66/5; xiang 163/10. This line should be
considered parallel to the preceding line.

The poem is unregulated: twice there is identity of tone category
of the respective even-numbered syllables of the lines in the same
couplets.

15. Misery Pavilion 勞勞亭 Lɑu-lɑu Dheng (Láo-láo Tíng)

ten hǎ shiɑng sim chiὺ   天 下 傷 心 處

lɑu-lɑu sὺng kæk dheng   勞 勞 送 客 亭

chuin biung dji bhiɛt kǒ   春 風 知 別 苦

biət kiěn liǒu dheu tseng   不 遣 柳 條 青

                                    (Five-syllable regulated quatrain)

     Title: lɑu 19/10 here is a descriptive (GS 4) "(sad)", which
possibly is related to the word usually represented by this graph mean-
ing "labor, troublesome". The reduplicative modifies the following
word, dheng 8/7, and the whole phrase is the name of an actual place,
famous as a favorite spot for partings.

     15.1 ten 37/1 and hǎ 1/2 form a place expression (GS 17), but
this expression, which literally means "below heaven", has become a
common idiom, via the extension "all that which is below heaven", mean-
ing "the world". shiɑng 9/11 "hurt, wound" is transitive. chiὺ 141/5
"place" is a noun modified by the preceding words in the line, and is
the main word of a topic, to which the following line is the comment.
The context seems to demand a superlative here, which is really an ex-
tension of the English "the", associated with "given" information spec-
ified in the topic: "The heart-wounding place in the world..." becom-
ing "The most heart-wounding place in the world...."

     15.2 sὺng 162/6 is transitive. kæk 40/6. The first four syl-
lables modify the last word in the line, as in the preceding line.
This last word, a noun, is the head word of a nominal comment (GS 31),
which is identificational.

     15.3 chuin 72/5; biung 182/0, personified, and the actor of dji;
bhiɛt 18/5; kǒ 140/5, here a noun, object of dji.

     15.4 kiěn 162/10 "send out, produce, cause to appear" is another
verb to which biung is the actor. liǒu 75/5 modifies dheu 75/7 "twig",
and that phrase modifies the object of kiěn which is tseng 174/0.
Willow branches resemble streaming tears and are symbols of parting.

16-17. <u>From</u> Old airs 古風 Gŏ biung (Gŭ fēng)

Title: gŏ 30/2 "old, ancient times". <u>biung</u> is extended here to
"air, song" and "mood, style, custom". In this set of poems, Lĭ Bhæk
tries to recapture the spirit of the <u>Book of songs</u> (see "General back-
ground",p.vii). According to tradition, Confucius collected folk
songs and other poems composed by mostly anonymous Chinese poets and
selected about three hundred of them to form the classic now known as
the <u>Book of songs</u>. He is said to have done this in order to bring the
attention of the ruler of China to the thoughts and aspirations of his
subjects so that he could take their feelings into account and govern
them wisely.

16. <u>No. 1</u>

Here Lĭ Bhæk gives a capsule critical history of poetry and a
statement of his purpose. His treatment is elliptical and allusive,
and it would be well to introduce the main events, people, and literary
forms referred to before presenting the poem itself.

16.1-4 The three-hundred-odd poems of the <u>Book of songs</u> are
divided into four sections: the "Airs 風 Biung (Fēng)", the "Greater
odes 大雅 Dhài ngǎ (Dà yǎ)", the "Lesser odes 小雅 Siěu ngǎ (Xiǎo
yǎ)", and the "Hymns 頌 Ziŏng (Sòng)". A typical view in Chinese
traditional literary criticism holds that the moral and political prin-
ciples permeating the <u>Songs</u> were ignored during the period of the "War-
ring states 戰國 Jiɛn guǝk (Zhàn guó)", B.C. 403-221, when the ruling
house of Jiou (see Table 1,p.viii) held only nominal sway over its sub-
ject states.

16.6 The period of the "Warring states" ended when the powerful
western state of Dzhin, having gradually subdued all the other states
ruled a unified China for about fifteen years. In the traditional
Chinese view, the Dzhin Dynasty is regarded as insufferably strict and
anti-intellectual. In an attempt to achieve conformity with official
government thought, the first Dzhin emperor ordered the suppression of
most literary works, and all but one copy of each suppressed work was
destroyed. These single remaining copies were deposited in a library
in the capital, but that library too was destroyed during the fighting
in the capital when the Dzhin Dynasty was overthrown.

16.8 Kiuǝt Ngiuæn 屈原 (Qū Yuán), a high official in the
southern state of Chriŭ (see "General background",p.viii) during the
fourth century B.C., was also a great poet. What remains of his out-
put are found in the <u>Songs of the state of Chŭ</u>. One of the poems re-
liably associated with his name is the "Encountering sorrow 離騷
Li sau (Lĭ sāo)", a long poem of spiritual discontent and search.

16.9 The poetic style of Kiuǝt Ngiuæn influenced two poets of
the Xǎn Dynasty, Si-mǎ Siang-njiu 司馬相如 (Sī-mǎ Xiāng-rú, B.C.
179-117) and Iang Hiung 揚雄 (Yáng Xióng, fl. first century B.C.).
The rulers of the Xǎn Dynasty, which succeeded the Dzhin, modified the
strict measures instituted by the Dzhin and began many of the political
institutions that lasted for two thousand years.

16.13 It became the practice in the Xàn Dynasty to adopt official reign names to be used in identifying years. These names were regularly changed whenever a new emperor ascended the throne, as well as at other times, whenever it was thought that a change in reign name might bring good fortune. Reign names are usually two syllables long and have some laudatory or auspicious meaning. The last important reign period of the Xàn Dynasty has the name "Establish peace 建安 Giàn qɑn (Jiàn ān)", and it lasted from 196 to 220. This reign name is used to identify an important group of poets that flourished then, and in the following period of disunion.

16.15 It is a custom almost universally followed by Chinese poets to refer to their own dynasty and to the reigns of emperors contemporary with them by indirect means and in complimentary terms. Here, Lǐ Bhæk refers to the Dhɑng Dynasty as an "August era".

16.18 The founding of the Dhɑng Dynasty is referred to here as a carrying out of the dictates of fate.

16.24 Another classical text whose compilation is traditionally ascribed to Confucius is the Spring and autumn annals 春秋 Chuin tsiou (Chūn qiū), a chronicle of events from 722 to 481 B.C. The last words of the chronicle are: "In the spring of the fourteenth year, at a hunt in the west, a unicorn was trapped." Why did Confucius stop the chronicle with the words "a unicorn was trapped"? One early account explains that when this happened the hunters did not recognize the animal as a unicorn, an animal associated with good luck. On the contrary, they thought it was a bad omen and gave it away. Only after Confucius identified it as a unicorn was it retrieved. Thereupon, disgusted at the ignorance and moral decay of his time, Confucius stopped writing the Annals.

dhài ngǎ giǒu biət tzɑk	大雅久不作
ngo shrui giàng zhui djhin	吾衰竟誰陳
iuɑng biung quǐ miàn tsǎu	王風委蔓草
jiàn guək dɑ giæng jrin	戰國多荆榛
5 liong xǒ siɑng dhǒm jhiək	龍虎相啖食
biæng guɑ dhài ghiuɑng dzhin	兵戈逮狂秦
jiàng shiæng hɑ miəi-mɑng	正聲何微茫

qəi qiuæn kǐ sɑu njin	哀怨起騷人
iɑng mǎ gek dhuəi bɑ	揚馬激頹波
10 kəi liou dhǎng mio ngin	開流蕩無垠
biǎi xiəng sui miǎn biɛn	廢興雖萬變
xiǎn jiɑng iæk ǐ luin	憲章亦已淪
dzhǐ dzhiong giǎn qɑn ləi	自從建安來
kǐ lěi biət tziok djin	綺麗不足珍
15 shiǎng dhǝi bhiuk ngiuæn gǒ	聖代復元古
zhui qiəi giuǝi tsiæng jin	垂衣貴清真
ghiuən dzhəi zhiok xiou miæng	羣才屬休明
jhiəng iuǝn ghiɒng iɑk lin	乘運共躍鱗
miən jit siɑng biǎng xuàn	文質相炳煥
20 jiǔng seng lɑ tsiou min	眾星羅秋旻
ngǎ jǐ dzhǝi shran jhuit	我志在刪述
zhui xiuəi qiǎng tsen chuin	垂輝映千春
xiəi shiǎng njiu iǒu lip	希聖如有立
dzhiuɛt bit qiu huæk lin	絕筆於獲麟

(Five-syllable old-style poem)

16.1 <u>dhài</u> 37/0 "big, great"; <u>ngǎ</u> 172/4 "elegant, elegant piece of writing, ode"; <u>giǒu</u> 4/2 "long time", here an adverb to the following verbal phrase: "for a long time"; <u>tzɑk</u> 9/5 is a transitive verb, but its object has been topicalized (GS 40).

16.2 <u>ngo</u> 30/4 is a first person pronoun, usually pre-verbal or modifying a noun: "I, my, we, our"; <u>shrui</u> 145/4 "downfall". <u>giàng</u> 117/6 "in the end, finally, after all" and <u>zhui</u> 149/8 are both in adverbial position here. The adverbial quality of <u>zhui</u> can be brought out in English by using the passive to translate the verb, and by using an adverbial phrase, "by whom?", to translate <u>zhui</u>. However, it is perhaps better to keep the verb active in English, and to turn <u>zhui</u> into the actor: "who?". <u>djhin</u> 170/8 "spread, tell about, narrate" is another transitive verb, again with a topicalized object.

16.3-4 The lines of this couplet are parallel. <u>iuɑng</u> 96/0, here "princely, royal". The "Airs" section of the <u>Book</u> <u>of</u> <u>songs</u> has fifteen subdivisions, each with a title identifying the geographical region with which the poems of that subdivision are associated. <u>iuɑng</u> is such a title. The ten poems in this subdivision are associated with the small royal precinct actually controlled by the dynastic house of Jiou. This area surrounds the city known then as well as in Dhɑng times as Lɑk-iɑng (the Eastern Capital of the Dhɑng). <u>quǐ</u> 38/5 "be abandoned to"; <u>miæn</u> 140/11 "vine, creeper"; <u>tsǎu</u> 140/6. <u>jièn</u> 62/12 "battle, contest"; <u>guək</u> 31/8 "nation, state"; <u>da</u> 36/3 "many, much, be overgrown with"; <u>giæng</u> 140/6 "thornwood, bramble"; <u>jrin</u> 75/10 "thicket".

16.5 <u>liong</u> 212/0 "dragon"; <u>xǒ</u> 141/2 "tiger"; <u>siɑng</u> 109/4 (cf. 5.3); <u>dhǒm</u> 30/8 "eat"; <u>jhiək</u> 184/0 "eat".

16.6 <u>biæng</u> 12/5 "weapon"; <u>guɑ</u> 62/0 "lance"; <u>dhèi</u> 162/8 "arrive at, until"; <u>ghiuɑng</u> 94/4 "crazy"; <u>dzhin</u> 115/5 "(dynasty)". Notice the vague relationship here between the topic and the comment: "About the (use of) weapons, my comment is that it went on until..."

16.7 <u>jiàng</u> 77/1 "correct, right"; <u>shiæng</u> 128/11 "sound"; <u>ha</u> 9/5 "how...!"; <u>miəi</u> 60/10 "tiny" combines with the meaningless syllable <u>mɑng</u> 140/6 to form an alliterative descriptive "(indistinct)" (GS 4). During the troubles at the end of the third century B.C., the tradition of writing literature correctly, as in the <u>dhài</u> <u>ngǎ</u> of Line 1, was beginning to fade.

16.8 <u>gəi</u> 30/6 "sadness"; <u>kǐ</u> 156/3 "arouse"; <u>sɑu</u> 187/10 "sorrow".

16.9 <u>iɑng</u> 64/9 "(surname)"; <u>mǎ</u> 187/0 for si-mǎ "(surname)"; <u>gek</u> 85/12 "incite, urge"; <u>dhuəi</u> 181/7 "collapse"; <u>ba</u> 85/5. The poetry of Kiuət Ngiuæn inspired a form of prose-poem known as <u>biò</u> 賦 , whose popularity among the literati was greatly enhanced when Si-mǎ Siɑng-njiu and Iɑng Hiung became its proponents. <u>ba</u> is here a symbol for this <u>biò</u> form, whose development had declined until it had nearly collapsed after Kiuət Ngiuæn, until the time of Si-mǎ and Iɑng.

16.10 <u>kəi</u> 169/4 is "begin" here; <u>liou</u> 86/7 "flow"; <u>dhǎng</u> 140/12 "spread (as water)"; <u>mio</u> 86/8, here: "without", a common extension;

ngin 32/6 "shore, bank". Lǐ Bhæk disapproves of the development of
wordiness and frivolity in literature during the Xàn.

   16.11-12 The lines of this couplet are parallel: topic, two
adverbs, and a verb. biæi 53/12 "decline, decadence" and xiəng 134/9
"revive, revival" form a compound (GS 6) meaning "the course of his-
tory", here referring to the history of poetry. sui 172/9 "although"
regularly appears in adverb position and connects the sentence it ap-
pears in with the one that follows. miæn 140/9 is here used as an
adverb: "in ten thousand ways"; bièn 149/16 "change, be changeable",
here, an intransitive verb. xiæn 61/12 "law, pattern", frequently
associated with legal documents, here refers to the traditional pro-
sodic values that Lǐ Bhæk finds in the dhɑ̀i ngǎ but misses in later
poetry. It forms a synonym compound with jiɑng 117/6 "pattern". iæk
8/4 "also" and ǐ 49/0 "already" are both adverbs. luin 85/8 "sink, be
submerged".

   16.13 dzhǐ 132/0 here forms a synonym compound with dzhiong 60/8
"head away from", an intransitive verb of motion. giæn 54/6 "build,
establish"; qɑn 40/3 "peace": this verb-object construction is a reign
name, the time object (GS 21) of dzhǐ dzhiong. The verb-object con-
struction dzhǐ dzhiong giæn qɑn modifies ləi; (GS 16); dzhǐ dzhiong
is seen here as a co-verb (GS 26). The combination dzhǐ dzhiong X ləi
means "from the time of X up to now". The whole line is time topic
(GS 36) to the following line.

   16.14 kǐ 120/8, here extended to mean "intricately decorated",
forming with lèi 198/8 "pretty" a synonym compound with derogatory
overtones. The logical subject, "poetry", has been omitted. tziok
157/0 "sufficient" is here an auxiliary verb (GS 25) with this meaning
extended to "be worth (doing the action of the verb that follows)".
The verb in this case is djin 96/5 "prize, esteem", usually a noun,
here a transitive verb with a topicalized object.

   16.15 shiæng 128/7 "inspiring respect because of a morality de-
veloped to the highest degree, august"; dhəi 9/3 "era". These words
form the time topic and the rest of the line is its comment. bhiuk
60/9, with the concrete meaning "return to". The actor is an implied
"we" or "China". ngiuæn 10/2 "of the beginning, primal".

   16.16 zhui 33/5 "let...hang"; qiəi 145/0 "upper garment, clothing".
This phrase alludes to a passage from the Book of changes 易 經 Iæk
geng (Yì jīng), a classic on divination, which, like the Book of songs
and the Spring and autumn annals, is attributed to Confucius. In its
"Appended commentary", Part 2, Paragraph 2, mention is made of three
sage rulers who are said to have "...allowed the upper and lower gar-
ments to hang down, and the world was in order" (Wilhelm-Baynes 1967,
p. 332). A quiet inactivity, without any interference in the natural
order of things, is regarded as the best kind of government. The
phrase zhui qiəi refers to a government characterized by such valued
inactivity; it is another time topic and the rest of the line is its
comment: "Now that we have a 'letting the garments hang' sort of gov-
ernment..." giuèi 154/5 "esteem, value"; tsiæng 85/8 is possibly a
noun here; jin 109/5 "true, truth". These last two words suggest

qualities valued by the Taoists. The Taoists trace the origin of their school of thought to a man called Venerable Master 老子 Lǎu Tzǐ (Lǎo Zǐ, or Lao Tzu), whose surname, Lǐ 李 , was the same as that of the Dhɑng imperial house. So it is likely that the poet is making a connection between Taoist values and qualities which he hopes will characterize the Dhɑng government (Aoki 1965, p. 279).

The last two words of Lines 15 and 16 could be either coordinate, or the first word could be subordinate to the second. If the lines are treated as parallel, as they most likely should be, the decision as to the grammatical relationship between these two words should apply to both lines.

16.17 ghiuən 123/7 "flock"; dzhəi 64/0 "talent, one possessing talent, talented person". See GS 2. zhiok 44/18 "belong to, be subsumed under"; xiou 9/4 "beauty, excellence"; miæng 72/4 is here in a common extension of its meaning: "clear vision, enlightened intelligence".

16.18 jhiəng 4/9 "ride, take advantage of"; iuən 162/9 "turn of fate"; ghiɔng 12/4 "make go together, synchronize"; iɑk 157/14 "leap"; lin 195/12 "scales (of a fish)", a synecdoche for "fish", which is in turn a metaphor for the ghiuən dzhəi of the preceding line.

The two lines should probably be analyzed as follows: ghiuən dzhəi is the topic to three comments. The first two, zhiok xiou miæng and jhiəng iuən, are verbal (verb-object). The last is nominal, with lin as the main word modified by iɑk, then iɑk lin is in turn modified by ghiɔng: "scaly things that leap in harmony".

16.19 miən 67/0 "refinement of (literary) style"; jit 154/8 "substance, content (of a literary work)". biæng 86/5 and xuɑn 86/9 both mean "bright", and this synonym compound is changed from an intransitive verb to a transitive one, because of siɑng (see 1.1). When an intransitive verb of quality becomes transitive, it often changes its meaning to a causative: "make bright, illuminate".

16.20 jiɔng 143/6 "crowd, multitude"; seng 72/5 "star". See GS 2. lɑ 122/14 "net, spread like a net over"; tsiou 115/4; min 72/4.

Lines 14-20 comprise a series of exhortations discreetly couched in descriptive terms--a frequent device.

16.21 ngǎ 62/3; jl 61/3 "ambition, aim"; dzhǒi 32/3, here used abstractly; shran 18/5 "delete (from a literary corpus)"; jhuit 162/5 "narrate". These two coordinate intransitive verbs comprise the place object of dzhǒi. Confucius is said to have "edited" the Book of songs, selecting the three hundred poems of the classic from about 3,000 songs that were actually collected. In the Spring and autumn annals, Confucius "narrates" events of the past.

16.22 zhui 33/5, here best regarded as modifying the following word: "down-streaming"; xiuəi 159/8 "brilliance, glory", referring to the reputation of Lǐ Bhæk's own works; qiæng 72/5 "illuminate, shine";

tsen 24/1 "thousand"; chuin, here a synecdoche for "year".

    16.23 xiəi 50/4 "hope" has a sentence object; shiɔng refers to Confucius; njiu 38/3 "if", a conjunction in English but an adverb in Chinese; iŏu 74/2; lip 117/0 "stand, establish": iŏu lip is a verb-object compound: "have an establishing, have success in getting established". Lĭ Bhæk aspires on the one hand to be a Confucius in passing on literary works to later generations, and on the other hand to have his literary talent recognized by the present ruler.

    16.24 dzhiuɛt 120/6 "stop", a transitive verb here; bit 118/6 "writing brush"; qiu 70/4 "at" (GS 22); huæk 94/14 "capture"; lin 198/12, for 麒 ghi-lin "fabulous one-horned elk, unicorn". Between "at" and the following verb-object phrase, supply "(the words)". Again, Lĭ Bhæk aspires to emulate Confucius by stopping writing only when morality sinks to the low point symbolized by the words huæk lin. From the general panegyric tone of the poem, we may assume that he thinks that this low point will never again occur.

17. No. 47.

The source of this comparison of peach blossoms with pine trees is possibly the following passage attributed to the philosopher Suin-tzǐ 荀子 (Xún-zǐ, fl. B.C. 298-238):

> Peach and plum trees are beautiful for a while, but (their blossoms) wither after their time has come. Pines and cypresses, on the other hand, pass through hard winters without fading, and are covered with frost and snow without changing: they can be said to maintain their integrity.

[Quoted in Lǐ Zhiěn 李善 (Lǐ Shàn, d. 689), note to Tzǎ Si 左思 (Zuǒ Sī, d. ca. 306), "Summoning a recluse 招隱 Jieu qiěn (Zhāo yǐn)", No. 2 of two, in Seu Tǔng 蕭統 (Xiāo Tǔng, 501-531), ed., Collection of literary works 文選 Miən siuěn (Wén xuǎn)]

dhɑu xua kəi dung iuæn	桃花開東園
hom sieu kua bhæk njit	含笑誇白日
ngǒu mung chuin biung iuæng	偶蒙春風榮
shræng tsǐ iem iɑng jit	生此艷陽質
5 kiəi mio gai njin shriək	豈無佳人色
dhǎn kiǒng xua biət jhit	但恐花不實
qiuæn-djiuěn liong xuǎ biəi	宛轉龍火飛
leng lɑk tzǎu siɑng shit	零落早相失
ghiǔ dji nom shran ziong	詎知南山松

10   dhuk lip dzhì seu shrit   獨 立 自 蕭 瑟

(Five-syllable old-style poem)

17.1 dhɑu 75/6 "peach tree"; xua 140/4. These two words com-
prise the topic to a series of comments that extend to the last couplet.
For the special meaning of kəi see 7.4. dung 75/4 "eastern"; iuæn
31/10 "garden", the chief word of the place object.

17.2 hom 30/4 "wear (a smile)"; siɛu 118/4 "smile"; kua 149/6
"show off, brag"; bhæk 106/0, here: "bright".

17.3 ngǒu 9/9 "accidentally, by chance"; mung 140/10 "receive";
iuæng 75/10 "flowering", the main word of the direct object of mung.
The two words preceding iuæng tell the source from which the flowering
was received.

17.4 shræng 100/0 "cause to appear, produce"; tsǐ 77/2 "this,
these"; iɛm 151/21 "radiant"; iɑng 170/9, here in its basic meaning:
"sunny". iɛm and iɑng form a coordinate compound: "late spring-
time". jit 154/8 is "object, thing" here.

17.5 kiǒi 151/3 is a rhetorical interrogative: How can it be
that...!"; gai 9/6 "excellent"; shriək 139/0 "color, appearance,
beauty." In this line, the poet connects the symbol with the symbolized.

17.6 kiǒng 61/6 "fear", an auxiliary verb; jhit 42/11 "bear
fruit".

17.7 qiuǎn-djiuǎn 40/5, 159/11 "(turning)": GS 4. liong here
stands for 蒼龍 tsɑng liong "Green Dragon", a name for the seven east-
ern zodiacal constellations. xuǎ 86/0 stands for xuǎ seng 星 "Fire
Star", referring either to the planet Mars, or to the middle star of
the three that constitute the constellation "Heart" 心 sim, one of
the seven eastern zodiacal constellations. This middle star is Antares,
a reddish, variable supergiant, the brightest star in the southern sky.
In China it is seen in the east during the last month of spring and the
first month of summer. Under the latter interpretation, liong xuǎ
would thus refer to the end of spring and the beginning of summer. biəi
183/0 "to fly". This line is a time topic with the following line as
its comment.

17.8 leng 173/5 "in bits"; lɑk 140/9. This alliterative phrase
is a quasi-descriptive, not a genuine one, because each syllable has
meaning apart from the sound. Another comment (still to dhɑu xua in
Line 1) completes the line: tzǎu 72/2 "soon", modifying the rest of
the comment; shit 37/2 "lose", probably intended to recall the phrase
shit qì 失意   "fail in attaining one's ambition", referring to a
disappointed official, one whose talents are ignored. Here the peach
blossoms lose their positions of eminence on the branches.

17.9 ghiǔ 149/5 is another rhetorical interrogative: "How...!"
The object of dji is a pivot (GS 43), and comprises the rest of the
line: nom 24/7 "south": "South Mountain" is a frequently-occurring

place name, usually referring to the mountains south of the Western
Capital, Djhiang-qan. ziong 75/4 "pine" is the chief word of the pivot.

17.10 This line comprises two coordinate comments to ziong.
dhuk 94/13 modifies lip, which here has its basic meaning. The rest
of the line constitutes the second of the two comments. For the mean-
ing of dzhl here, see 5.3; but a likely extension is "according to (the
pine tree's) own nature". seu-shrit 140/13, 96/9: both syllables had
the same initial in the older language, namely, s-. In the second syl-
lable, the s- was followed by a medial which combined with it to give
shr- in Dhang times, where it still functions as an alliterative de-
scriptive: "(wind whistling in trees)". With dzhl, it is a verb:
"...and makes a seu-shrit sound according to its own nature".

18. First of four poems entitled Pouring a drink alone under the
moon 月 下 獨 酌 Ngiuæt hǎ dhuk jiɑk (Yuè xià dú zhuó)

xua gan qit ho tziǒu	花 間 一 壺 酒
dhuk jiɑk mio siɑng tsin	獨 酌 無 相 親
giǔ bəi qiɛu miæng ngiuæt	舉 杯 邀 明 月
duəi qiǎng zhiæng som njin	對 影 成 三 人
5 ngiuæt giəi biət gǎi qǐm	月 既 不 解 飲
qiǎng dho zui ngǎ shin	影 徒 隨 我 身
dzhòm bhǎn ngiuæt tziɑng qiǎng	暫 伴 月 將 影
hæng lɑk sio ghip chuin	行 樂 須 及 春
ngǎ gɑ ngiuæt bhəi-huəi	我 歌 月 徘 徊
10 ngǎ miǒ qiǎng leng luàn	我 舞 影 零 亂
sěng zhi dhung gau xuɑn	醒 時 同 交 歡
tzuì hòu gɑk biən sàn	醉 後 各 分 散
iuǎng get mio dzhiæng iou	永 結 無 情 遊
siɑng ghi mak iuən xàn	相 期 邈 雲 漢

(Five-syllable old-style poem)

Title: jiɑk 164/3 "pour wine". Drinking is a frequent subject of
Chinese poetry; overindulgence is more likely to provoke a smile than
a scandal. Lǐ Bhæk is especially known for his love of wine.

18.1 gan 169/4 is a place noun (GS 17) meaning "interval, space
between, position at or among". Here it forms a place expression with

xua, functioning as a place topic (GS 37). qit 1/0; ho 33/9 "wine jar"; tziǒu 164/3. For this measured noun construction see 8.3. Though it would be possible to consider these three words as constituting a comment to the first two (supplying "there is", or the like), it is probably preferable to take the two half-lines as coordinated place topics to the next line as comment.

18.2 tsin 147/9 "be friends with". This comment is in two co-ordinated parts, separated at the caesura.

18.3 bəi 75/4; qiɛu 162/13 "invite". Again, two coordinate comments.

18.4 duəi 41/11 "to face"; qiæng 59/12 "shadow" also appears in 3/3, but written differently, and with an extension of meaning; zhiæng 62/2, but here "make a total of" is smoother; som 1/2. Again, two comments.

18.5 giəi 71.7 "from the beginning", an adverb, here combining with the following adverb to mean "has never"; gǎi 148/6 "understand" qǐm 184/4 "drink".

18.6 dho 60/7 "only", an adverb; zui 170/13 "follow"; shin 158/0.

18.7 dzhòm 72/11 "for the time being"; bhǎn 9/5 "make...one's companion"; tziɑng 41/8 "together with, and"--an unusual instance of a coordinating conjunction, lending a leisurely prosiness to the style.

18.8 hæng 144/0 "make...happen" derives from a primary meaning "walk, go"; lɑk 75/11. This verb-object phrase is topic to what fol-lows: sio 181/3 "must" is an auxiliary; ghip 29/2 "meet...in time". The persona complains that if he waited for a more appropriate drinking companion, spring would be gone, and the season would no longer be right for such a party.

18.9 gɑ 76/10 "sing"; bhəi huəi 60/8, 60/6, "(going back and forth)", a descriptive anciently built (cf. 17.7) on a word huəi 回 "go back" (cf. 4.3);   bhəi is a meaningless syllable added to make a rhyming descriptive.

18.10 miǒ 136/8 "dance"; luàn 5/12 "be in a chaotic state" forms an alliterative, and hence quasi-descriptive, compound with leng "be in bits" (cf. 17.8).

The lines of this couplet have identical grammatical structures: each line consists of two sentences, separated at the caesura. The first sentence consists of an actor topic followed by an intransitive verb; the second sentence is a topic followed by a (quasi-) descriptive. In the parallel couplets of regulated poetry, the repetition of words in identical line positions is not permitted; in this old-style poem, however, the repetition of ngǎ is perfectly normal in otherwise par-allel lines.

18.11 sěng 164/9 "sober"; zhi 72/6 "time" (GS 18); dhung 30/3
"alike, similarly"; gau 8/4 "mix, exchange"; xuɑn 76/18 "joy". sěng
zhi is time topic (GS 36) to the rest of the line.

18.12 tzuì 164/8 "intoxicated"; hòu 60/6 "time afterward". This
phrase is another instance of a time expression functioning as time
topic to the rest of the line, where X-hòu, which is literally "at the
time-afterward of X", is best translated "after X". gɑk 30/3 "each";
biən 18/2 "divide, separate"; sàn 66/8 "scatter, separate".

18.13 iuěng 85/1 "for a long time, forever, eternally"; get 120/6
"tie, bind, contract to", an auxiliary; iou 162/9 "travel, wander,
stroll" is modified by mio dzhiæng. The persona now feels that pas-
sionless wandering, such as that of the moon and the shadow are more
valuable than ordinary human attachments. The theme of retreat from
the world is common in Chinese poetry, and is especially prominent in
the poetry of Lǐ Bhæk.

18.14 ghi 74/8 "appointed time, meet at an appointed time, meet";
mak 162/14 "far"; iuən 173/4 "cloud", and xàn 85/11 "(name of a river)"
form a subordinate compound, an epithet for the Milky Way. The last
three words of the line constitute a place object to ghi.

19. With some wine in my hand, I put a question to the moon
把 酒 問 月   Bǎ tziǒu miən ngiuæt (Bǎ jiǔ wèn yuè); Original
note: My old friend Gǎ Zhuin had me put the question to it 故 人 賈
淳 令 余 問 之   Gò njin Gǎ Zhuin liæng iu miən ji (Gù rén Jiǎ
Chún lǐng yú wèn zhǐ)

tseng ten iǒu ngiuæt   青 天 有 月 來 幾 時
   ləi giǎi zhi

ngǎ gim dheng bəi   我 今 停 杯 一 問 之
   qit miən ji

njin pan miæng ngiuæt   人 攀 明 月 不 可 得
   biət kǎ dək

ngiuæt hæng kiɑk iǔ   月 行 卻 與 人 相 隨
   njin siɑng zui

5 gěu njiu biəi giæng   皎 如 飛 鏡 臨 丹 闕
   lim dɑn kiuæt

liok qen miɛt dzhǐn   綠 烟 滅 盡 清 輝 發
   tsiɑng xiuəi biæt

dhǎn gèn siɛu dzhiong   但 見 宵 從 海 上 來
   xǒi zhiàng ləi

neng dji xěu xiàng   寧 知 曉 向 雲 間 沒
   iuən gan mət

bhæk tò dǎu iɑk   白 兔 擣 藥 秋 復 春
   tsiou bhiuk chuin

10 həng nga go sei   姮 娥 孤 棲 與 誰 鄰
        iǔ zhui lin

    gim njin biət gèn   今 人 不 見 古 時 月
        gǒ zhi ngiuæt

    gim ngiuæt dzhəng geng   今 月 曾 經 照 古 人
        jiɛu gǒ njin

    gǒ njin gim njin   古 人 今 人 若 流 水
        njiɑk liou shuǐ

    ghiòng kàn miæng ngiuæt   共 看 明 月 皆 如 此
        gai njiu tsǐ

15 ui ngiuæn dɑng gɑ   惟 願 當 歌 對 酒 時
        duài tziǒu zhi

    ngiuæt guɑng djhiɑng jiɛu   月 光 長 照 金 樽 裏
        gim tzuən lǐ

                            (Seven-syllable old-style poem)

        Title: bǎ 64/4 "grasp, have in the hand"; miàn 30/8 "ask...a question".

        "Original note ":   It is not known who the poet's friend Gǎ Zhuin (154/6, 85/8) is. liæng 9/3 "cause" is here followed by a pivot (cf. 12.11): iu 9/5 "(first person pronoun), I, my, me, we, our, us"; ji 4/3, here "(third person pronoun, object of the preceding verb) him, her, it, them".

        19.1 ləi is basically coordinate with the sentence that pre-cedes it, and which consists of a place topic, a verb, and an object: "...and come (up to the present)", but here extended in a special con-struction to "Since..." (cf. 16.13). These five words then form a topic to a comment comprising the following two words. giǒi 52/9 "how much?" combines with zhi to give the English "how long?", which in turn combines with ləi to give a phrase which in English must come at the beginning of the sentence: "How long has it been since...?"

19.2 gim 9/2 "today, now"; dheng 9/9 "stop", transitive here.

19.3 pan 64/15 "climb, try to climb, climb toward", here the goal
of the action is not achieved. The auxiliary kǎ (GS 41) has another
auxiliary, dək 60/8 "get, achieve" as its object. The verb-object ex-
pression pan miæng ngiuæt is the topicalized object of dək.

19.4 hæng is here "move, motion" (cf. 18.8). kiɑk 26/7 is the
adversative adverb that appeared at 11.13, where it was written differ-
ently: 26/5. iǔ 134/7 "accompany, together with, along with" (GS 14).
zui is transitive, and siɑng replaces the object.

19.5 gěu 106/6 "(moon-)white"; njiu appears here in its basic
meaning "resemble, be like"; giæng 167/11 "mirror", modified by the
preceding word, is a pivot; lim 131/11 "look down from"; dɑn 3/3
"cinnabar, red"; kiuæt 169/10 "tower erected outside the city gate,
watchtower", but here in a specialized sense: "gate of a royal palace",
such gates being painted red. The moon is evidently set in a sky lit
by sunset colors.

19.6 liok 120/8 "green"; qen 86/6 "mist, haze", referring to haze
at dusk; miɛt 85/10 "extinguish, be dissipated"; dzhǐn 108/9 (GS 15);
biæt 105/7 has its basic meaning here: "emerge".

19.7 siɛu 40/7 "night"; dzhiong (GS 26); xǎi 85/7 "sea".   The
sentence siɛu... ləi is the object of gěn. siɛu is a time topic; the
implied actor of dzhiong and ləi is the moon.

19.8 neng 40/11 "how?"; xěu 72/12 "morning"; xiàng 30/3 "head
for" is a co-verb: "toward", but with the place word gan best trans-
lated by the English "into, among". mət 85/4 "sink, disappear".

19.9 tò 10/6 "rabbit"; dǎu 64/14 "pound (in a mortar)"; iɑk 140/5
"medicine", here referring to an elixir of immortality. This same
sentence is found in a work by Biò Huen 傅玄 (Fù Xuán, 217-278)
called "Imitating the 'Heavenly questions' (a work attributed to Kiuət
Ngiuæn)":

        What is in the middle of the moon?

        A white rabbit pounding medicine.

bhiuk is best extended here to "return to...(in endless cycles)".

19.10 həng ngɑ (38/6, 38/7) is the name of the wife of the leg-
endary archer Ngèi 羿 (Yì). One story about her is that she stole
an elixir of immortality from her husband, consumed it, turned into an
immortal, and fled to the moon. go 39/5 "alone", an adverb; sei 75/8
"perch, alight, stop on a branch away from the home nest, sojourn"; iǔ
is here best translated by the English preposition "to"; lin 163/12 is
an intransitive verb: "be neighbors".

19.12 dzhəng 73/8 "to experience" and geng 120/8 "pass through,
to experience" form a synonym compound which is a specialized auxiliary

verb indicating that the action of the following verb has been com-
pletely experienced. jitu 86/9 "illuminate, shine on", so dzhəng geng
jitu would be "has shone on".

19.13 njiɑk 140/5 "resemble" liou modifies shuǐ (GS 16).

19.14 ghiɔ̀ng is here in its usual adverbial use: "together",
perhaps slightly extended to "with someone"; gai 106/4. The first four
words of the line constitute a verb-object clause which is the topic to
the last three words of the line, another verb-object construction.

19.15 ui 61/8; ngiuæ̀n 181/10 "want", an auxiliary verb; dɑng
102/8 "be right in the process of"; gɑ "song" is a noun here, rather
than "sing", a verb, because of the parallelism with tziǒu. After the
collapse of the Xɑ̀n in 220, China was divided into three kingdoms. In
the north, the Ngiuə̀i 魏 (Wèi) Dynasty ruled from 220 to 264. It
was founded by the great general Dzhɑu Tsɑu 曹操 (Cáo Cāo, 155-220),
who was also one of the Giæ̀n Qɑn poets (see 16.13). His famous "Verse
of a song on transitoriness 短歌行 Duǎn gɑ hæng (Duǎn gē xíng)"
contains these lines:

Facing wine, right in a song--

man's life: how long?

The object of ngiuæ̀n is the long sentence that ends the poem. This sen-
tence begins with a time topic that ends with zhi (cf. 18.11).

19.16 djhiɑng 168/0 (cf. 6.2); gim 167/0 "gold"; tzuən 65/12
"goblet"; lǐ 145/7 "inside, in".

Prosodic note 8: Changing rhymes

Old-style poems over eight lines often change rhymes. In Poem 18,
there are rhymes on alternate, even-numbered lines: tsin, njin, shin,
and chuin, then a change of rhyme: luɑ̀n, sɑ̀n, and xɑ̀n.

In Poem 19, the option of having the first line rhyme is taken.
The rhyme changes three times, and every time there is a change of
rhyme, the first line of the new rhyme group also rhymes. Below are
transcriptions of the last words of every line in Poem 19, grouped
according to rhyme:

zhi, ji, (dək), zui;

kiuæt, biæt, (ləi), mət;

chuin, lin, (ngiuæt), njin;

shuǐ, tsǐ, (zhi), lǐ.

Notice that in the second rhyme group listed above, mət seems not
to rhyme perfectly with kiuæt and biæt. However, according to even the
strictest rhyming conventions, this rhyme is permitted (see Table 4,
p. 6 : Group 14).

20. First of two poems entitled Long Gully song 長干行
Djhiang Gan hæng (Cháng Gān xíng)

tsiɛp biæt chriu piɒu ngæk	妾 髮 初 覆 額
jiɛt xua mən dzhen ghiæk	折 花 門 前 劇
lang ghi djiuk mǎ ləi	郎 騎 竹 馬 來
njiʮu jrhiang lǔng tseng məi	繞 床 弄 青 梅
5 dhung giu djhiang gan lǐ	同 居 長 干 里
liǎng siɛu mio hem tsəi	兩 小 無 嫌 猜
zhip sì ui giuən bhiǒu	十 四 為 君 婦
siou ngan miði zhiang kəi	羞 顏 未 嘗 開
dei dhou xiàng qòm bek	低 頭 向 暗 壁
10 tsen huàn biət qit huəi	千 喚 不 一 回
zhip ngǒ shǐ djiěn mi	十 五 始 展 眉
ngiuæn dhung djhin iǔ xuəi	願 同 塵 與 灰
zhiang dzhuən bhǎu djhiǒ sìn	常 存 抱 柱 信
kiði zhiǎng miàng bio dhəi	豈 上 望 夫 臺
15 zhip liuk giuən iuæn hæng	十 六 君 遠 行
ghio dhang iʮm iɒ duəi	瞿 唐 灩 澦 堆
ngǒ ngiuət biət kǎ chiok	五 月 不 可 觸

iuæn shiæng ten zhiàng qəi	猿 聲 天 上 哀
mən dzhen djhi hæng tziæk	門 前 遲 行 跡
20 qit qit shræng liok dhəi	一 一 生 綠 苔
dhəi shim biət nəng sǎu	苔 深 不 能 掃
lɑk iɛp tsiou biung tzǎu	落 葉 秋 風 早
bat ngiuæt ho-dhep ləi	八 月 蝴 蝶 來
shrang biəi sei iuæn tsǎu	雙 飛 西 園 草
25 gǒm tsǐ shiɑng tsiɛp sim	感 此 傷 妾 心
dzhuǎ jrhiou hung ngan lǎu	坐 愁 紅 顏 老
tzǎu miěn hɑ̀ som ba	早 晚 下 三 巴
iù tziɑng shiu bàu ga	預 將 書 報 家
siɑng ngiæng biət dhàu iuǎn	相 迎 不 道 遠
30 djhiək jì djhiɑng biung shra	直 至 長 風 沙

(Music Bureau poem)

Title: gɑn 51/0 represents several different words. In this place name, it is perhaps a dialect variant of "gully" 澗 gàn. Djhiɑng-gɑn is the name of a village five lǐ south of the modern Nán-jǐng 南京 (or Nanking). In the various collections of Music Bureau poems (see "Prosodic note 6", p. 51), several poems have as their titles the name of this village followed by a word that means "words of a song, verse", such as hæng 144/0 here. Such poems usually have love as their theme. Thus the title of this poem by Lǐ Bhæk identi-fies it as a Music Bureau poem; the text of the poem is scarcely dis-tinguishable from a five-syllable old-style poem in its prosody.

20.1 tsiɛp 38/5 "secondary wife" is often used, as here, as a deprecatory first person pronoun said by a married woman: "I, me, my". biæt 190/5 "hair (on top of human head)"; chriu 18/5 "first", an ad-

verb; <u>piɒu</u> 146/12 "cover", a transitive verb; <u>ngæk</u> 181/9 "forehead".
The line is time topic to what follows: "When...first...."

20.2 <u>jiɛt</u> 64/4 "break off, pick (a flower)"; <u>mən</u> 169/0; <u>ghiæk</u>
18/13"to play". The line consists of two coordinate comments, sepa-
rated at the caesura.

20.3 <u>lɑng</u> 163/7 "young man", but often, as here, used as a
second person pronoun by a wife to her husband: "you, your"; <u>ghi</u>
187/8 "ride (astride)"; <u>djiuk</u> 118/0; the basic meaning of <u>mǎ</u> is "horse";
for <u>ləi</u> here, see GS 15.

20.4 <u>njiɛu</u> 120/12 "wind around, go (galloping) around"; <u>jrhiɑng</u>
53/4 "bed" (cf. the appearance of this word at 14.1, where it is writ-
ten differently); <u>lùng</u> 55/4 "play with, use...as a toy"; <u>məi</u> 75/7 is
here a metonym for a branch of the tree, used as a play whip.

20.5 <u>giu</u> 44/5 has its basic meaning here: "dwell" and takes a
place object: <u>lǐ</u> 166/0 "village".

20.6 <u>liǎng</u> 11/6 "two"; <u>siɛu</u> 42/0 "small", but here a metonym:
"small people"; <u>hem</u> 38/10 and <u>tsəi</u> 94/8 both have two meanings, either of
which would apply here: "suspicion, loathing". This synonym compound
is the object of <u>mio</u>, and this verb-object phrase is perhaps best trans-
lated "innocent, easygoing, passionless".

20.7 <u>zhip</u> 24/0 "ten"; <u>sì</u> 31/2 "four". <u>zhip sì</u> is a coordinate
compound: "fourteen". It is a time topic here: "when I was in my
fourteenth year of age, at thirteen". <u>ui</u> 87/8 "become"; <u>giuən</u> 30/4;
<u>bhiǒu</u> 38/8 "wife".

20.8 <u>siou</u> 123/5 "embarrassed, shy"; <u>ngan</u> 181/9 "face, expression;
<u>miəi</u> 75/1 "not yet" combines with the auxiliary verb <u>zhiɑng</u> 30/11
"taste, experience" to form an adverb: "never"; <u>kəi</u> is extended here:
"open (the face in a smile)". Notice the topicalization of the object
of <u>kəi</u>.

20.9 <u>qɒm</u> 72/9 "dark"; <u>bek</u> 32/13 "wall".

20.10 <u>tsen</u> is an adverb here: "a thousand times"; <u>huàn</u> 30/9
"call"; <u>huəi</u> 31/3. The implied actor of <u>huàn</u> is different from that
of the surrounding verbs.

20.11 <u>ngǒ</u> 7/2 "five"; <u>shǐ</u> 38/5 "begin"; <u>djiɛn</u> 44/7 "spread", but
with a special application here: "spread...(from a frown)".

20.12 <u>dhung</u> is an intransitive verb here: "be together (with
you)"; <u>djhin</u> 32/11 "dust"; for <u>iǔ</u> as a conjunction, see GS 14; <u>xuəi</u> 86/2
"ash". <u>djhin iǔ xuəi</u> is the time object (GS 21) of <u>dhung</u> and may be
introduced by such words as "until we become...." "Dust and ashes" as
a figure for death recalls these lines from a "Coffin-bearer's song
挽 歌 Miǎn gɑ (Wǎn gē)", by Liuk Giəi 陸 機 (Lù Jī, 261-303):

Before, you were seven feet of a human form;

now you've become dust and ashes.

20.13 zhiɑng 50/8 "forever"; dzhuən 39/3 "remain, cause...to re-
main, keep, preserve"; bhǎu 64/5 "wrap the arms around and hold";
djhiǒ 75/5 "pillar, stanchion, upright wooden support". bhǎu djhiǒ
is from the Jriɑng-tzǐ (see 10.7), ch. 29, "Robber Jiɑk 盜 跖
Dhǎu Jiɑk (Dào Zhí)":

Master Tail made a date with a girl to meet below a

bridge. The girl didn't show up. When the water

rose, he didn't leave, but held on to a bridge

stanchion until he died.

sìn 9/7 "trust", the main word of the direct object of dzhuən. It is
modified by the verb-object phrase that precedes it: "a hold-stanchion
trust, a trust like the one Master Tail had".

20.14 zhiǎng 1/2 is transitive here: "mount, climb"; bio 37/1 is
here used in a common extension: "husband"; dhəi 133/8 "watchtower,
platform (for looking off into the distance)". The wife is distressed
that in spite of the mutual faith she shared with her husband, she is
now driven to a loneliness because of his absence, such that she seems
always to be gazing into the distance, hoping to catch sight of him
returning.

20.15 liuk 12/2 "six"; iuǎn 162/10 "far", here, an adverb; hæng
"travel".

20.16 ghio 109/13 "(name of a place)"; dhɑng 30/7 "embankment".
Ghio Embankment is the name of a gorge through which the Yangtze passes,
in the eastern part of the modern district of Fèng-jié 奉 節 , in
the province of Sì-chuān 四 川 (or Szechwan), where the Three Gorges
begin. iɛm-iò (85/28, 85/13) "(name of a place)"; duəi 32/8 "pile".
Iɛm-iò Pile is the name of a rock at the beginning of Ghio Embankment,
in the middle of the Yangtze, rising over a hundred feet during the
winter low-water season, but only eight feet or so in the summer, when
the water in the river runs high. The rock makes dangerous eddies in
the Yangtze, and boatmen take special care to avoid it. The names of
both places in this line form a coordinate phrase, place object to
hæng in the preceding line.

20.17 ngiuæt here means "month". The Chinese year starts in
spring, and the fifth month occurs in midsummer. biət kǎ is injunc-
tive: "you had better not...!" chiok 148/13 "hit", the implied direct
object being Iɛm-iò Pile (GS 28).

20.18 iuæn 94/10; shiæng is here "voice, cry". The sad cry of
gibbons is associated with the western area of China corresponding to
modern Sì-chuān Province. qəi is an intransitive verb here: "be sad,

mournful". Notice the word order: subject, place topic, comment.

20.19 djhi 162/11 "late, delay"; hæng has yet another meaning
here: "leave, departure"; tziæk 157/6 "footprint", the main word of the
topic (to which the next line is the comment): "Footprints that you
left in front of our gate when you made your reluctant departure...."

20.20 qit qit "one by one" (GS 3); dhəi 140/5 "moss".

20.21 shim is here "thick, dense"; nəng 130/6 "can, be able to",
an auxiliary; sằu 64/8 (GS 28).

20.22 lɑk modifies iɛp 140/9 "leaf", chief word of a topic that
is vaguely related to the comment (GS 30). This comment is itself
another topic-comment construction:

      Fallen leaves--the autumn wind is early.
Cf. 8.2.

20.23 bat 12/0 "eight". The eighth month occurs in mid autumn.
ho-dhep (both characters 142/9) "butterfly". When both place or time
topic and subject are present, the usual order is as in this line
rather than as in line 18 above.

20.24 shrang 172/10 "pair, in pairs"; sei 146/0 is a modifier
here: "western". tsằu is the main word of a place object.

20.25 gồm 61/9 "respond emotionally to, be moved by".

20.26 jrhiou 61/9 "sadness, be sad, grieve". There are several
possible relationships between dzhuǎ and jrhiou: coordinate: "I sit
and grieve that..."; subordinate (extending "sit" to "deep-seatedly,
deeply"): "I grieve deeply that...", or (extending "sit" to a special
meaning: "without being able to do anything about it, unaccountably,
somehow") "I am somehow sad that..."; or verb-object: "I sit in grief
that..." A "red face" is a figure for youth. lằu 125/0 "become old,
show signs of old age".

20.27 tzằu miǎn are in a coordinate relationship, with an im-
plied "or" between them (GS 12). This phrase is a time topic: "(At a
time that will come) sooner or later...." hà 1/2 has a place object
here and means "proceed down". The Three Ba's are three commanderies
set up in the Xằn Dynasty. The area corresponds to the eastern part of
Sì-chuān Province.

20.28 iħ 181/4 "beforehand"; tziɑng here means "take"; shiu 73/6
"letter"; bằu 32/9 "inform, let...know"; ga 40/7 "family". Notice the
irregular placement of the caesura, caused by the position of the two
coordinate verb-object phrases.

20.29 ngiæng 162/4; dhằu 162/9 "say", with a one-word sentence as
its object: "About my welcoming you, I do not say that it will be a
matter of traveling very far to do so."

20.30 djhiək 109/3 "only"; ji 133/0 "go as far as"; shra 85/4.
Long Wind Sands is about seven hundred lǐ away from Long Gully, in the
modern province of An-hui 安徽

21. The road to Zhiok is difficult 蜀道難 Zhiok dhǎu nan
(Shǔ dào nán)

Title: zhiok 142/7 is an ancient name for the region in western
China roughly corresponding to the modern province of Sì-chuān (20.16).
dhǎu 162/9 "road"; nan 172/11 "difficult, difficulty". This title is
a standard one for Music Bureau poems that describe the rugged scenery
southwest of the Chinese heartland. Like many Music Bureau poems, this
poem has lines of varying length, with seven-syllable lines predomi-
nating.

The journey described in the poem begins in Djhiang-qan (see
above, p.22), proceeds through difficult mountain country to the west
and south, and ends in Gǐm-zhiæng 錦城 (Jǐn-chéng, literally,
"Brocade City"; the city is now called Chéng-dū 成都 and is the cap-
ital of Sì-chuān Province). It is important to know that Djhiang-qan
is in the region of the ancient state of Dzhin (16.6). In the earliest
period of Chinese history, this area was non-Chinese, and the people
living there were uncivilized, from the Chinese point of view. By the
middle of the first millennium B.C., Dzhin was sinified, and by the
third century B.C. its ruler had accomplished the unification of China.
Though the Dzhin Dynasty is judged harshly by later historians, the
name Dzhin is also associated with the positive results of the new uni-
fication and the new Chinese order developed in succeeding dynasties.
In the present poem, the name "Dzhin" appears only once, in Line 6, but
the opposition of the peace, civilization, and control associated with
the name, to the dangers, barbarism, and abandon associated with the
name "Zhiok" is central to the poem.

21.3 According to the traditional account of the origin of Zhiok,
the reigns of its first five rulers extended over a period of 34,000
years. The names of the first and third rulers are Silkworm Thicket
and Fish Mallard.

21.6 Dzhin, neighboring Zhiok to the northeast, was considered
more thoroughly Chinese than Zhiok, by the middle of the first millen-
nium B.C.

21.9 There is a story about how in the fifth century B.C., a
prince of Dzhin tried to subvert the stability of Zhiok. He knew
that the prince of Zhiok had a weakness for feminine beauty, so he
sent him a present of five young ladies. The prince of Zhiok sent
five young men to meet them on the Zhiok road and to escort them back
to the Zhiok capital. The men and the young ladies met, and on the
way back they came upon a huge snake, which disappeared into a hole in
the mountain. One of the men took hold of the snake's tail, but was
unable to pull it out. Then all five men pulled, and they caused a land-
slide so great that the single mountain which the snake entered was
reshaped into five new mountains. The five men and the five women were
crushed to death.

21.11 According to Chinese myth, six dragons carry the sun across
the sky in a chariot. The highest mountain in Zhiok is marked with a
flag. When the charioteer sees this marker, he knows that he has taken

the sun far enough west, and that it is time to return.

    21.17 The Chinese zodiacal constellations number twenty-eight, and each is assigned a geographical area. Plow (comprising some of the southern stars of Orion, and some neighboring stars) is assigned to Zhiok, and Well (comprising some of the eastern stars of Gemini) is assigned to Dzhin. At the border of these two regions are the Blue Mud Mountains.

    21.23 The cuckoo is a nocturnal bird native to Zhiok. Its mournful cry is said to resemble the Chinese words for "Better go home!" In the third century B.C., a prime minister of Zhiok developed flood control measures that saved the country from disaster. In recognition of his achievement, Emperor Miǎng 望 (Wàng) of Zhiok abdicated in his favor, and, in mid-spring, when the cuckoos cry most, the emperor retired into the mountains. The people of Zhiok, when they hear the cry of the cuckoo, remember this emperor and grieve for him.

qi-xio-xî   噫吁嚱危乎高哉
   ngui ho gɑu tzəi

zhiok dhǎu ji nɑn   蜀道之難難於上青天
   nɑn qiu zhiǎng tseng ten

dzhom dzhung   蠶叢及魚鳧
   ghip ngiu bhio

kəi guək   開國何茫然
   hɑ mɑng-njiɛn

5 njĭ ləi sî miɐn   爾來四萬八千歲
   bat tsen siuɛi

biət iǔ dzhin səi   不與秦塞通人烟
   tung njin qen

sei dɑng tɑ̀i bhæk   西當太白有鳥道
   iǒu děu dhǎu

kǎ ǐ huæng dzhiuet
    ngɑ mi den

可 以 横 絶 峨 眉 巓

dhǐ bəng shran dzhuəi
    jriàng jrhǐ sǐ

地 崩 山 摧 壯 士 死

10 njiɛn hòu
    ten tei zhiæk jrhàn
    siɑng gou liɛn

然 後 天 梯 石 棧 相 鉤 連

zhiàng iǒu
    liuk liong huəi njit
    ji gɑu biɛu

上 有 六 龍 回 日 之 高 標

hǎ iǒu
    chiong bɑ ngiæk jiɛt
    ji huəi chiuɛn

下 有 衝 波 逆 折 之 回 川

huɑng hɑk ji biəi
    zhiàng biət dək guà

黄 鶴 之 飛 尚 不 得 過

iuæn nɑu iok dhò
    jrhiou pɐn iuæn

猿 猱 欲 渡 愁 攀 援

15 tseng nei
    hɑ bhɑn bhɑn

青 泥 何 盤 盤

bæk bhò giǒu jiɛt
    qiuæng ngam luɑn

百 步 九 折 縈 巖 巒

mən shrim lek tziǎng
    ngiǎng xiæp siək

捫 參 歷 井 仰 脅 息

ĭ shiǒu piǒ qiɐng
    dzhuǎ djhiɑng tɑn

以手撫膺坐長嘆

miɐn giuɐn sei iou
    hɑ zhi huan

問君西遊何時還

20 qiuɐi dho jrhɑm-ngɑm
        biɐt kǎ pan

畏途巉巖不可攀

dhǎn gɛn bi děu
    hɑu gǒ muk

但見悲鳥號古木

hiung biɐi tsi dzhiong
    njiɛ̀u lim gan

雄飛雌從繞林間

iɒu miɐn tzĭ-gui
    dhei ià ngiuæt

又聞子規啼夜月

jrhiou kung shran

愁空山

25 zhiok dhǔu ji nɑn
        nɑn qiu zhiǎng tseng ten

蜀道之難難於上青天

shrĭ njin teng tsĭ
    deu jio ngan

使人聽此凋朱顏

liɛn piong kiǔ ten
    biɐt iæng chiæk

連峯去天不盈尺

ko ziong dɑu guài
    qi dziuɐt bek

枯松倒挂倚絕壁

biəi tuɑn bhuk liou
   jræng xiuæn xuəi

飛湍瀑流爭喧豗

30 pæng ngai djiuèn zhiæk
   miàn xɑk luəi

砯崖轉石萬壑雷

ghi xiěm iǎ njiɑk tsɪ̌

其險也若此

tzia njɪ̌ iuǎn dhǎu ji njin
   ho ui ho ləi tzəi

嗟爾遠道之人胡爲乎來哉

giuæn gɑk jrhæng-huæng
   nji ngai-nguəi

劍閣崢嶸而崔嵬

qit bio dɑng guan

一夫當關

35 miàn bio mɑk kəi

萬夫莫開

shriǔ shiǒu
   huək piǎi tsin

所守或匪親

xuà ui
   lɑng iǔ jrhai

化爲狼與豺

djieu bhɪ̌ mǽng xǒ

朝避猛虎

ziæk bhɪ̌ djhiɑng jhia

夕避長蛇

40 mɑ nga jhuɪ̌n xuet

磨牙吮血

shrat njin njiu ma

殺人如麻

gɪ̌m zhiæng
   sui iuən lɑk

錦城雖云樂

biət njiu   不 如 早 還 家

    tzău huan ga

zhiok dhău ji nɑn   蜀 道 之 難 難 於 上 青 天

    nɑn qiu zhiăng tseng ten

45 jriək shin sei miǎng   側 身 西 望 長 咨 嗟

    djhiɑng tzi-tzia

                     (Music Bureau poem)

21.1 qi-xio-xì (30/13, 30/3, 30/17) is an exclamation of amaze-
ment: "whee! wow!"; ngui 26/4 "dangerous"; ho 4/4 "(particle at the
end of an interrogative sentence)"; gɑu 189/0 "high place"; tzəi 30/6
"(particle at the end of an exclamatory sentence)". One of the ex-
ceptions to the usual order-- first: topic, second: comment--involves
the use of certain rhetorical particles like ho and tzəi. (comment)
ho (topic) tzəi means "How (comment) the (topic) is!"

21.2 The locative particle qiu (16.24) has an extension in a
comparative construction, where it means "than": nɑn qiu X means "is
more dangerous than X". zhiǎng here has a place object (cf. 20.14) and
means "go up to".

21.3 dzhom 142/18 and dzhung 29/16 "thicket" comprise a man's
name; ghip 29/2 "and" is a coordinate conjunction (GS 14) joining two
halves of a topic; ngiu 195/0 and bhio 196/2 "mallard" comprise another
name, the second half of the topic.

21.4 kəi here has the extended meaning "to found"; guək 31/8
"nation"; mɑng 140/6 in mɑng-njiɛn "(indistinct)", where njiɛn 86/8
is a manner suffix (GS 5), mɑng is a one-syllable representation of
mɑng-mɑng, a reduplicating descriptive, meaning "(indistinct)" (see
below, 41.10), and the manner phrase is functioning like a descriptive.
This line is the comment to the preceding, and itself consists of a
topic and a comment. The founding of the Zhiok nation is viewed as
happening so far in the past that knowledge about it can only be faint.

21.5 njì 89/10 "approach (the present time)" forms a coordinate
expression with ləi "from then coming toward the present time to". In
numerical expressions, miæn is multiplied by the number that precedes
it; similarly with tsen. siuèi 77/9 "year", the unit that is counted
by the numerical expression. siuèi is the main word of a place object
of ləi. The whole line is a time topic to what follows.

21.6 səi 32/10 "frontier region". iŭ 134/7 is here a co-verb
(GS 26): "with". tung here: "let...through, exchange". qen here
is "smoke (from a chimney or stove), and njin qen is a metonym for
njin.

Paraphrasing the couplet: "It wasn't until forty-eight thousand years later that there was human communication with the Dzhin frontier regions."

21.7 dɑng here: "right where...is"; tɑ̀i 37/1 "great". tɑ̀i bhæk is the name of a snowcapped mountain rising 4,000 meters high about 125 km.WSW of Djhiɑng-qɑn. dĕu 196/0 "bird, suitable only for birds".

21.8 Y "take, use...as an instrument, by means of, with" replaces Y dhɑ̌u (GS 27). The combination kɑ̌ Y is effectively a two-syllable auxiliary meaning "can". It differs from kɑ̌ alone in that its topic is generally the actor of the main verb (and the voice of the English verb translating the main verb is active), whereas the topic of kɑ̌ alone is generally the recipient of the action of the main verb (and the voice of the English verb translating it is passive). huæng 75/12 "in a crosswise manner, right across"; dzhiuet is here "cut across", with a place object. ngɑ 46/7 mi "(name of a place)" refers to a mountain about 230 km.SSW of Gĭm-zhiæng; because this mountain lies far from the route described in the poem, it is to be taken as a metonym for the whole Zhiok area. ngɑ mi is homonymous with the Chinese for "moth eyebrow" (13.2); possibly the name refers to the way two of the main peaks slope out like moth antennae. den 46/19 "(mountain) peak".

21.9 bəng 46/8 "collapse"; dzhuəi 64/11 "be crushed"; jriɑ̀ng 33/4 "young and able-bodied"; jrhĭ 33/0 "officer, soldier"; sĭ 78/2 "die". The line consists of three short topic-comment constructions.

21.10 njiɛn is here a one-syllable verb-object phrase: "resembles it", by extension: "it is like that"; here it modifies a time noun (GS 18) with which it forms a time expression in topic position: "After it was like that", with an important extension of the meaning of hòu "Only after it was like that..., Only then...." tei 75/7 "ladder"--"ladders so long that they seem as though they would stretch to the sky" connect impassable places on the road. zhiæk 112/0; jrhæn 75/8 "reinforced road"-- this phrase is coordinate with ten tei. gou 167/5 "hook up to"; liɛn 162/7 "connect to".

21.11 zhiɑ̀ng is place topic: "above"; gɑu here means "situated in a high place"; biɛu 75/11 "marker". The four words liuk...njit comprise a subject-verb-object sentence modifying gɑu biɛu: "a high marker, where...."

21.12 chiong 144/9 basically means "dash against, pound"; here, it modifies bɑ, and the combination may be translated "billow". ngiæk 162/6 "roll back against the current"; jiet, here, "turn back", coordinate with ngiæk; huəi, intransitive here: "go back", and modifying chiuen. The line is nearly parallel to Line 11; only the four words of the modifying clause are organized differently.

21.13 huɑng 201/0 "yellow, brown"; hɑk 196/10 "(crane)", the bird the immortals ride. It is white or huɑng, both colors associated with old age. zhiɑ̀ng 42/5 "still, even so"; dək is an auxiliary verb here, indicating successful completion of the action of the following verb;

guἀ here is "pass over, cross".

21.14 nɑu 94/9 "(gibbon)" forms a synonym compound with iuæn;
iok 76/7 "want, wish", an auxiliary verb; dhὸ 53/6 "to cross"; jrhiou
here another auxiliary: "be sad about (how hard it is to)"; iuæn 64/9
"drag, pull oneself up, climb" forms a synonym compound with the pre-
ceding word.

21.15 nei 85/5 "mud". The Blue (Green, or Gray) Mountains are
about 150 km.WSW of Great White along the main route connecting the
Dzhin and Zhiok areas. bhɑn 108/10 "writhe, have many turns", here,
reduplicated to form an intensive (GS 3). tseng nei is the place
topic, not the subject, of hɑ bhɑn bhɑn; the implied subject is the
mountain road.

21.16 bæk 106/1 "hundred"; bhὸ 77/3 "step"; giŏu 5/1 "nine".
The first four words of this line constitute a second comment, co-
ordinate with hɑ bhɑn bhɑn in the previous line. This comment is
itself composed of a place topic: "In (every) hundred steps..." and
a comment. A third comment ends the line: qiuæng 120/10 "wind around";
ngam 46/20 "cliff" and luɑn 46/19 "mountain range" are coordinate
place objects.

21.17 mən 64/8 "lay hands on, touch"; shrim 28/9 "Plow (name of
the 21st of the 28 Chinese zodiacal constellations)"; lek 77/12 "pass
through"; tziǎng 7/2 "Well (22nd of the 28 zodiacal constellations)";
ngiǎng 9/4 "raise the head to look"; xiæp 130/6 "hold in (the breath)";
siək 61/6 "breath". The line consists of four comments (three verb-
object and one single-verb), all to the unmentioned topic, which is the
traveler.

21.18 ї is here used in its basic, co-verbal function (GS 26;
cf. 21.8 above), with shiŏu 64/0 "hand" as its object. piŏ 64/12
"touch gently"; qiɑng 130/13 "chest, breast"; dzhuἀ here has the same
possibilities of translation as it had in 20.26; tɑn 30/11 "sigh".
The implied actor is still the traveler.

21.19 miὸn takes two objects: first, giuɑn, the one to whom the
question is put; second, the rest of the line, which is the question.
hɑ, here: "what?", modifies zhi, and the phrase is an interrogative
time topic, with huan 162/13 "return", the comment. The implied actor
to miὸn is the persona; giuɑn refers to the traveler (cf. 2.1).

21.20 qiuὸi 102/4 "fear, fearsome, precipitous"; dho 162/7 "path,
road"; jrham 46/17 "steep and dangerous". For the kǎ-verb construction,
cf. 20.17.

21.21 bi 61/8 "sad"; hɑu 141/7 "call, cry", followed by a place
object. gŏ, here: "ancient, old".

21.22 hiung 172/4 "male bird"; tsi 172/5 "female bird".

21.23 iɔu 29/0 "and what is more", an adverb connecting the sen-
tence it occurs in with the previous sentence. miən 128/8 "hear ".
tzĭ-gui (39/0, 147/4) "(cuckoo)", a pivot; dhei 30/9 "call, cry", with
a place object.

21.24 This line is parallel to the last three words of Line 23.

21.26 The pivot (GS 43) has a comment consisting either of two coordinated elements, or of two elements the first of which is time topic to the second: <u>teng</u> 128/16 "hear" then becomes "when he hears...." <u>deu</u> 15/8 "cause to become withered"; <u>jio</u> 75/2 "red, ruddy", said of a youthful appearance.

21.27 <u>liɛn</u> takes the following word as object and means here "pass through one...after another"; <u>piong</u> 46/7 "mountain peak", a pivot; <u>kiù</u> 28/3 "leave, be distant from"; <u>iæng</u> 108/4 "fill"; <u>chiæk</u> 44/1 "Chinese linear foot". The peaks are described as being less than one foot away from the sky.

21.28 <u>ko</u> 75/5 "withered"; <u>dàu</u> 9/8 "upside down", an adverb; <u>guài</u> 64/8 "be suspended"; <u>qì</u> 9/8 "be set in"; <u>dzhiuɛt</u> is here "stopping, blocking, precipitous, impassable".

21.29 <u>biəi</u> modifies <u>tuɑn</u> 85/9 "rapids"; <u>bhuk</u> 85/15 "waterfall, cascading" modifies <u>liou</u>, here: "stream"; <u>jræng</u> 87/4 "compete in", an auxiliary; <u>xiuæn</u> 30/9 "yell"; <u>xuəi</u> 152/3 "clash". The rapids and streams below the road vie with each other to see which can make the loudest noise.

21.30 <u>pæng</u> 112/5 "make a loud sound"; <u>ngai</u> 46/8 "cliff"; <u>djiuɛ̀n</u> "make...turn" (cf. 17.7 and GS 4, where the same character represents <u>djiuɛ̌n</u>, an etymologically related, intransitive correlate to <u>djiuɛ̀n</u>); <u>xɑk</u> 32/14 "gulley"; <u>luəi</u> 173/5 "thunder". The break between the topic and the comment in this line is after <u>zhiæk</u>, and the meaning of the topic-comment relationship here is "The effect of (topic) is (comment)". <u>miæ̀n xɑk</u> modifies <u>luəi</u>: cf. <u>qit bəi tziǒu</u> in 8.3.

21.31 <u>ghi</u> 12/6 is an attributive pronoun: "his, its, their..."; <u>xiɛ̌m</u> 170/13 "danger"; <u>ià</u> 5/2 is a pause particle frequently occurring in prose, here separating the topic from the comment.

21.32 <u>tzia</u> 30/10 is an interjection: "Alas!"; <u>njì</u> 89/10 is a second person pronoun: "you"; for the apposition here, see GS 46. The rest of the line is a comment, itself consisting of a topic and a comment, but in reverse order, for rhetorical effect (cf. Line 1, above): <u>ho</u> 130/3 "why?", regularly precedes a verb: <u>ui</u> here means "do", and the following <u>ho</u> reinforces the force of the rhetorical question: "How 'why-do-you-do-it?' your coming is! How questionable your journey is!"

21.33 <u>giuæm</u> 18/13 "two-edged sword"; <u>gɑk</u> 169/6 "tall building"; <u>jrhæng-huæng</u> (46/8, 46/14) "(high mountain)"; <u>nji</u> 126/0 is a conjunction, frequent in prose, that usually occurs between comments, where the first comment modifies the second--but often this subordinate relationship changes to coordinate: "and" (GS 14); <u>ngai</u> keeps some of its original meaning in this descriptive, which <u>nguəi</u> 46/10 forms with it: "(cliff, high and rocky)". Sword Tower is about 190 km.SSW of Blue Mud. <u>Gìm-zhiæng</u>, the end of the journey, is about 200 km. farther to the SW.

21.35 mɑk 140/7, occurs preverbally and says that of the possible participants in the action of the following verb, "none" actually participate. Lines 34 and 35 are in a topic-comment relationship, meaning "If (topic), then (comment)."

21.36 shriŭ 63/4 is a pronoun that replaces an object, whether direct, place, or time, of the following verb, and at the same time with that verb forms a noun. Thus, shriŭ and shiŏu 40/3 "guard" together mean "where (someone) is standing guard". Here this phrase is a place topic: "At a place where (someone) is standing guard...." huək 62/4, is another preverbal element and says that of the possible participants in the action of the verb (and here the participants are not actually named), "someone or other" might actually participate. piǒi 22/8 "not be" is a negative used to negate a nominal comment (GS 31).

21.37 xuà 21/2 "transform"; ui is coordinate with xuà (GS 15): "(they) change into...." lɑng 94/7 "wolf"; jrhai 153/3 "(wild dog)". Again, the lines of this couplet are in an "if..., then..." relationship.

21.38 bhì 162/13 "avoid"; mæ̌ng 94/8 "ferocious".

21.39 ziæk 36/0 "evening, night"; jhia 142/5 "snake".

21.40 mɑ 112/11 "grind"; nga 92/0 "tooth"; jhuǐn 30/4 "suck"; xuet 143/0 "blood". The two actions are given in the same order as the animals performing them in the preceding line.

21.41 shrat 79/7 "kill"; ma 200/0 "hemp", a figure here for a large number of slender things strewn about in disorder.

21.42 gǐm 167/8 "brocade"; iuən 7/2 "say" takes a sentence as its object, and here the sentence is a single-word comment, lɑk, here: "full of joy, fun". Logically, the topic to this comment is gǐm zhiæng, which has been topicalized (GS 40), changing an original "Though they say that Gǐm-zhiæng is full of joy...," to "Gǐm-zhiæng-- though they say it is full of joy...."

21.43 njiu is here "resemble...in goodness", and biət njiu is an idiom: "not be as good as", a transitive expression, here with a comment as its object.

21.45 jriək 9/9 "bend, incline", a transitive verb; tsi 30/6 "sigh" makes a synonym compound with the following word.

Chapter 5

Note to the student: In two stages, this chapter encourages great-
er reliance on the glossary. The first stage comprises Poem 22 alone.
The second stage begins with Poem 23.

In Poem 22, English glosses for new characters and for new mean-
ings of old characters will no longer be regularly provided in the
text. Only codes will be given, and you should refer to the glossary
for the English meanings. When a character represents more than one
word or appears in this collection in more than one meaning of a word,
you should be able to determine the word or meaning appropriate to a
given line of a poem by the line codes appearing after the respective
words and meanings.

Beginning with Poem 23, radical-remainder codes for new characters
and for new meanings of old characters will be given only if the radi-
cal of the character is obscure. For details, see the "Note to the
student" before Poem 23.

Dhǒ Biǒ 杜甫 (Dù Fǔ, 712-770)

Of all Chinese poets, Dhǒ Biǒ probably ranks highest in the esteem
of later readers because of the broad range of his subject matter, his
control of style, the depth of his feeling, and his high-minded patri-
otism.

He was concerned that the government accord with orthodox Confu-
cian principles, that it totally supress the rebellions that were be-
ginning to tear the Dhang empire apart, and that it bring into posi-
tions of power only incorruptible and wise officials. Nevertheless,
he himself spent only a few years during his forties in a minor posi-
tion at Djhiang-qan and with the court in exile. The outbreak of the
Qan Liuk-shran rebellion (see the next poem, below) turned him into a
refugee, as it did many of his literary contemporaries, and he had no
official position from the third year of the rebellion until a few
years before his death, when he was for a short time a military adviser
to a governor-general in the west.

The rest of his adult life he spent traveling, trying to muster
support for his applications for official appointment, fleeing war and
famine, settling and resettling his wife and children, growing his own
fruit and vegetables, visiting friends (which included his older con-
temporaries Iuang Ui and Lǐ Bhæk), and writing.

Unlike Iuang Ui and Lǐ Bhæk, and indeed unlike most Chinese poets,
Dhǒ Biǒ finds poetry a suitable and powerful medium to express his re-
actions to current national events and to convey his concern for his
family. Many of his best poems are on these themes.

22. Northward journey 北 征 Bək jiæng (Běi zhēng)

This five-syllable old-style poem is one of the longest of the genre. The rhyming is loose; the only requirement is that the rhymes end in -t, and once even this rule is broken.

The time of the poem is 757. At the end of 755, Qan Liuk-shran 安 祿 山 (Ān Lù-shān, d. 756) began a momentous rebellion. His ancestors were of northern, non-Chinese stock. Because of successful military campaigns in the northeast, he became a favorite in the court of the emperor Huen-tzong 玄 宗 (Xuán-zōng, or Hsüan-tsung, r. 713-756). The rebellion that he began was itself unsuccessful, but it rocked the Dhang government to its foundations, and later historians have marked it as the beginning of the eventual downfall of the dynasty.

In 757, the most shocking events of the rebellion are recently past. The rebel forces are occupying the two capitals. Huen-tzong and a small part of the imperial court have fled to the west, and during this journey, Iang Guək-djiung 楊國忠 (Yáng Guó-zhōng) chief minister of state, whom loyal officers blame for the rebellion, is murdered (or executed); in addition, the Emperor is forced to order the execution of Iang Giuəi-piəi 楊貴妃 (Yáng Guì-fēi, literally, "Iang the Honored Consort"), the Emperor's favorite concubine, a cousin of Guək-djiung and his entrée into the inner circle of the Emperor's most intimate associates. Huen-tzong has abdicated in favor of his son, Siuk-tzong 肅宗 (Sù-zōng, r.756-763), a month after the death of the Iangs.

As for recent events in Dhǒ Biǒ's life, they include the removal of his family from the dangers of Djhiang-qan, over a year earlier, to a place in Pio 鄜 (Fū) County, in the central part of the modern province of Shǎn-xī (or Shensi). Shortly afterward, he tries to rejoin the court of Siuk-tzong but is captured by the rebels and held in occupied Djhiang-qan. He soon escapes, and joins the court in exile at Bhiung-ziang 鳳翔 (Fèng-xiáng, literally "The Phoenix Soars"), about 160 km.east of Djhiang-qan. His official duties as "Reminder" to the Emperor are interrupted when he offends the Emperor by supporting a general whom the Emperor feels ought to be punished. His dismissal is put in the form of Imperial permission to leave his post and rejoin his family. The northward journey to Pio, some 350 km. away, and the reunion with his wife and children are the main events of this poem.

In Line 43, Dhǒ Biǒ refers to a famous story, which goes as follows: A certain fisherman travels along unfamiliar streams, when suddenly he comes upon a beautiful grove of flowering peach trees. He follows the trees until he arrives at a strange land occupied by people wearing clothes that he has never seen before. The people receive him hospitably, and they turn out to be as curious about him as he is about them. They exchange news, and he finds out from them that they are descendents of refugees of the historical disorder surrounding the collapse of the Dzhin Dynasty (16.6). They left their original homes at that time and formed an ideal community separated from the rest of civilization. Until the intrusion of the fisherman, they have lived their lives on their orderly farms in complete seclusion. After a time, they let the fisherman return, enjoining him never to reveal his discovery. Later the fisherman tries to find his way back to the land of the Peach Spring, but without success.

huɑng dɛi njì tzɛi tsiou	皇帝二載秋
njuìn bat ngiuæt chriu git	閏八月初吉
dhǒ tzǐ tziɑng bək jiæng	杜子將北征
tsɑng-mɑng miən ga shit	蒼茫問家室
5 ui zhi tzɑu gan ngio	維時遭艱虞
djhiɛu iǎ shiěu hà njit	朝野少暇日
gò dzhom qən si bhǐ	顧慙恩私被
jiɛu xiǔ giuəi bhung bit	詔許歸蓬蓽
bài zi ngèi kiuæt hǎ	拜辭詣闕下
10 tjuit tek giǒu miəi chuit	怵惕久未出
sui bhiæp gàn jræng tzi	雖乏諫諍姿
kiǒng giuən iǒu ui shit	恐君有遺失
giuən zhiæng djiùng xiəng jiǒ	君誠中興主
geng iuəi gò mit miət	經緯固密勿
15 dung ho biǎn miəi ǐ	東胡反未已
zhin biǒ bhiǎn shriǔ tset	臣甫憤所切
xiuəi tèi liuɛn hæng dzhǎi	揮涕戀行在
dhǎu dho iou xuǎng-xuət	道途猶恍惚

ghiɛn kuən hom chriɑng i	乾坤含瘡痍	
20 qiou ngio hɑ zhi bit	憂虞何時畢	
mǐ-mǐ iu tsen mæk	靡靡踰阡陌	
njin qen miěu seu-shrit	人煙眇蕭瑟	
shriǔ ngiɒ dɑ bhǐ shiɑng	所遇多被傷	
shin ngim gæng liou xuet	呻吟更流血	
25 huəi shiǒu bhiɒng ziɑng huɐn	迴首鳳翔縣	
tziæng ghi miǎn miæng miɛt	旌旗晚明滅	
dzhen dəng hɑn shrɑn djhiong	前登寒山重	
liɒ dək qǐm mǎ kuət	屢得飲馬窟	
bin gau njip dhǐ děi	邠郊入地底	
30 geng shuǐ djiung dhǎng guet	涇水中蕩潏	
mæng xɒ lip ngǎ dzhen	猛虎立我前	
tsɑng ngai xɒu zhi liɛt	蒼崖吼時裂	
giuk zhui gim tsiou xuɑ	菊垂今秋花	
zhiæk dəi gǒ giu djhiɛt	石戴古車轍	
35 tseng iuən dhǔng gɑu xiɒng	青雲動高興	
qiou jrhǐ iæk kǎ iuɛt	幽事亦可悅	

shran guǎ dɑ suǎ sèi	山 果 多 瑣 細
lɑ shræng dzhop ziǎng lit	羅 生 雜 橡 栗
huək hung njiu dɑn shrɑ	或 紅 如 丹 砂
40 huək xək njiu děm tsit	或 黑 如 點 漆
iǒ lò ji shriǔ njio	雨 露 之 所 濡
gom kǒ dzhəi get jhit	甘 苦 齊 結 實
miěn si dhɑu ngiuæn nuèi	緬 思 桃 源 内
qiæk tǎn shin shièi jiuɛt	益 歎 身 世 拙
45 pɑ-dhɑ miàng pio djhǐ	坡 陀 望 鄜 時
ngam guk hò chuit mət	巖 谷 互 出 沒
ngǎ hæng ǐ shuǐ bin	我 行 已 水 濱
ngǎ bhuk iou muk mɑt	我 僕 猶 木 末
chi děu miæng huɑng sɑng	鴟 鳥 鳴 黄 桑
50 iǎ shiǔ giǒng luàn huet	野 鼠 拱 亂 穴
iǎ shim geng jièn djhiɑng	夜 深 經 戰 場
hɑn ngiuæt jièu bhæk guət	寒 月 照 白 骨
dhung guɑn bæk miæn shri	潼 關 百 萬 師
iuǎng jiǎ sàn hɑ tsuət	往 者 散 何 卒

55 zuì liæng bæn dzhin min   遂令半秦民

dzhɑn hɒi ui ì miet   殘害為異物

xiuɒng ngɑ̌ dhuɑ̌ ho djhin   況我墮胡塵

ghip giuəi dzhǐn hua biæt   及歸盡華髮

geng nen jì mɒu quk   經年至茅屋

60 tsei tzǐ qiəi bæk get   妻子衣百結

dhʌng kuk ziong shiæng huəi   慟哭松聲迴

bi dzhiuɛn ghiɒng qiou qet   悲泉共幽咽

bhiæng shræng shriǔ giɛu nji   平生所嬌兒

ngan shriək bhæk shiɒng siuɛt   顏色白勝雪

65 gèn ia bɒi miɛn dhei   見耶背面啼

gǒu nì giɑk biət miæt   垢膩腳不襪

jrhiɑng dzhen liɑng siɛu niǔ   牀前兩小女

bǒ djhæn dzhəi guɑ sit   補綻才過膝

xǒi dho tjæk bɑ dhɑu   海圖坼波濤

70 ghiɒu siɒu i kiok jiɛt   舊繡移曲折

ten ngo ghip tzǐ bhiʌng   天吳及紫鳳

den dɒu dzhǒi zhiǒ hɑt   顛倒在裋褐

lǎu bio dzhiæng huai qɑk	老 夫 情 懷 惡
qǒu siɛt nguɑ̀ shriɒ njit	嘔 泄 臥 數 日
75 nɑ mio nɑng djiung bhæk	那 無 囊 中 帛
giɒu njiǔ hɑn lǐm lit	救 汝 寒 凜 慄
biǎn dhɘi iæk gǎi bau	粉 黛 亦 解 苞
kim djhiou shrɑ̀u lɑ liɛt	衾 裯 稍 羅 列
shriɒu tsei miɛn bhiuk guɑng	瘦 妻 面 復 光
80 tjǐ niǔ dhou dzhǐ jrit	癡 女 頭 自 櫛
hak mǒu mio biət ui	學 母 無 不 為
xěu jriɑng zui shiǒu mɑt	曉 妝 隨 手 抹
i zhi shi jio iuɛn	移 時 施 朱 鉛
lɑng-dzhiæk huɑ̀i mi kuɑt	狼 籍 畫 眉 闊
85 shræng huan duɒi dhung djhǐ	生 還 對 童 稚
zǐ iok miɑ̀ng gi kɑt	似 欲 忘 飢 渴
miɒn jrhǐ ghiɑ̀ng miǎn sio	問 事 競 挽 鬚
zhui nəng tziək chin xɑt	誰 能 即 嗔 喝
piæn si dzhɘ̀i dzhək jrhiou	翻 思 在 賊 愁
90 gɑm zhiǒu dzhop luɑ̀n guɑt	甘 受 雜 亂 聒

sin giuəi tsiǎ qiuəi qì   新 歸 且 慰 意

shræng lǐ qiɛn dək shiuɛt   生 理 焉 得 說

jì tzuən zhiàng mung djhin   至 尊 尚 蒙 塵

giǎi njit xiou lɛn tzuət   幾 日 休 練 卒

95 ngiǎng guɑn ten shriək gǎi   仰 觀 天 色 改

dzhuǎ gak qiɛu piən xuɑt   坐 覺 妖 氛 豁

qim biung sei bək ləi   陰 風 西 北 來

tsǒm-dhǒm zui huəi-huət   慘 澹 隨 回 紇

ghi iuɑng ngiuǎn jrhiǔ jhuǐn   其 王 願 助 順

100 ghi ziok xǐ djhi tuət   其 俗 喜 馳 突

sùng biæng ngǒ tsen njin   送 兵 五 千 人

kio mǎ qit miæn pit   驅 馬 一 萬 匹

tsǐ bəi shiǔu ui giuəi   此 輩 少 爲 貴

sì biɑng bhiuk iǒng guet   四 方 服 勇 決

105 shriǔ iòng gai qiəng dhəng   所 用 皆 鷹 騰

pà dhek guà tziɛn dzhit   破 敵 過 箭 疾

shiæng sim pɑ xiu djhiǔ   聖 心 頗 虛 佇

zhi ngì kiəi iok dhuət   時 議 氣 欲 奪

qi lɑk jǐ jiǎng shiou	伊 洛 指 掌 收
110 sei giæng biət tziok bhat	西 京 不 足 拔
guɑn giuən tsiǎng shim njip	官 軍 請 深 入
xiuk iuɛi kǎ gio biæt	蓄 銳 可 俱 發
tsǐ giǔ kəi tseng ziu	此 舉 開 青 徐
ziuɛn jiɛm liɑk həng ghiæt	旋 瞻 略 恆 碣
115 hǎu ten tziæk shriɑng lɔ	昊 天 積 霜 露
jiæng kiəi iǒu siuk shrat	正 氣 有 肅 殺
huǎ djiuěn miɑng ho siuɛi	禍 轉 亡 胡 歲
shiɛi zhiæng ghim ho ngiuæt	勢 成 擒 胡 月
ho miæng ghi nəng giǒu	胡 命 其 能 久
120 huɑng gɑng miəi ngi dzhiuɛt	皇 綱 未 宜 絕
qiək dzhɑk lɑng bɑ̀i chriu	憶 昨 狼 狽 初
jrhì iǔ gǒ sen bhiɛt	事 與 古 先 別
gan zhin giæng jriu xǒi	姦 臣 竟 菹 醢
dhung qɑk zui dhǎng sek	同 惡 隨 蕩 析
125 biət miən hǎ qiən shrui	不 聞 夏 殷 衰
djiung dzhì djio bɑu dɑt	中 自 誅 褒 妲

jiou xɑ̀n   huæk tzəi xiəng   周 漢 獲 再 興

siuɛn guɑng   guɑ̌ miæng djiɛt   宣 光 果 明 哲

huɑn-huɑn   djhin tziɑ̀ng giuən   桓 桓 陳 將 軍

130 djhiɑ̀ng iuæt   biən djiung liɛt   仗 鉞 奮 忠 烈

miəi njǐ   njin dzhǐn biəi   微 爾 人 盡 非

io gim   guək iou huɑt   于 今 國 猶 活

tsei liɑng   dhɑ̀i dhung dhèn   淒 涼 大 同 殿

dzhek mɑk   bhæk shiɑ̀u tɑt   寂 寞 白 獸 闥

135 do njin   miɑ̀ng tsuǐ hua   都 人 望 翠 華

gai kiəi   xiɑ̀ng gim kiuæt   佳 氣 向 金 闕

iuæn liəng   gɔ̀ iɔ̌u jhin   園 陵 固 有 神

sɑ̌u shrɑ̌   shriɔ̀ biət kuet   掃 灑 數 不 缺

huɑng-huɑng   tɑ̀i tzong ngiæp   煌 煌 太 宗 業

140 zhiɔ̌ lip   zhǐm huæng dhɑt   樹 立 甚 宏 達

                                      (Five-syllable old-style poem)

     Title: bək 21/3; jiæng 60/5.

          22.1-2 huɑng 106/4 and dèi 50/6 form a synonym compound, which
     here is a metonym: "(the present) emperor('s reign)"; njǐ 7/0; tzəi
     159/6. njuǐn 169/4; git 30/3. This couplet comprises a time topic and
     consists of phrases standing in a series of subordinate relationships.
          Siuk-tzong's first reign period (see 16.13) is called Jǐ Dək
     至 德   (Zhì Dé, literally, "Ultimate Virtue") and corresponds
     roughly to the Western years 756-757. It happens that the second year
     of this period has thirteen months. The practice of adding an extra,
     or intercalary, month every two or three years was developed to keep

the relationship between the months and the seasons stable. In this way, the Chinese were able to have months that always start exactly with a new moon and a year where the first three months coincide with the spring season, the next three with summer, and so on, except when there is an extra month. Any month of a thirteen-month year may be designated extra, except the first.

The other months regularly have names according to their order: "First Month", "Second Month", and so on. The month that is designated extra in a given year is considered an extra occurrence of the month that precedes it, and takes its name from that month, being called, for example, "Extra Eighth", if it follows the eighth month. Thus the addition of an intercalary month does not disturb the numbering of the regular months. The extra month of the second year of the Jì Dək reign period occurs after the regular eighth month, in autumn, and the first day of that month corresponds to September 18, 757, in the Western calendar.

Dhǒ Biǒ is about to begin his journey during a period of the month that he calls "When Good´Luck First Begins", a term used in ancient times for the first part of the month.

The caesura in Line 2, which according to the usual prosodic rules should fall between bat and ngiuæt, fails to correspond to the grammatical break, which would naturally fall between ngiuæt and chriu. Thus the poet has created a tension between poetic convention and the natural workings of the Chinese language. When there is a string of modifying expressions in Chinese, it is often expedient in English to translate beginning with the last Chinese element, which is the main word in the string, and work backwards, using phrases with "of" (or clauses with "that"): "In the 'When-Good-Luck-First-Begins' period of the Extra Eighth Month of the autumn of the second year of our present Emperor's reign..."

22.3 dhǒ 75/3; tzǐ 39/0. See the note to the title of Poem 8 for the word order here, which is the reverse of the English: "Master Dhǒ", the poet speaking of himself in the third person. A less honorific translation, using the basic meaning of tzǐ, is also possible: "a child of the Dhǒ's". tziang 41/8 and bək modify jiæng.

22.4 tsang 140/10 forms a rhyming descriptive with mang, describing the great distance from his family that the poet finds himself as he is performing the action of the verb, or else describing the vagueness of his knowledge about his family. shit 40/6.

22.5 ui 120/8 is an archaic demonstrative; tzau 162/11; gan 138/11; ngio 141/7. The implied actor of tzau is "we officials".

22.6 djhiɛu 74/8 and iǎ 166/4 are coordinate topics, figures for "officials" and "common people", respectively. shiěu 42/1; hà 72/9.

22.7 gò 181/12. dzhom 61/11 modifies the following comment, telling under what circumstances the comment occurs. The comment itself consists of a topic: gən 61/6, modifying si 115/2; and a comment: bhǐ 145/5. Paraphrase: "Yet, to my embarrassment, the Emperor's personal consideration, which is due to his favor, has been bestowed on

me." The line glosses over the fact that the poet has offended the
Emperor.

22.8 jiɛu 149/5; xiŭ 149/4; giuəi 77/14; bhung 140/11 and bit
140/11 stand for the gate made of these poor materials bound together,
which in turn stands for the house behind the poor gate--a double
metonym--and the compound is the place object of giuəi.

22.9 bə̀i 64/5 and zi 160/12 are coordinate and comprise the
topic, giving the reason for the action in the comment. ngə̀i 149/6
has as its place object kiuæt hă, which stands for "Imperial audience
hall".

22.10 tjuit 61/5 and tek 61/8 form a synonym compound which de-
scribes the persona; the persona is also the implied actor topic of
chuit 17/3.

22.11 bhiæp 4/4; gə̀n 149/9 and jræ̀ng 149/8 form a synonym com-
pound that modifies tzi 38/6.

22.12 ui 162/12 modifies shit 37/2.

22.13 zhiæng 149/6; djiṳng 2/3 and xiəng 134/9 form a verb-object
compound that means "restoration (of order and prosperity in the na-
tion)". The compound modifies jiŏ 3/4, the chief word of a nominal
comment (GS.31). zhiæng modifies the predication; in other words, it
modifies an implied "is".

22.14 geng 120/7 and iuə̀i 120/9 are terms from weaving, here used
as a figure for "the ins and outs of government". gò 31/5 modifies the
comment, mit 40/8 and miət 20/2, a synonym compound describing the im-
plied subject, which is the Emperor.

22.15 ho 130/5 throughout the poem refers to the rebels. biăn
29/2; ɪ̆ 49/0.

22.16 zhin 131/0 is in apposition with biŏ 101/2 (GS 46), and
the two words stand for "I" in the context of an official report to
the Emperor. bhiăn 61/12; tset 18/2, with the preceding shriṳ, forms
a noun clause ("wherein it is keen, what is keen") which is another
nominal comment. Literally, "As for me, Biŏ, my zealous dissatisfac-
tion is what is keen (because of it)". More smoothly: "This is what
I resent so keenly."

22.17 xiuəi 64/9; tə̀i 85/7; liuɛn 61/19; hæng dzhŏi: "(place
where when the Emperor) travels he is at, the Emperor's temporary
headquarters".

22.18 iou 94/9; xuăng-xuət (61/6, 61/8) describes the state of
mind of the persona.

22.19 ghiɛn 5/10 and kuən 32/5 are metonyms for "heaven" and
"earth", respectively. For an explanation of how hexagrams are used
in divination, see Wilhelm/Baynes 1950-68, especially pp. xlix-liv and

721-24.   hom 30/4; chriang 104/10; i 104/6.

22.20   qiou 61/11; bit 102/6.

22.21   mǐ 175/11; iu 157/9; tsen 170/3 and mæk 170/6 form a co-ordinate compound (GS 6).

22.22   qen 86/9, a common variant writing for the same word that appears in 21.6. For njin qen, see the note to that line, p. 86. miěu 109/4. The meaning of the descriptive seu-shrit (140/13, 96/9) is extended here; cf. 17.10.

22.23   ngiò 162/9 forms a noun clause with shriǔ, with a personal referent: "those whom we meet". bhǐ 145/5 is an auxiliary, marking the following verb as passive.

22.24   shin 30/5; ngim 30/4; gæng 73/3.

22.25   huəi 162/6, a common variant writing of the same word that appears in 21.11. bhiùng 196/3--the usual translation for this word, "phoenix", is, strictly speaking, inaccurate. ziang 124/6; huən 120/10. Notice the placement of the two objects (GS 24).

22.26   tziæng 70/7; ghi 70/10; miæn 72/7, the time topic; miæng 72/4. The flags of the provisional capital are seen as flickering in the evening like fires.

22.27   dzhen 18/7; dəng 105/7; han 40/9; djhiong 166/2, the main word of the place object.

22.28   liò 44/11; dək 60/8; qìm 184/4; kuət 116/8, modified by the verb-object clause qìm mǎ, is the object of dək.

22.29   bin 163/4; gau 163/6; děi 53/5, modified by dhì, is the object of njip 11/0.

22.30   geng 85/7; shuǐ 85/0; djiung 2/3, the place topic; dhǎng 140/12; guet 85/12.

22.29-30 About a third of the way along on his journey, Dhǒ Biǒ passes through the town of Bin, through which flows the Geng. Accord-ing to the poet's own explanatory note in another poem, it is at Bin that his party is finally issued horses. Up to then, they have been traveling on foot.

22.32   tsang 140/10 describes lichen or moss growing on the cliff. xòu 30/4; liɛt 145/6.

22.33   giuk 140/8; gim 9/2. gim tsiou modifies xua.

22.34   dəi 62/14; giu 159/0 (giu has a colloquial variant reading: chia); djhiɛt 159/12.

22.35   tseng iuən "blue cloud(-bearer), blue sky, clear day".

dhŭng 19/9 is followed by a place object: gɑu 189/0, modifying xiə̀ng 134/9. The implied recipient of the action of the verb is the mood of the persona.

22.36   qiou 52/6; jrhì 6/7; iuɛt 61/7.

22.37   guǎ 75/4; suǎ 96/10; sè̀i 120/5.

22.38   lɑ 122/14; dzhop 172/10; ziǎng 75/12; lit 75/6.

22.39   huək 62/4; shra 112/4, a common variant for the same word appearing in 20.30. It is unclear whether the poet is referring to a cosmetic powder or rouge, or to the elixir of immortality.

22.40   xək 203/0; dě̀m 203/5; tsit 85/11.

22.41   ji 4/3 (GS 42). shriǔ makes a "what" clause. njiu 85/14. The whole line is a topic: "What the rain and dew moisten...."

22.42   The comment to the previous line is itself a topic-comment construction. The topic is a coordinate construction, consisting of gom 99/0 and kǒ 140/5 in an "or" relationship. dzhei 210/0; get 120/6; jhìt 40/11.

22.43   miě̀n 120/9; si 61/5; ngiuæn 85/10; nuə̀i 11/2, a place word.

22.44   qiæk 108/5; tɑ̀n 76/11, a graphic variant of the same word in 21.18--the word has an alternate pronunciation: tɑn. shin 158/0; shiè̀i 1/4; jiuɛt 64/5, the main word of the object of tɑ̀n: "the clumsiness of the way I personally have gotten along in the world".

22.45   pɑ 32/5; dhɑ 170/5. This rhyming descriptive is a place topic here. pio 163/11; djhǐ (or jǐ) 102/6. pio djhǐ is the name of a sacrificial mound near the town where Dhǒ Biǒ settled his family.

22.46   guk 150/0; hò̀ 7/2; chuit 17/3. The mutual activity here is that the cliffs emerge out of the valleys, and the valleys disappear at the bottom of the cliffs.

22.47   ї 49/0 modifies a nominal place comment (GS 33), the main word of which is bin 85/14.

22.48   bhuk 9/12; mɑt 75/1. This line is parallel to the preceding line.

22.49   chi 196/5; miæng 196/3 has a place object. sɑng 75/6. The tree is brown because it is dead.

22.50   iǎ 166/4; shiǔ 208/0; giǒng 64/6; luɑ̀n 5/12; huet 116/0. This line is also parallel to the preceding line.

22.51   shim 85/8 is the comment to iǎ, and iǎ shim is the time topic to the rest of the line. geng 120/7; djhiɑng 32/9.

22.52 <u>guət</u> 188/0.

22.53 <u>dhung</u> 85/12 is the name of a mountain pass where several
tens of thousands of government troops were routed by rebels in 756.
<u>bæk</u> multiplies <u>miæn</u> (cf. 21.5); <u>shri</u> 50/7, the main word of the actor.

22.54 <u>iuæng</u> 60/5; <u>jiǎ</u> 125/4, a nominalizing suffix, here makes a
time topic with <u>iuǎng</u>: "at a time that has happened in the past;
recently; just a while ago". <u>sɑn</u> is the last topic. <u>hɑ</u> 9/5, inter-
rogative adverb to <u>tsuət</u> 24/6 here asking "why?"
      The effect of the string of topics (actually a topic followed by
a comment which is itself a topic-comment construction, of which the
comment is again another topic-comment construction, and so on) in
these two lines is something like: "At Dhung Pass: the million sol-
diers: just recently: their scattering: why was it so hurried?"

22.55 <u>zuǐ</u> 162/9; <u>bɑn</u> 24/3; <u>min</u> 83/1, the main word of the pivot
(cf. <u>liæng</u> in the original comment after the title of No. 19).

22.56 <u>dzhɑn</u> 78/8; <u>hɑi</u> 40/7, forming with <u>dzhɑn</u> the first of two
coordinate comments; <u>ì</u> 102/6; <u>miət</u> 93/4. The second comment, "...and
became different things" means "and became things different from living
human beings--died".

22.57 <u>xiuæng</u> 85/5 is a conjunction, appearing in the second of
the two sentences it connects. It invites a comparison of the amount
of a certain quality shared by the things described in the two sen-
tences: "If (first sentence) has a certain quality, how much more does
(second sentence) partake of the same quality!" It is like a verb in
that the following word can be a pivot, as here. <u>dhuǎ</u> 32/12.

22.58 <u>ghip</u> 29/2 is a verb here   (cf. 21.3). <u>dzhǐn</u> 108/4;
<u>hua</u> 140/8.
      What quality in the two sentences is being compared? Possibly it
is futility: "At Dhung Pass, a million soldiers perished, their forma-
tions broken in sudden panic, with no apparent result in stemming the
tide of rebellion. Even more futile is my situation. A loyal adviser,
eager to serve my Emperor, I try to join the court in exile, only to
be captured on the way. And when I do manage to escape the rebels and
join the court, my advice offends the Emperor who in consequence sends
me on this trip home. My hair has turned white--that is the only thing
I have to show for my recent efforts."

22.59 <u>jì</u> 133/0; <u>mau</u> 140/5; <u>guk</u> 44/6. The two half lines are
comments, probably in a coordinate relationship, though the English
seems to demand that one be subordinate to the other: either "After
passing through a year, I arrive..." or "A year has gone by before...."

22.60 <u>tsei</u> 38/5 ; <u>tzǐ</u> 39/0; <u>bæk</u> 106/1; <u>get</u> 120/6.

22.61 <u>dhɑng</u> 61/11; <u>kuk</u> 30/7. The weeping of the reunited family
is answered by the soughing of wind in the pine trees.

22.62 <u>dzhiuɛn</u> 85/5; <u>ghiɔng</u> 12/4; <u>qiou</u> 52/6; <u>qet</u> 30/6.

22.63 bhiæng 51/2; shræng 100/0; giɛu 38/12; nji 10/6, the main
word of a topic to which there are at least five comments distributed
in the next three lines, is modified by the preceding four words, which
constitute a shriǔ-clause.

22.64 shiə̀ng 19/10; siuɛt 173/3. The comparative of the adjec-
tive would be appropriate in English.

22.65 ia 128/3; bə̀i 130/5; miɛ̀n 176/0; dhei 30/9.

22.66 gǒu 32/6; nǐ 130/12; giɑk 130/7; miæt 145/15, ordinarily a
noun, is here turned into a verb by the preceding negative.

22.67 niǔ 38/0.

22.68 bǒ 145/7 and djhə̀n 120/8 constitute a metonym for "clothes".
dzhəi 64/0; sit 163/11.

22.69 dho 31/11; + jæk 32/5; dhɑu 85/14.

22.70 ghiə̀u 134/12; siə̀u 120/12; i 115/6; kiok 73/2 and jiɛt
refer to the crooked and broken arrangement of lines, shifted as a
result of turning the old embroidery into patches for the clothes of
the little girls.

22.71 ngo 30/4--"Heaven Ngo" is the name of a sea divinity having
a tiger's body, eight heads with human faces, eight legs and eight
tails. tzǐ 120/5.

22.72 den 181/10; zhiǒ 145/7; hɑt 145/9.

22.73 lǒu 125/0; huai 61/16; qɑk 61/8. Possibly the poet is
depressed because of the duties he feels he should be attending to
at court.

22.74 qǒu 30/11; siɛt 85/5; nguə̀ 131/2, with a time object
(16.13); shriə̀ 66/11.

22.75 nɑ 163/4; nɑng 145/17; bhæk 50/5.

22.76 giə̀u 66/7; njiǔ 85/3, a pivot; lǐm 15/13; lit 61/10.
These two lines constitute a rhetorical question put by the poet to
his family.

22.77 biə̀n 119/4 and dhə̀i 203/5 are topicalized objects (GS 40)
of the following verb. bau 140/5 would modify the objects if they
appeared in their original position following the verb. For the op-
posite direction of modification in English, cf. "cup of wine" at 8.3.

22.78 kim 145/4 and djhiou 145/8 are also topicalized here;
shrə̀u 115/7; lɑ 122/14; liɛt 18/4.

22.79 shriə̀u 104/10; guɑng 10/4.

22.80 t̲j̲ì̲ 104/14; d̲h̲o̲u̲ 181/7; d̲z̲h̲ì̲ 132/0; j̲r̲i̲t̲ 75/15.

22.81 h̲a̲k̲ 39/13; m̲ŏ̲u̲ 80/1. The effect of the two negatives here is to create a universal: "everything".

22.82 j̲r̲i̲a̲n̲g̲ 38/4; z̲u̲i̲ s̲h̲i̲ŏ̲u̲, itself a verb-object construction, is an adverb here: "free-handedly, randomly"; m̲a̲t̲ 64/5.

22.83 i̲ z̲h̲i̲, verb object, is a time topic here: "at another time, in a moment"; s̲h̲i̲ 70/5; j̲i̲o̲ 75/2; i̲u̲ɛ̲n̲ 167/5.

22.84 l̲a̲n̲g̲ 94/7; d̲z̲h̲i̲æ̲k̲ 118/14. l̲a̲n̲g̲-d̲z̲h̲i̲æ̲k̲ is a two-syllable word, of which the syllable l̲a̲n̲g̲ occurs alone in the same meaning as l̲a̲n̲g̲-d̲z̲h̲i̲æ̲k̲ (but dzhiæk does not). The word is adverbial to h̲u̲à̲i̲ 102/7. m̲i̲ is a pivot; k̲u̲a̲t̲ 169/9 (and see GS 15).

22.85 s̲h̲r̲æ̲n̲g̲ 100/0; d̲h̲u̲n̲g̲ 117/7; d̲j̲h̲ì̲ 115/8.

22.86 z̲ì̲ 9/5 and i̲o̲k̲ 76/7 are auxiliaries; m̲i̲à̲n̲g̲ 61/3; g̲i̲ 184/2; k̲a̲t̲ 85/9.

22.87 g̲h̲i̲à̲n̲g̲ 117/15 is an auxiliary; m̲i̲ă̲n̲ 64/7; s̲i̲o̲ 190/12.

22.88 t̲z̲i̲ə̲k̲ 26/7, another auxiliary; c̲h̲i̲n̲ 30/10; x̲a̲t̲ 30/9.

22.89 p̲i̲æ̲n̲ 124/12; s̲i̲ 61/5; d̲z̲h̲ə̲k̲ 154/6.

22.90 g̲o̲m̲ 99/0; z̲h̲i̲ŏ̲u̲ 29/6; g̲u̲a̲t̲ 128/6.

22.91 s̲i̲n̲ 69/9; t̲s̲i̲ă̲ 1/4; q̲i̲u̲è̲i̲ 61/11 and q̲ì̲ 61/9 form a verb-object expression, meaning "improve the feelings, get into a better mood".

22.92 s̲h̲r̲æ̲n̲g̲ and l̲ì̲ 96/7 form a compound: "way of life, how to subsist". q̲i̲ɛ̲n̲ 86/7; s̲h̲i̲u̲ɛ̲t̲ 149/7, with a topicalized direct object.

22.93 j̲ì̲ 133/0 and t̲z̲u̲ə̲n̲ 41/9 refer to the Emperor. z̲h̲i̲à̲n̲g̲ 42/5. m̲u̲n̲g̲ 140/10 and d̲j̲h̲i̲n̲ form a euphemism: "be in exile, be away from the capitals".

22.94 g̲i̲ŏ̲i̲ 52/9; x̲i̲o̲u̲ 9/4, an auxiliary; l̲ɛ̲n̲ 120/9; t̲z̲u̲ə̲t̲ 24/6.

22.95 g̲u̲a̲n̲ 147/18; s̲h̲r̲i̲ə̲k̲ is the main word of a pivot; g̲ŏ̲i̲ 66/3.

22.96 g̲a̲k̲ 147/13; q̲i̲ɛ̲u̲ 38/4; p̲i̲ə̲n̲ 84/4; x̲u̲a̲t̲ 150/10.

22.97 q̲i̲m̲ 170/8. s̲e̲i̲ b̲ə̲k̲ "northwest" is an adverb: "from the northwest".

22.98 t̲s̲ŏ̲m̲-d̲h̲ŏ̲m̲ (61/11, 85/13); h̲u̲ə̲i̲-h̲u̲ə̲t̲ (31/3, 120/3). The Uighurs are a Turkic people, who lived in what is now Mongolia during Dhang times, and who had a reputation for great ferocity. In 756, they helped Dhang government forces in a successful campaign, and in recognition of this help, Siuk-tzong adopted as his ceremonial brother

the prince who led the Uighur troops. The poet is not entirely happy
that it has become necessary to engage the help of these unreliable
tribesmen.

22.99 jrhiù 19/5; jhuĭn 181/3.

22.100 ziok 9/7; xĭ 30/9; djhi 187/3; tuət 116/4. djhi tuət
refers to a fast ambush on horseback.

22.101 sŭng 162/6. In 8.3, the number-measure expression pre-
ceded the noun that it modified. Here the order is reversed. biæng
12/5 is the noun measured. ngo tsen, the number, and njin, the measure,
are in apposition with biæng (GS 46): "soldiers, five thousand men",
or, more smoothly, "five thousand soldiers".

22.102 kio 187/11. It is a peculiarity of Chinese that there
are standard measures used in counting certain nouns. Such a measure
is pit 23/2, for counting horses.

22.103 bə̀i 159/8. shiĕu is a topicalized pivot.

22.104 biɑng 70/0. sì biɑng is a metonym: "people on all four
sides, everyone". bhiuk 74/4; iŏng 19/7; guet 85/4.

22.105 iŏng 101/0; qiəng 196/13; dhəng 187/10. qiəng and dhəng
are in a topic-comment relationship. Then "eagles leap" serves as an
epithet for "brave soldiers": those whose gallantry is like an eagle-
overtaking leap. This compound is the nominal comment to the first
two words of the line, and the predication is modified by gai (cf.
22.13).

22.106 pà 112/5; dhek 66/11; guà 162/9; tzièn 118/9; dzhit 104/5.
The verb-object topic has dzhit as the main word of its comment, and
dzhit is modified by another verb-object phrase. The whole comment is
best translated as an English comparative adjective construction.

22.107 shiæng sim is a metonym for the Emperor. pɑ 181/5; xiu
141/6; djhiù 9/5.

22.108 ngì 149/13 is the main word of a time topic, zhi ngì, a
vague phrase with several possible interpretations, among them the
following: "during scheduled conferences (of the military commanders),
during deliberations (by high officials) about the timing (of military
operations), according to public opinion". kiə̀i 84/6; dhuɑt 37/11.
Dhŏ Biŏ is describing afterthoughts about accepting Uighur help.

22.109 qi 9/4 and lɑk 85/6 are the names of two rivers near
Lɑk-iɑng, the Eastern Capital, and constitute a metonym for the city.
jĭ 64/6 and jiɑ̆ng 64/8 are in a verb-object relationship and form an
ancient epithet for "something easily done". The compound is ad-
verbial to shiou 66/2, whose object is topicalized.

22.110 giæng 8/6; bhat 64/5. The two capitals were in fact re-
covered soon after this poem was written, but in the reverse order.

22.111 guɑn 40/5; giuən 159/2; tsiǽng 149/8 has a comment as its
object here; shim 85/8. The poet thinks that after the capitals have
been recovered, the troops will ask to penetrate deeply into the heart-
land of the rebels.

22.112 xiuk 140/10; iuɛi 167/7; gio 9/8, adverb; biæt 105/7.
The poet cautions that concentrated and coordinated government action
would be best.

22.113 tsɨ 77/2; giŭ 134/10; kəi 169/4; tseng 174/0 and ziu 60/7
are ancient names for territories in eastern China.

22.114 ziuɛn 70/7; jiɛm 109/13; liɑk 102/6; həng 61/6 and ghiæt
(or ghiɛt) 112/9 are the names of mountains recalling another ancient
state northeast of Tseng, near the home territory of the rebels.

22.115 hǎu 72/4; tziæk 115/11.

22.116 jiɛng 77/1; siuk 129/7. Autumn kills plants and is
associated with the meting out of justice.

21.117 huǎ 113/9; miɑng 8/1. The line consists of a two-word
sentence, topic and comment, followed by a three-word sentence, a
topicless nominal comment, where the implied topic is perhaps "now"
or "this year".

22.118 shiɛi 19/11; zhiæng 62/2; ghim 64/13.

22.119 miæng 30/5; ghi 12/6, adverb; giǒu 4/2. When Qɑn Liuk-
shran took the Eastern Capital early in 756, he shortly thereafter
proclaimed himself Emperor of China. In the orthodox view, the rule
of China is validated by a mandate that comes from heaven itself.
When there is a revolution, it is regarded as a sign that this mandate
has terminated. It would appear that Dhǒ Biǒ considers the mandate to
have shifted, at least temporarily, to the rebels.

22.120 gɑng 120/8; ngi 40/5, an auxiliary. The object of
dzhiuɛt has been topicalized.

22.121 qiək 61/13 takes a sentence as its object. dzhɑk 72/5; lɑng-
bɑ̀i (94/7, 94/7), cf. lɑng-dzhiæk at 22.84; chriu 18/5. lɑng-bɑ̀i
modifies chriu, the main word of a time topic.

22.122 iŭ 134/7; sen 10/4; bhiɛt 18/5.

22.123 gan 38/6; jriu 140/9; xǝi 164/10. Dhǒ Biǒ is referring to
the killing of Iɑng Guək-djiung, whose body was cut into eight pieces
by the loyal soldiers.

22.124 dhung qɑk, an adverb-adjective construction meaning
"similarly evil", is a metonym for "those who were like him in evil,
his cohorts in crime". zui 170/13; dhǎng 140/12; sek 75/4. sek does
not rhyme as it should. The character representing this syllable in-
cludes the element 彳 . There are several other characters that

also contain this element but represent syllables that end in -t, such
as the one that appears at the end of 22.70. Perhaps Dhǒ Biǒ was mis-
led by this similarity into thinking that the syllable represented by
the character at the end of this line rhymed properly. See Stimson
1973.

22.125 miən 128/8 takes a sentence as its object. hǎ 35/7;
qiən 79/6; shrui 145/4, the head word of a time topic.

22.126 djiung 2/3 is a place noun, standing alone as a place
topic, and acting as a double metonym: "within (the royal palace)"
standing for "(people) within (the royal palace)". djio 149/6; bɑu
145/9; dɑt 38/5. bɑu stands for Bɑu Zĭ 妲 (Bāo Sì), a favorite
consort of King Qiou 幽 (Yōu) of the Jiou Dynasty, who reigned 781-
70 B.C. dɑt stands for Dɑt Gĭ 己 (Dá Jĭ), a favorite consort of
King Djhiǒu 紂 (Zhòu) of the Shiɑng Dynasty, who reigned 1154-1122
B.C., and who was the last, infamous ruler of that dynasty. Both
women were associated with the downfall of their respective courts,
and it is appropriate to allude to them in the context of the execution
of Iɑng Giuèi-piəi. Dhǒ Biǒ is pointing out that the course of events
in those ancient royal houses was different from what happened re-
cently in the Dhɑng Dynasty. Those women were not executed, and their
rulers' houses fell. Not so with the Dhɑng Dynasty: Iɑng Giuèi-piəi
was executed, so the Dhɑng Dynasty can be expected to survive the
disorder for which she has been blamed.
     In the context of the couplet there is an inconsistency. If the
first line of a couplet alludes to the downfall of the Hǎ Dynasty and
of the dynasty known as Shiɑng or Qiən, it is appropriate for the
second line to allude to the two women involved. Mention of Dɑt Gĭ is
therefore perfectly to be expected, whereas mention of Bɑu Zĭ is quite
unexpected, because she is associated with the fall of a Jiou ruler,
rather than with the fall of the Hǎ Dynasty. There is in fact a woman
who is blamed with the overthrow of the Hǎ, named Mɑt Xĭ 妹喜 (Mò
Xĭ), the favorite consort of the last ruler of the Hǎ. Perhaps Dhǒ
Biǒ changed mɑt dɑt to bɑu dɑt to avoid an undesirable internal rhyme.

22.127 jiou 30/5; xǎn 85/11; huæk 94/14; tzèi 13/4 .

22.128 siuɛn 40/6, (Xuān) the name of a Jiou king who reigned
827-781 B.C.; guɑng, for guɑng miǒ 武 (Guāng-wǔ), the name of
a Xǎn ruler who reigned A.D. 25-58. Both these rulers instituted re-
forms. guǎ 75/4; miæng 72/4; djiɛt 30/7.

22.129 huɑn 75/6; djhin 170/8. tziɑng 41/8 is a transitive verb
here, which with its object forms a compound meaning "General". For
the inverted order in this line, cf. GS 45. It was General Djhin who
had Iɑng Guək-djiung executed and who persuaded the Emperor to order
the execution of Iɑng Giuèi-piəi.

22.130 djhiɑng 9/3; iuæt 167/5; bièn 37/13; djiung 61/4; liɛt
86/6.

22.131 miəi 60/10; biəi 175/0.

22.132 io 7/1 is a prefix marking time or place expressions and is best left untranslated. huɑt 85/6.

22.133 tsei 85/8, a variant of the same word written differently in 12.9. liɑng 85/8; dhung 30/3; dhèn 79/9. "Great Unity Hall" is the name of a building in a palace in Djhiɑng-qɑn, in Dhɑng times.

22.134 dzhek and mɑk 40/11 form a synonym compound. shiòu 94/15; tɑt 169/13, a metonym for "hall". "White Beast Gate" refers to a hall in a palace, also in Djhiɑng-qɑn, but in Xɑ̀n times.
    In each of these parallel lines, there are several ways in which the first two words are grammatically related to the last three. To maintain the parallelism, a relationship determined for one line should also apply to the other. First, the two parts of the lines may be in a modifier-modified relationship, in which case the couplet constitutes two coordinate place topics to the following lines. Second, they may be in a topic-comment relationship: "What is chilly is...; what is quiet is..." Third, they may be in a comment-topic relationship, in the rhetorical inversion associated with descriptives. dzhek and mɑk are independent words, occurring alone elsewhere, but they do end in -k and might be considered near-rhyming quasi-descriptives. If this possibility is allowed, then the force of parallelism makes tsei liɑng participate in a similar inversion, too: "How chilly Great Unity Hall is! How quiet, White Beast Gate!"

22.135 do 163/9; tsul 124/8; hua 140/8, a metonym for "flag". The flags on the Emperor's carriage were decorated with blue-green kingfisher feathers.

22.136 gai 9/6. "Golden Towers" refers to the imperial palace.

22.137 iuæn 31/10 and liəng 170/8 refer to the mausolea of previous Dhɑng emperors. jhin 113/5 refers to the spirits of the dead emperors.

22.138 sɑ̌u and shrǎ 85/19 constitute a metonym for all the rituals honoring the imperial dead. shriò 66/11; kuet 121/4. When the Emperor returns to his capitals, the rituals at the tombs of former emperors will resume, and the continuation of the dynasty will be assured.

22.139 huɑng-huɑng 86/9; tzong 40/5. Tɑ̀i-tzong (Tɑ̀i-zōng) is the posthumous name of the second Dhɑng emperor, who reigned 627-50. He and his father, who became the first emperor, founded the dynasty. ngiæp 75/9.

22.140 zhiǒ 75/12; lip 117/0; zhǐm 99/4; huæng 40/4; dhɑt 162/9.

Note to the student: The presentation of Poem 23 begins the last stage of the introduction to traditional Chinese lexicography, which is one of the aims of this book. From Poem 23 on, no radical-remainder code will be given for new characters or for old characters with new meanings, if the analysis of the character into radical and remainder is obvious. See the beginning of the glossary for a list of the radicals considered to be obvious and to present no problems. Characters with obvious codes, already glossed but now occurring in a new meaning, have a raised circle (°) after their transcriptions in the text of the poem.

23. The officer at Stone Moat 石壕吏 Zhiæk-hɑu lì (Shí-háo lì)

mò dhou zhiæk hɑu tsuən	暮 投 石 壕 村
iŏu lì iᴧ jrak njin	有 吏 夜 捉 人
lɑ̌u qung iu dzhiɑng tzŏu	老 翁 踰 牆 走
lɑ̌u bhiŏu chuit mən kɑn	老 婦 出 門 看
5 lì xo qit hɑ nŏ	吏 呼 一 何 怒
bhiŏu dhei qit hɑ kŏ	婦 啼 一 何 苦
teng bhiŏu dzhen djì zi	聽 婦 前 致 詞
som nom ngiæp zhiæng shiò	三 男 鄴 城 戍
qit nom bhiò shiu jì	一 男 附 書 至
10 njì nom sin jiᴧn sɏ̌	二 男 新 戰 死
dzhuən jiǎ tsiǎ tou shræng	存 者 且 偷 生
sɏ̌ jiǎ djhiɑng ɏ ɏ	死 者 長 已 矣
shit djiung gæng mio njin	室 中 更 無 人

ui iðu njið hǎ suən   惟 有 乳 下 孫

15 iðu suən mǒu miði kiù   有 孫 母 未 去

chuit njip mio huɑn ghiuən   出 入 無 完 裙

lǎu qið liək sui shrui   老 嫗 力 雖 衰

tsiǎng dzhiong lì ià giuəi   請 從 吏 夜 歸

gip qiðng hɑ iɑng iuæk   急 應 河 陽 役

20 iou dək bhì zhin chui   猶 得 備 晨 炊

ià giðu ngiǔ shiæng dzhiuɛt° 夜 久 語 聲 絕

njiu miən kip qiou qet   如 聞 泣 幽 咽

ten miæng dəng dzhen dho   天 明 登 前 途

dhuk iǔ lǎu qung bhiɛt   獨 與 老 翁 別

(Five-syllable old-style poem)

Title: lì 30/3. Stone Moat is just south of the Yellow River, in the western part of the modern Hé-nán Province.

23.2 When iðu is followed by a pivot, it is often most conveniently translated by the English indefinite article: "a, an". ià 36/5.

23.3 dzhiɑng 90/13. tzǒu is a resultative (GS 15).

23.4 The last character in the line, 109/4, represents a word that has two pronunciations: kɑn and kɑ̀n. (kɑ̀n is the origin of the usual modern reading; the modern reading corresponding to kɑn occurs now only in a specialized sense.) kɑn is the preferred reading here, because -n and a level tone are all that are required for the rhyme in the first quatrain of this loosely rhyming poem.

23.5 qit 1/0 and hɑ are both in adverbial position: "entirely, how...!" Better English would reverse the order.

23.7 dzhen 18/7; djì 133/4.

23.8 Ngiæp City is about 500 km.NE of Stone Moat. Government forces engaged rebel forces there in 759. shiə̀ 62/2 is the main word of a nominal place comment (GS 31, 33).

23.9 jì 133/0, another resultative, like ləi in 20.3.

23.10 njì 7/0; jiɛ̀n 62/12.

23.11 dzhuən 39/3; tsiǎ 1/4.

23.12 djhiɑng 168/0; the second Y̌: 111/2.

23.14 njiǒ 5/7; suən 39/7.

23.15 iǒu suən mǒu may be analyzed in two ways. iǒu suən may be considered to modify mǒu: "The (young) mother, who has my grandson", or "The mother of my grandson". Or suən may be considered a pivot: "There is a grandson, whose mother..." Either analysis is supported by the placement of the caesura.

23.16 chuit njip is a phrase whose elements are in a coordinate "or" construction and which stand for the place "left" or "entered": "away from home or at home". The phrase is a time topic, but a convenient English translation might use the word "Whether...."

23.17 lǎu qiə̀ stands for "I, my". shrui 145/4.

23.18 lì stands for "you". giuəi 77/14.

23.19 qiə̀ng 61/13. hɑ iɑng is the name of a place about 200 km. down the Yellow River from Stone Moat. Government forces were encamped there in 759.

23.21 giǒu 4/2.

23.22 njiu has another verb as its object, and this verb has two objects, of which the second is preceded by a modifier.

23.23 dəng 105/7; dzhen 18/7.

23.24 dhuk, which is an adverb in the Chinese, is best translated in English as though it modified lǎu qung. iǔ 134/7.

24. Grieving about Green Slope 悲青坂 Bi° Tseng-biǎn
(Bēi Qīng-bǎn)

In the first month of winter, 756, government troops suffered a disastrous defeat at the hand of Qɑn Liuk-shran's rebel forces on a particular day and at a particular site, slightly east of Djhiɑng-qɑn. The histories mention a second defeat of the same government army two days later at an unspecified site, probably the Green Slope of this poem.

ngǎ giuən   tseng biǎn
    dzhǎi dung mən
我軍青坂在東門

ten hɑn   qìm mǎ
    tɑ̀i bhæk kuət
天寒飲馬太白窟

huɑng dhou   hei nji
    njit xiɑ̀ng sei
黃頭奚兒日向西

shriɓ° ghì   quan giung
    gǒm djhi tuət
數騎彎弓敢馳突

5 shran siuɛt° hɑ° biəng
    iǎ seu-shrit
山雪河冰野蕭瑟

tseng zhì   piong qen
    bhæk njin guət
青是烽煙白人骨

qiɛn dək   bhiɓ shiu
    iǔ ngǎ giuən
焉得附書與我軍

njǐn dhǎi   miæng° nen
    mɑk° tsɑng-tsuət
忍待明年莫倉卒

(Seven-syllable old-style poem)

24.1 Topic, place topic, comment. The attack on the government forces will come from the east (see below, Line 3).

24.2 Great White (see 21.7) is too far to the west to be meant literally here; it is a metonym for "mountainous area near Djhiang-qan.

24.3 "Yellow/brown-heads" is the name of a subdivision of a non-Chinese nation to the north; "Sons of Hei (37/7)" is the name of another northern non-Chinese nation. Together the two names refer to the rebels in general. njit 72/0.

24.4 quan giung (57/19; 57/0) is a metonym. djhi tuət: 22.100.

24.5 Three sentences, separated at the caesuras.

24.6 Two sentences, separated at the second caesura. The second sentence is nominal with njin guət as the comment. The line takes up tseng in Line 1 and bhæk in Line 2 and reinterprets them in terms of battle and death.

24.7 iǔ 134/7 introduces the beneficiary of the action of the verb.

24.8 tsɑng 9/8 builds a descriptive on tsuət (GS 4).

25. Spring view 春望 Chuin miɑng° (Chūn wàng)

guək° pɑ° shran hɑ dzhəi	國 破 山 河 在
zhiæng chuin tsău muk shim	城 春 草 木 深
gŏm zhi° xua tziɛn luɪ	感 時 花 濺 淚
hən bhiɛt dĕu giæng° sim	恨 別 鳥 驚 心
5 piong xuă liɛn som ngiuæt	烽 火 連 三 月
ga shiu dĕi miæn gim	家 書 抵 萬 金
bhæk dhou sɑu gæng duăn	白 頭 搔 更 短
huən iok biət shiəng jrim	渾 欲 不 勝 簪

(Five-syllable regulated poem)

Title: miɑng 74/7.

25.1 guək is probably a metonym for "capital city". dzhəi 32/3.

25.6 Notice that the topic is different from the actor, which is implied. gim 167/0.

25.7 gæng 73/3. bhæk dhou is a topicalized pivot; duăn is in a resultative relationship to sɑu (GS 15): "My head of white hair I have scratched so that it is even shorter."

25.8 shiəng 19/10.

26. I hear that government troops have recovered Hé-nán and Hé-běi 聞官軍收河南河北   Miən guan giuən shiou Ha-nom Ha-bək (Wén guān jūn shōu Hé-nán Hé-běi)

giuǎm nguǎi xuət djhiuɛn
  shiou gěi bək

劍外忽傳收薊北

chriu miən těi luǐ
  mǎn qiəi zhiɑng

初聞涕淚滿衣裳

kiɑk kɑn tsei tzǐ
  jrhiou hɑ° dzhěi

卻看妻子愁何在

mǎn giuěn shi shiu
  xǐ iok ghiuɑng°

漫卷詩書喜欲狂

5 bhæk njit biǎng gɑ
     sio tʑiòng tziǒu

白日放歌須縱酒

tseng chuin tzɑk° bhǎn°
  xǎu huan xiɑng

青春作伴好還鄉

tziək dzhiong° ba hap
  chiuɛn miò hap

即從巴峽穿巫峽

bhiɛn hà siɑng iɑng
  xiàng lɑk iɑng

便下襄陽向洛陽

iu dhen iuæn dzhěi dung giæng

余田園在東京
(Seven-syllable regulated poem)

Title: nom 24/7 and bək 21/3 are place nouns in these names of Dhang administrative regions north and south of the Yellow River. The two regions correspond roughly to the modern provinces of Shān-dōng and Hé-běi, and the northern half of Hé-nán Province. This is a large,

triangular area with an apex where the Yellow River bends east, and
spreading north and south of the Yellow eastward to the sea. It is
rebel territory. The poem was probably written in 763, when Dhǒ Biǒ
was in the Zhiok area.

26.1 giuǎm: 21.33. giuǎm nguǎi refers to Dhǒ Biǒ's present
place of residence. gèi is the name of a place corresponding to the
modern town of Jì in northern Hé-běi Province, about 30 km.E of Běi-
jīng (or Peking).

26.3 kiɑk 26/7.

26.4 xǐ 30/9 is the topic of a new sentence and specifies the
cause for what is mentioned in the comment.

26.5 bhæk 106/0; njit 72/0.

26.6 huan xiɑng, a phrase consisting of a verb and a place
object, is itself the place object of tzɑk. xǎu modifies huan xiɑng,
a pivot.

26.7 tziək 26/7 typically modifies a nominal comment: "is
namely". Here, since the topic of this nominal sentence is also the
place object of the verb that precedes it, the pivot quality is best
reflected by translating with a relative clause: "...which will be
namely...." mio 48/4. The Yangtze River passes through these two
famous gorges on its way out of the Zhiok area.

26.8 siɑng 145/11. Siɑng-iɑng (literally "Sunny Side of the
Siɑng River") corresponds to the modern city of Xiāng-yáng, in north-
ern Hú-běi Province, about 175 km.north or northeast of the Yangtze.

An original note appears after the last line. dhen 102/0.

Dhǒ Biǒ never actually made the trip projected in this poem.

Chapter 6: Poets of the Mid and Late Dhang (T'ang)

The remaining 29 poems in this anthology are by six poets from
the Mid and Late Dhang, as opposed to the High Dhang, which is the
period of the three poets read so far. Four of the six poets intro-
duced in this chapter are from Mid Dhang, which began in the middle
decades of the eighth century and lasted until some time in the second
quarter of the ninth. The first two of these, Mäng Gau and Iuang Giän,
are poorly known in the West.* The third is Bhæk Giu-ì, a poet whose
reputation is equal to those of the three High Dhang poets, and who is
well known in the West through the translations of Arthur Waley (e.g.
Waley 1918, 1919, 1946). The fourth poet is less well known: Lǐ Huà.
The last two of the six poets introduced here are from the Late Dhang,
which ended with the dynasty in 907. They are Dhǒ Miuk and Lǐ Shiang-
qiǎn, both fairly well known in the West.

----

* But see Owen 1975 on Mäng Gau.

A. Mäng Gau 孟郊 (Mèng Jiāo, 751-814)

Mäng Gau's official career began late in his lifetime. At age forty-five, he finally passed the national examinations on the third try. In his fiftieth year he finally received his first appointment, a minor one, which brought him near to the place of his birth in eastern China. He was not good at this job, and his superior replaced him, giving him half his salary while he gave his replacement the other half. After a few years, Mäng Gau resigned and moved, first to Djhiang-qan, then to Lak-iang, where he held a minor sinecure. He died in 814 of a sudden illness contracted while traveling to another post.

He belonged to a circle of literati centering around the great prose stylist and poet, Han Iǒ 韓愈 (Hán Yù, 768-824). It is evident that Han Iǒ and the other poets in the group appreciated Mäng Gau's poetry, but in later ages down to the present his reputation has fared less well, and his poems are badly represented in the most common anthologies currently available. His best poems bristle with difficult, violent images, which set them apart from most other Chinese poems, and it is perhaps this fact which has prevented all but a few mild examples of his work from being included in anthologies.

The nine poems by Mäng Gau collected here constitute a suite of connected poems. They are difficult, almost impenetrable. A convincing interpretation depends on an intimate knowledge of the oeuvres of Mäng Gau and his fellow poets. Stephen Owen seems to have such knowledge, and it is chiefly because his interpretation of this suite is so convincing and interesting that I have included it in this collection. In nearly every detail I have followed his interpretation, which can be found in Owen 1975, pp. 140-52.

27-35. Cold stream 寒溪 Han kei (Hán xī)--nine poems

In these poems, a continuous train of thought can be detected; they should therefore be regarded as constituting a single suite of nine consecutive parts.

27. No. 1

shriɑng sěi shuǐ shriək dzhǐn	霜 洗 水 色 盡
hɑn kei gɛn siɛm lin	寒 溪 見 纖 鱗
hǎɛng lim xiu kung° giǎng	幸 臨 虛 空 鏡
jiɛu tsǐ dzhɑn dzhuǐ shin	照 此 殘 悴 身
5 dzhiɛm huɑt biət dzhǐ qiěn	潛 滑 不 自 隱
lb° děi iuɛng gǎng sin	露 底 瑩 更 新
xuɑt njiu giuən tzǐ huai°	豁 如 君 子 懷
tzəng zhǐ ngui hǎm njin	曾 是 危 陷 人
shǐ miɛng° tsiěn ziok° sim	始 明 淺 俗 心
10 iǎ get° djiɛu ǐ tzin	夜 結 朝 巳 津
dzhiǎng shriðu qit giuk biɛk	淨 漱 一 掬 碧
iuěn siɛu tsen liǔ djhin	遠 消 千 慮 塵
shǐ dji nei bhð dzhiuɛn	始 知 泥 步 泉
mɑk° iǔ shran ngiuɛn lin	莫 與 山 源 隣

(Five-syllable old-style poem)

27.3 hæng 51/5 is an adverb, or possibly an auxiliary, here; lim 131/11; xiu 141/6.

27.4 jiɛu 86/9; dzhan 78/8.

27.6 iuæng 96/10.

27.7 xuɑt 150/10. giuən 30/4 and tzǐ "lord's son, gentleman's son" is a Confucian term for "ideal moral man".

27.8 tzəng 73/8; ngui 26/4.

27.12 liǔ, parallel to giuk in the previous line, must be treated as a measure.

27.14 iǔ 134/7 and lin (written differently) appear in the same grammatical construction at 19.10.

Paraphrase: Winter weather has cleansed the stream; it is now so clear that even the tiniest things in it can be seen. Like an Emperor making a visit, I came down to this mirror, which is empty of anything that would interfere with our encounter. It has revealed things about me that are unpleasant, but true. It has also revealed things about it- self, and its own vacillation cannot hide in the winter clarity. The revelation is gemlike in clarity and preciousness. At first, however, the stream dissembled, welcoming me with a gentlemanly civility. Then it showed something of its true self, which includes a power strong enough to bring a man down. Only after I found out the truth about my- self and the stream did I begin to understand about the vulgar mind, to which such revelations are meaningless, and which also vacillates like the stream, now freezing, now melting. I had a purifying wash in what seemed like jade; it caused the spiritual dust accumulated by my anxious consideration of material things to disperse into the far distance. Now I know that a stream like this one, which shows its inconstancy not only by freezing and melting but also by sometimes being muddied by the activities of people living near it and other times being clarified by the winter weather, as now, is to be preferred over a stream that is constant in its clarity and in always being unfrozen.

28. No. 2

lɑk iɑng ngàn ben dhǎu	洛 陽 岸 邊 道
mæng zhǐ jriang dzhen kei	孟 氏 莊 前 溪
jiou hæng sò biəng° tjæk°	舟 行 素 冰 坼
shiæng tzɑk tseng iɛu sei	聲 作 青 瑤 嘶
5 liok shuǐ get° liok ngiok	綠 水 結 綠 玉
bhæk bɑ shræng bhæk guei	白 波 生 白 珪
miæng miæng bǎu giæng djiung	明 明 寶 鏡 中
miət miət ten jiɛu dzhei	物 物 天 照 齊
jriək bhò hà ngui kiok	仄 步 下 危 曲
10 pan° ko° miən shriang dhei	攀 枯 聞 孀 啼
shriang piən shràu siɛu xiæt	霜 芬 稍 消 歇
ngiəng giǎng miəi-mang dzhei	凝 景 微 茫 齊
tji° dzhuǎ djhiək zhǐ teng	癡 坐 直 視 聽
djǎng hæng shit tziong hei	戀 行 失 蹤 蹊
15 ngàn djhiòng djiok giək lɑu°	岸 重 斸 棘 勞
ngiǔ ngiæn dɑ bi° tsei	語 言 多 悲 悽

(Five-syllable old-style poem)

28.2 zhỉ 83/0. This line is nominal comment to Line 1.

28.3 jiou 137/0.

28.4 tseng 174/0.

28.5 ngiok 96/0.

28.8 miət miət: GS 3. ten 37/1. dzhei 210/0, an intransitive
verb, is a comment here, to the first four words of the line as topic.
This topic consists of a topicalized object, an actor topic, and a
transitive verb: "All things: Heaven's reflecting them is impartial".

28.9 jriək 9/2 occurred at 21.45, written differently.

28.10 shriang 38/17, basically "widow", is here probably "mate-
less female birds". From the time of the earliest literature on, good
government and well-ordered society are associated with the proper care
of the helpless and destitute, including widows and orphans. For ex-
ample, here is a passage from "Great field 大 田 Dà tián", No.
212 in the Book of songs:

> Over there, there is young grain not cut;
> here, there are sheaves not yet gathered.
> Over there, there are leftover handfuls;
> here, there is left-behind grain:
> these are the gain of the widowed woman!

Here the widowed bird calls because she is not properly cared for: she
becomes a symbol of things gone amiss.

28.12 dzhei 210/0 is here used in a bad sense: the winter land-
scape has flattened the distinctions between things and made them
blurry. It is all very well for an abstract heaven to view things as
if there were no distinctions of good and evil, beautiful and ugly,
but a man must see these differences clearly, or disorder (like the
abandonment of the destitute) will ensue. The persona realizes that
he must not be fooled by an easy vagueness.

28.13 djhiək 109/3; teng 128/16.

28.14 hæng 144/0.

28.15 djhiong 166/2; djiok 69/21 "hoe", here probably in a sec-
ondary meaning "use a hoe on, cut". giək 75/8. djiok giək is either
a verb-object construction: "to cut brambles", or a modifier-modified
construction: "brambles that cut (me)".

28.18 ngiæn 149/0.

Paraphrase: The way to get to Lok-iang is to take this stream,
flowing between high banks in front of my village. The ice breaks as
a boat goes along, sounding like tinkling jade (but sometimes there is
a sob). The jewelly scene is beautiful: all things are made equal in
this winter scene. But as I descend to the stream, the difficulty of
the path and sad bird calls remind me that this blurring of distinc-
tions, visual and moral, is not desirable: difficulty and distress are,
after all, bad. Beguiling fragrances disappear and lack of differen-
tiation blurs value--exactly the opposite of what I came to the stream
to achieve: clarity. I must achieve that enlightenment by focusing my
attention on present events--never mind that I may not find again the
way I took to get to the stream. My encounter with the stream is be-
ginning to be difficult; my words describing the revelation that has
resulted will be full of sorrow.

29. No. 3

xěu qǐm qit bəi tziǒu	曉飲一盃酒
top siuɛt guà tsiæng° kei	踏雪過清溪
bɑ lɑn dǔng ui dɑu	波瀾凍爲刀
jiuɛ̀n gɑt bhio iǔ qei	剸割鳧與鷖
5 siuk iǒ gai tziěn kɨ̀	宿羽皆剪棄
xuet shiæng djhim shra nei	血聲沉沙泥
dhuk lip iok hɑ ngiǔ°	獨立欲何語
mək nɛ̀m sim suɑn sei	默念心酸嘶
dǔng xuet mɑk tzɑk chuin	凍血莫作春
10 tzɑk chuin shræng biət dzhei	作春生不齊
dǔng xuet mɑk tzɑk xua	凍血莫作花
tzɑk xua biæt shriɑng dhei	作花發孀啼
qiou qiou giək jim tsuən	幽幽棘針村
dǔng sǐ nɑn° gæng lei	凍死難耕犂

(Five-syllable old-style poem)

29.3 dɑu 18/0, a pivot.

29.5 iǒ 124/0 is modified by the preceding verb.

29.12 biæt 105/7.

29.14 gæng 127/4.

Paraphrase: My intention had been, after some alcohol to heighten
the perceptions, to seek enlightenment from a stream that consisted of
clear, running water. Instead, the stream reveals itself to me in its
most hideous, destructive aspect: the expected clear water has treach-
erously become ice. River birds that, like me, expected water rather
than ice flew down during the night, and instead of landing safely on
water, they landed on knifelike blades of ice, covering the frozen sur-
face with blood and feathers. And I am deceived too, for instead of
the safe sounds of reasoned discourse whereby I could find enlighten-
ment in the stream, I seem to hear the sound of the birds' blood sink-
ing into the sand, and I am unutterably sad.

The blood is now frozen and presents itself to me in a horrible
vision that demands explanation. It does not signify springtime--
rain is for that; and if we make a springtime out of a season watered
with blood, we shall cause a state of inequality to arise: when such
a spring is measured against a normal spring, it is found to fall short
of the mark. The frozen blood does not signify flowers, either; water-
ing flowers with blood is unnatural, more likely to be associated with
a society that is in a state of moral disarray, as when widows are left
destitute. The ground is frozen to death and it is impossible to em-
ploy ordinary means of food production; this portends more than just
this single destructive event, but a chain of such events, as famine
spreads because of the cold.

30. No. 4

gɑu gung duəi ngiok seng	篙 工 碰 玉 星
qit lɓ zui bæng hueng	一 路 隨 迸 螢
shrak dʉng qəi tjiɛt dĕi	朔 凍 哀 徹 底
lʉu jrham iuæng dzhiɛmᵒ seng	獠 饞 咏 潛 鯉
5 biəng chĭ siɑng mɑ ngǎu	冰 齒 相 磨 嚙
biung qim suɑnᵒ dhɑk leng	風 音 酸 鐸 鈴
tsiæng bi biət kǎ dhɑu	清 悲 不 可 逃
sĕi chuit siɛm sit teng	洗 出 纖 悉 聽
biæk liɛm giuěn ĭ dzhĭn	碧 潋 卷 已 盡
10 tsʉi shrang biəi piɛu lengᵒ	彩 雙 飛 飄 零
hǎ niɛp huatᵒ biət dhæng	下 躡 滑 不 定
zhiǎng sei jiɛtᵒ nɑn dhengᵒ	上 樓 折 難 停
xau-gau xap chrap qiuæn	哮 嘐 呷 嘛 寃
ngiǎngᵒ sɓ hɑ zhi neng	仰 訴 何 時 寧

(Five-syllable old-style poem)

30.1 <u>gung</u> 48/0.

30.2 <u>qit</u> 1/0.

30.5 <u>chĭ</u> 211/0.

30.6   qim 180/0.

30.8   chuit 17/3.

30.9   giuĕn 26/6.

30.10   tsĕi 59/8.

Paraphrase: The boat-poler poles his boat through the ice making
the ice break into jade stars, so that the route behind him seems to
follow a shower of fireflies. This beauty contrasts with the destruc-
tive aspect of the stream: it brings a freeze from the north, whose
sadness I see at the bottom of the stream; and it brings an unnatural
craving for food, a gluttony typical of certain southern tribes whose
song I hear in the smell of rotting fish. The northern freeze has
turned the beautiful ice into teeth which bite each other; the south-
ern song sounds in the wind, ringing bells hung on the eaves of houses.
These revelations bring an inescapable sadness, but they also have the
clarity that I have been seeking. The sadness prepares me for further
revelations by cleaning out even the smallest receivers of perception.
Now I am no longer deceived into expecting safe answers to my questions:
the waves no longer remind me of beautiful green jade, and the colorful
pairs (shrang) of birds that I had hoped would provide happy reminders
of the prevalance of morality have flown, and fluttering they have fal-
len (and have been replaced by the shriang "widow, mateless bird",
28.10 and 29.12; shriang is nearly homophonous with shrang "pair").
On the ground, animals find no sure footing on the slippery ice; in
the air, birds cannot alight on broken branches. The victims of all
this uncertainty howl, gasp their grievances: when will their com-
plaints be answered?

31. No. 5

qit kiok qit djhiək shuǐ	一 曲 一 直 水
bhæk liong hɑ linº lin	白 龍 何 鱗 鱗
dǔngº biɛu dzhop suəi hɑu	凍 飚 雜 碎 號
tzei qim kæng guk sin	齏 音 坑 谷 辛
5 go tzen giət mio liək	枷 櫛 吃 無 力
biəi tzǒu gæng siɑng njin	飛 走 更 相 仁
mæng giung qitº jiɛtº hen	猛 弓 一 折 絃
iu chiuěn jræng ləi bin	餘 喘 爭 來 賓
dhɑi ngiæm tsǐ ji lip	大 嚴 此 之 立
10 siɛu shrat biət bhiuk djhinº	小 殺 不 復 陳
gěu gěu hɑ gěu gěu	皎 皎 何 皎 皎
qiuən qiuən bhiuk qiuən qiuən	盦 盦 復 盦 盦
zhuǐ dzhiæng shruat njit ngiuæt	瑞 晴 刷 日 月
gɑu biækº kəiº seng zhin	高 碧 開 星 辰
15 dhuk lip liǎng giɑk siuɛt	獨 立 兩 脚 雪
go ngimº tsen liǔ sinº	孤 吟 千 慮 新
ten jrham dho jiɛu jiɛu	天 讒 徒 昭 昭

gi jhiɛt xiu ngiən ngiən   箕 舌 虛 斷 斷

ngeu shiǎng biət teng njiǔ   堯 聖 不 聽 汝

20 kǔng miəi° iæk iǒu zhin   孔 微 亦 有 臣

gǎn° shiu giǎng zhiæng jiɑng   諫 書 竟 成 章

gǒ ngî jiung nɑn djhin   古 義 終 難 陳

(Five-syllable old-style poem)

31.1 The first two words are a time topic to the last three, a
nominal place comment, which is also a topic to bhæk liong in the next
line--the last three words of Line 1 are therefore a pivot.

31.2 bhæk liong is also a pivot.

31.4 tzei 179/10; sin 160/0.

31.6 biəi 183/0 metonym for "bird"; similarly tzǒu 156/0 has a
basic meaning "walk", but here it is a metonym for "animal".

31.7 The first two words are the topicalized modifier of the last
word, hen. The result of the topicalization here is to change "As soon
as I have broken the string of my ferocious bow..." to "My ferocious
bow: as soon as I have broken its string...." The whole line is a
time topic to the following.

31.8 jræng 87/4.

31.9 tsĭ 77/2. ji 4/3 "it", substituting for dhǎi ngiæm. In
prose, when an object of a verb is topicalized, often ji or another
pronoun appears after the verb, where the object was originally. Thus
tsĭ lip dhǎi ngiæm would become dhǎi ngiæm tsĭ lip ji. But here the
ji comes before the verb: placement of pronoun objects of verbs be-
fore the verb is a characteristic of the earliest period of the lan-
guage.

31.10 shrat 79/7.

31.12 qiuən 84/10, bhiuk 60/9, in combination with the intensified
adjectives, is a further intensive: "and again...!"

31.14 zhin 161/0.

31.15 The line consists of two sentences. The first ends at the
caesura and is a topicless comment. The second is a nominal sentence;

siuɛt is a place comment.

31.17 "Heaven's Slander-detector" is one of the six stars of the constellation Giuěn-jhiɛt 卷舌 (Juǎn-shé) Curled Tongue (part of Perseus, at about 4^h +40°). The star is said to govern shamanism and medicine and the ability to discriminate flattery and slander.

31.18 jhiɛt 135/0. "Winnowing-fan" is one of the 28 zodiacal constellations (part of Sagittarius, at about 18^h -30°), whose four stars are thought of as representing the outline of a widemouthed winnowing fan. The two stars that are the farthest apart of the adjacent stars constitute the mouth of the fan, and are called "Tongue"-- a metonym for "mouth". xiu 141/6.

31.19 ngeu 32/9.

31.20 kǔng 39/1; iæk 8/4; zhin 131/0.

31.21 shiu 73/6; giæ̀ng 117/6; zhiæng 62/2; jiɑng 117/6.

31.22 ngḭ 123/7.

Paraphrase: After rounding a bend in the stream, I see ice-filled water stretching out like a white, scaly dragon. A freezing whirlwind howls, mixed with pieces of ice; sounds of the wind-driven ice smashing against what stands in its way cause a painful sadness in the valley.
Notepaper in hand, I am ready to compose a petition to Heaven protesting the unnatural destruction in proper Confucian terms, but it is so cold and I am still so pained by what I see that I shiver and stammer, my words without efficacy. Birds and beasts come together, kind to each other in their mutual calamity. Their misery presents me with an opportunity to kill them for food--the cold weather of the stream having stopped normal food production. But I make a crucial decision to have compassion for these living beings, and as a sign of forsaking the opportunity to kill them, I break the string of my bow. They then accept me as their host, and they come to me, even though the cold has reduced them to their last breath. Killing wild animals for food is a petty, wanton affair, even in desperate circumstances; a larger, stricter morality must instead prevail. My decision not to kill the animals will stem the course of destruction begun by the cold weather.
The universe approves my decision, brought thus painfully about by the various revelations at the stream: the white-filled scene made unclear by quantities of mist begins to clear up, and the sun, moon, and stars all appear, while I stand, feet still in the snow that refuses to leave, anxious now about the effect of my decision to adhere to this compassionate morality. Against this morality, the stars, especially ones associated with words or mouths, argue vehemently for a primordial pragmatism that would lead to my killing an animal for food. However, I reply: "Ngeu was august and would not have listened to you; like Confucius, whose official position was tiny, yet he had underlings who were his disciples, I am of no particular consequence in officialdom,

yet I play host to these animals. Any practical considerations are
outweighed by classical precedent."

    The text of my admonition to Heaven about the consequences of the
cold and about what I hope has been a proper Confucian reaction on my
part is at last complete. It has been difficult for me to expound my
position, based as it is on classical attitudes; perhaps it will be so
unpersuasive as to have no effect at all.

32. No. 6

qin dùng° sǐ dǝk jhiǝk   因凍死得食

shrat biung njiǝng biǝt xiou   殺風仍不休

ǐ biæng ui njin ngì   以兵為仁義

njin ngì shræng dɑu dhou°   仁義生刀頭

5 dɑu dhou njin ngì seng   刀頭仁義腥

giuǝn tzǐ biǝt kǎ ghiou   君子不可求

bɑ lɑn tjiou giuæm biǝng   波瀾抽劍冰

siɑng pek njiu ghiou zhiou   相劈如仇讎

(Five-syllable old-style poem)

32.1 jhiǝk 184/0. The first two words are in a verb-object rela-
tionship, and they stand in a topic-comment relationship to the next
word: "Because of the freezing, they die". dǝk is an auxiliary here,
with jhiǝk as its object; the implied actor shifts: "...and they get
to eat" would make no sense; better "...and I get to eat (if I should
so choose)".

32.3 ngì 123/7. njin and ngì are two central virtues in Confu-
cian ethics. The combination may as well be translated "morality".

32.5 seng, appearing here written with the "meat" radical, ap-
peared at 30.4 written with the "fish" radical. Perhaps the poet meant
to indicate a difference in the word's shade of meaning by graphic
means.

35.6 ghiou 85/2.

35.7 giuæm modifies biǝng: "ice which has turned into swords"
reflects the grammatical relationship; "swords of ice" abandons it in
favor of smoother English.

35.8 zhiou 149/16.

Paraphrase: It is still freezing, and animals are still dying--
the possibility arises that I might eat what the freeze has already
killed. But these animals came to me because of a morality which they
expected to find in me. To kill one of them with a weapon would be to
cause that weapon to become the morality, in their eyes, and the mo-
rality would seem to the survivors like a knife point, reeking of car-
rion. A man of ideal moral character, according to Confucian ethics,
would not find himself in such a situation, and I continue to refuse
therefore to kill and eat any of the beasts.

The waves of the stream, however, draw out their swords of ice
and slice each other like enemies.

33. No. 7

tziɛm siuɛt njip ngiu sim	尖 雪 入 魚 心
ngiu sim miæng tsiou-tsiou	魚 心 明 愀 愀
xuǎng njiu° miǎng-liǎng shiuɛt°	怳 如 囷 兩 説
zǐ sò° gɑt° tset iou	似 訴 割 切 由
5 zhui shrǐ ì biɑng kiəi	誰 使 異 方 氣
njip tsǐ djiung tǒ liou	入 此 中 土 流
tziěn dzhǐn qit ngiuæt chuin	剪 盡 一 月 春
bèi ui bæk guk qiou	閉 爲 百 谷 幽
ngiǎng huai sin tzèi guɑng	仰 懷 新 霽 光
10 hà jièu ngi qiou jrhiou	下 照 疑 憂 愁

(Five-syllable old-style poem)

33.1 tziɛm 42/3.

33.2 miæng modifies tsiou-tsiou. A "change of the color of the face" that can be described as "bright" is most likely a "flush or red", the color of the blood of the stabbed fish spreading in the water.

33.3 xuǎng appeared at 22.18, written differently. Here it is part of a descriptive (GS 4). miǎng-liǎng (122/3, 11/6) was originally a descriptive: "Something that makes the sound 'miǎng-liǎng'", but it functions here as a noun.

33.4 tset 18/3; iou 102/0 .

33.5 biɑng 70/0.

33.6 djiung 2/3; tǒ 32/0.

33.7 ngiuæt 74/0. Cf. another number-measure expression at 8.3.

33.8 bèi ui: two verbs in a coordinate relationship, the second of which is a resultative (GS 15). qiou 52/6.

33.10 hà 1/2; ngi 103/9.

Paraphrase: The stream adds another revelation of itself as a destructive force and shows me that my admonition has been in vain: it sends one of the snowy knives mentioned in the previous poem into a fish, whose blood spreads red in the water. There must be some water spirit causing these events, teasing me with an explanation of this latest one, taunting me with the ineffectiveness of my plaint, leading me on by the blurriness of his own statement. Who caused this unnatural spirit from a strange land to come to a stream here in the heart of the civilized world and extend winter into the first month of spring, blocking the passage of winter so that it turns into a hundred valleys of gloom?

But now the sky begins to clear up and the light shines so that I have doubts about the appropriateness of my grief.

34. No. 8

kei lǎu kuk zhǐm hɑn	溪 老 哭 甚 寒
tèi sì biəng sɑn-sɑn	涕 泗 冰 珊 珊
biəi sǐ tzǒu sǐ heng	飛 死 走 死 形
siuɛt liɛt° piən° sim gɑn	雪 裂 紛 心 肝
5 giuæm njìn dùng biət gɑt	劍 刃 凍 不 割
giung hen giàng nɑn dhɑn	弓 絃 彊 難 彈
zhiɑng miən giuən tzǐ miǒ	常 聞 君 子 武
biət jhiək ten shrɑt dzhɑn	不 食 天 殺 殘
djiok ngiok qiěm gæk tsi	斸 玉 掩 骼 觜
10 dèu ghiuæng qəi lɑn gɑn	弔 瓊 哀 闌 干

(Five-syllable old-style poem)

34.1 lǎu 125/0--the poet is referring to himself. kuk 30/7 is transitive here. zhǐm 99/4 modifies hɑn 40/9, which is most conveniently considered a noun.

34.2 tèi and sì constitute the topic, biəng the comment in this nominal sentence; but since biəng is also topic to the descriptive that follows, it is a pivotal comment, another kind of pivot.

34.3 heng 59/4 is the main word of the topic, a topicalized object of liɛt in the next line.

34.4 The sentence comprising Line 3 and the first two words of this line constitutes the topic to which the rest of this line is the comment: "The splitting by the snow of the shapes of the dead bodies of the birds and beasts flurries my heart and liver." sim gɑn may form a compound with the extended meaning: "true feelings".

34.5 njìn 18/1.

34.7 zhiɑng 50/8; miǒ 77/4.

34.8 dzhɑn 78/8.

34.9 gæk 188/6. In the Book of rites 禮記 Lǐ jì (one of the
Confucian canonical works), Book 4, Chapter 21, almost identical words
are used: "One covers dead bones and buries carrion (of animals, out
of pity)."

34.10 dèu 57/1; qəi 30/6. "Poles supporting the railing of a
balcony" is a common figure for tears streaming down the face.

Paraphrase: I have wept about the cold, tears tinkling as they
fall. I have grieved about the bodies exposed on the frozen waste.
Hunting with sword or bow is impossible, and anyway I have rejected
it as a means to appease my hunger. As a gentleman should, I have
refused to eat even those bodies destroyed naturally. Now there is
one last act to accomplish. I must show my pity for the dead animals
by covering them in a ritual Confucian burial. The dirge I sing for
them brings a latticework of tears from my eyes, frozen to carnelian.

35.   No. 9

kei biung bǎi iu dǔng°	溪風擺餘凍
kei giǎng ham miæng chuin	溪景銜明春
ngiok siɛu xua dek dek	玉消花滴滴
kiou gǎi° guɑng lin lin	虹解光鱗鱗
5 huen bhò hǎ tsiæng kiok	懸步下清曲
siɛu ghi djhak piɑng tzin°	消期濯芳津
tsen lǐ biəng liɛt chiù	千里冰裂處
qit zhiɑk nuǎn iæk njin°	一勺暖亦仁
ngiəng tziæng hò siɑng sěi	凝精互相洗
10 qi-liɛn ghiǎng tziɑng sin	漪連競將新
xuət njiu giuæm chriɑng dzhǐn°	忽如劍瘡盡
chriu kǐ bæk jiɛn shin	初起百戰身

(Five-syllable old-style poem)

35.2 **ham** 167/6.

35.6 **ghi** 74/8.

35.7 **lǐ** 166/0.

35.8 **zhiɑk** 20/1

35.12 **jiɛn** 62/12. Lines 11 and 12 form one complex sentence.
xuət njiu are adverb and verb, with the rest of the two lines object
of **njiu**. The sentence that is the object of **njiu** is analyzable in at
least two ways. First, **giuæm chriɑng dzhǐn** (itself a topic-comment
construction) is actor topic to Line 12 as comment, **kǐ** being in this
case a transitive verb: "...the fact that the sword wounds are gone

arouses now for the first time a body that has endured a hundred bat-
tles." Second, we can assume an underlying sentence with the words in
this order: bæk jièn shin, giuæm chriang dzhĭn, chriu kĭ: "The sword
wounds of the body that has endured a hundred battles are gone, and
now for the first time the body rises." In this case, kĭ is intransi-
tive. This sentence is changed to the one in the poem by topicaliza-
tion, the effect of which is to focus on bæk jièn shin: "...its sword
wounds are gone; what rises for the first time now is a body that has
endured a hundred battles."

     Paraphrase: At last the cold spell has broken, and the wind
shakes loose the remaining frozen things from the trees, and the whole
scene at the stream shows signs of the beginning of spring. Jade-
white ice melts, and its flower-shaped formations drip; the stream-
dragon, its size and age diminished, has melted and its radiance
sparkles in a riot of scaliness.
     My footsteps from the long journey of this revelatory experience
descend to bends in the stream that are now pure. At this time of the
melting of the stream, it washes a fragrant ford. Anywhere in the
area of the splitting ice, for a thousand miles, you can dip up a
ladle of water and it will be warm and kind. The spirits of the stream,
my own spirit, once frozen, now wash each other in mutual enlightenment.
Ripples vie to see which will start bobbing again.
     It is suddenly as though, sword wounds gone, what rises now for
the first time is a body that has endured a hundred battles.

B. Iuang Giàn   王建   (Wáng Jiàn, 768?-830?)

Not much is known about Iuang Giàn's life. After passing the national civil service exam, he held minor positions, including one that took him on a military expedition, before retiring.

He is known as a writer of new Music Bureau poems and of new Palace poems--short poems that tell of events in the palace, otherwise unrecorded.

36. Song of the newly-wed bride 新嫁娘詞 Sin gà niang zi° (Xīn jià niáng cí)--third of three poems

som njit njip djhio muài	三 日 入 廚 内
sěi shiǒu tzɑk° gæng tɑng	洗 手 作 羹 湯
miài qom go jhiək siàng	未 諳 姑 食 性
sen kiěn siěu go zhiɑng	先 遣 小 姑 嘗

(Five-syllable unregulated quatrain)

36.1 som 1/2.

36.2 gæng 123/13.

36.4 sen 10/4. siěu go "husband's younger sister"; zhiɑng 30/11.

37. I sent away my son's wife   去婦 Kiù bhiǒu° (Qù fù)

sin° bhiǒu kiù nen
   bhen shiǒu tziok

新婦去年胼手足

qiəi biət hà° bhiong
   dzhom biæi° tsuk

衣不暇縫蠶廢簇

bhæk dhou shrǐ ngǎ
   qiou ga jrhì

白頭使我憂家事

huan° njiu ià lǐ
   shiɛu dzhɑn jiok

還如夜裏燒殘燭

5 dɑng chriu ui sìn°
     bhɑng njin ngiǔ°

當初為信傍人語

kiǎi dhàu njiu° gim
   dzhì sin kǒ

豈道如今自辛苦

dzhǎi zhi tziòng° hem°
   jiək giuɛn djhi

在時縱嫌織絹遲

iǒu si biət zhiǎng
   lin° ga giəi

有絲不上鄰家機

(Seven-syllable old-style poem)

Title: kiù 28/3 is transitive here, used in a causative sense:
"cause to go".

37.1 "new wife" is a term for one's son's bride. kiù 28/3;
tziok 157/0. This nominal sentence breaks at the caesuras: actor
topic, time topic, nominal comment--supply "have" in English.

37.2 qiəi is topicalized object of bhiong; hà is an auxiliary.

tsuk is a place object.

   37.3 bhæk dhou is probably time topic: "When (I have) white
hair...", "In my old age...."   The actor topic is unspecified; it is
most likely the fact that the daughter-in-law was not getting the
chores done in the family silk business.

   37.4 lï 145/7. dzhan 78/8 is in a resultative relationship to
the previous verb. jiok, chief word of the object of njiu, is modified
by the intervening words.

   37.5 ui 87/8 is an auxiliary here, probably best left untrans-
lated. Perhaps what the neighbor said was that the daughter-in-law
was being lazy or purposely delinquent in doing her chores.

   37.6 njiu gim "when you get to the present" is best translated
simply "now". sin 160/0.

   37.7 tziòng is an auxiliary here; hem takes a sentence as its
object.

   37.8 zhiǎng 1/2 is causative here; its topicalized object is si;
the main word of its place object is giəi. The daughter-in-law may
have been a slow worker, but at least when she was still at her mother-
in-law's house, there were enough people at home so that the silk could
be woven there rather than farmed out to neighbors.

   Note: this poem is also classed as a Music Bureau poem.

38. Seeing the moon while traveling   行見月   Hæng gèn ngiuæt
(Xíng jiàn yuè)

ngiuæt chriu shræng	月初生
giu° njin gèn ngiuæt qit ngiuæt hæng	居人見月一月行
ngiuæt hæng qit nen zhip njì ngiuæt	月行一年十二月
ghiɑng bàn mǎ zhiàng kàn iɛng° kuet	強半馬上看盈缺
5 bæk nen xuɑn lɑk nəng giěi hɑ	百年歡樂能幾何
dzhěi gɑ gèn shiěu hæng gèn dɑ	在家見少行見多
biət iuɛn qiəi jhiək siɑng kio° kiěn°	不緣衣食相驅遣
tsǐ shin zhui ngiuæn djhiɑng bən bɑ	此身誰願長奔波
kep djiung iǒu bhæk tsɑng iǒu siok	篋中有帛倉有粟
10 kiěi xiàng ten ngai° tzǒu luk-luk	豈向天涯走碌碌
gɑ njin gèn ngiuæt	家人見月望我歸

miàng ngǎ giuəi

jiàng zhǐ   dhǎu zhiàng   正 是 道 上 思 家 時

   si ga zhi

(Music Bureau poem)

38.1 shræng 100/0.

38.2 The implied actor topic to hæng is the traveler.

38.3 zhip njì ngiuæt is in apposition to qit nen.

38.4 ghiɑng bàn is a time topic: "over half the time". kuet 121/4.

38.5 bæk nen is the longest a man can expect to live: "life-time". nəng 130/6. The compound interrogative giǒi hɑ is simply "how much...?"

38.6 shiěu 42/1 is comment to the preceding three words. ngiuæt is implied as object after both occurrences of gèn. dɑ 36/3.

38.7 This line is an "if" clause, topic to the next line.

38.8 tsǐ shin is a time topic: "While inhabiting this body...", "While one is alive..." bən 37/6 modifies bɑ, chief word of the nom-inal comment; the predication is modified by djhiɑng.

38.9 tsɑng 9/8; siok 119/6. The line constitutes two more "if" clauses, coordinate topics to the next line.

38.10 tzǒu 156/00.

38.11 miàng 74/7.

38.12 jiàng 77/1.

C. Bhæk Giu-ì 白居易 (Bái Jū-yì or Bó Jiū-yì, 772-846)

Over two thousand six hundred poems by Bæk Giu-ì survive; his
extant oeuvre is the largest of any Dhɑng poet.

He passed the national civil service examinations in his twenty-
sixth year and pursued a long official career, mostly in the capitals.
He kept aloof from the political quarrels that plagued China during
his lifetime; this fact, combined with his deep appreciation of Bud-
dhism, probably accounts for the general cheerfulness of his poetry.
Even harangues about social evils and superstition have the lightness
and clarity of language that characterize all his poetry, and that
have made him one of the best loved poets outside of China.

Much biographical detail can be extracted from his poetry as well
as from outside sources; a masterly biography has been written by
Arthur Waley (Waley 1949).

39. Simplicity's song 簡簡吟 Gǎn-gǎn ngim° (Jiǎn-jiǎn yín)

so ga siěu niǔ
    miæng gǎn-gǎn

蘇家小女名簡簡

bhio-iong xua səi
    liǒu iɛp ngǎn

芙蓉花腮柳葉眼

zhip qit bǎ giæng
    hak děm jriɑng

十一把鏡學點粧

zhip njì tjiou jim
    nəng siɵu° zhiɑng

十二抽針能繡裳

5 zhip som hæng dzhuǎ
    jrhì dheu pǐm

十三行坐事調品

biət kěng mei dhou
    bhæk dhì dzhɑng

不肯迷頭白地藏

leng-lung iuən gèi
    shræng tsɜ̀i iɑ̀ng

玲瓏雲鬢生菜樣

pieu-ieu biung ziǒu
     dzhiɑng-miəi xiɑng

飄颻風袖薔薇香

zhio tzi° ì° təi
     biət kǎ jrhiɑng

殊姿異態不可狀

10 xuət xuət djiuěn dhǔng
         njiu iǒu guɑng

忽忽轉動如有光

njì ngiuæt bhiæn shriɑng

         shrat dhɑu lǐ

二月繁霜殺桃李

miæng nen iok° gà
         gim nen sǐ

明年欲嫁今年死

djhiǎng njin qɑ-mǒu
         miət bi° dhei

丈人阿母勿悲啼

tsǐ niǔ biət zhǐ
         bhiæm bio tsei

此女不是凡夫妻

15 kiǒng zhǐ ten siɛn
         djæk njin shiɛi

恐是天仙謫人世

jǐ hop njin gan
         zhip som siuɛi

只合人間十三歲

dhài do xǎu miət
         biət gen lɑu

大都好物不堅牢

tsěi iuən i sàn
     liou-li tsiuɛi

彩雲易散琉璃脆

(Seven-syllable old-style poem)

Title: The name is appropriate for a young girl. The reduplication is for intensification of the meaning, if indeed any meaning other than what might be called up by sound association is intended.

39.1 siĕu 42/0.

39.2 səi and ngǎn are the chief words of two nominal comments to niŭ: "About niŭ...and it is a case of səi and ngǎn"--again, supply "have" in English.

39.3 hak 39/13, an auxiliary.

39.5 "walking and sitting" means "in all that she did". jrhî 6/7 is an auxiliary.

39.6 kə̆ng 130/4, another auxiliary. dhou is a pivot: it is object of the causative verb mei and topicalized object of dzhang. bhæk 106/0 and dhî in the immediate context seem to have secondary meanings "without reason, vain" and "territory, quarters", where "gay section of a city" would be the implication. The line would then read: "She had no intention of letting her head/herself be deluded into being hidden by the gay quarters"--she is determined to perfect her training so that she can find a decent husband. But I think there is the possibility of a double meaning, the second of which makes sense in the context of the whole poem. If we take the primary meanings of bhæk dhî, we get: "She had no intention of letting herself be led astray from the path of a lifetime that runs the normal length into a situation where she would be buried by white earth--earth associated with death"--and the line simply says that during her training to be a young lady, she did not expect an early death.

39.7 shræng 100/0. iɑ̆ng is the main word in a nominal comment, and it is modified by shræng tsə̆i: "is in the manner of green vegetables", "is like green vegetables", for "is as beautiful as green vegetables".

39.8 xiɑng 186/0. Parallel to Line 7.

39.12 gim 9/2.

39.13 djhiǎng 1/2 forms a compound with njin meaning "wife's father". qɑ-mou is an affectionate term of address to a mother. miət 20/2.

39.14 bhiæm 16/1.

39.15 siɛn is another pivot: object of zhî and topicalized object of djæk. Following djæk is its place object. shiɛ̆i 1/4.

39.16 siuɛ̆i is the main word of a nominal comment that tells the duration of the topic.

39.17 gen 32/8; lɑu 93/3.

40. Lady True's tomb 真娘墓 Jin niɑng mɔ̀ (Zhēn niáng mù)--
original note: The tomb is in Tiger Hill Temple   墓在虎丘寺
Mɔ̀ dzhɛ̌i Xɔ̌-kiou Zì (Mù zài Hǔ-qiū Sì)

jin niɑng mɔ̀

真娘墓

xɔ̌ kiou dhɑ̌u

虎丘道

biət shiək   jin niɑng
    giæng djiung miɛn

不識真娘鏡中面

ui gɛn   jin niɑng
    mɔ̀ dhou° tsɑ̌u

唯見真娘墓頭草

5 shriɑng dzhuəi°   dhɑu lǐ
    biung jiɛt len

霜摧桃李風折蓮

jin niɑng sǐ zhi
    iou shiɛu nen

真娘死時猶少年

ji bio   dhei shiɔ̌u
    biət lɑu gɔ̀°

脂膚蔑手不牢固

shiɛi gan iou miət
    nɑn liou° liɛn°

世間尤物難留連

nɑn liou liɛn

難留連

10 ì siɛu xiæt

易消歇

sɔ̀i bək xua

塞北花

gang° nɑm siuɛt

江南雪

(Music Bureau poem)

Title: Lady True was a beautiful entertainer of Dhang times, re-
nowned in eastern China. Her tomb became a famous sight-seeing spot
in what is now Wú 吳 District (or Soochow) in Jiāng-xī (or Kiangsi)
Province, and it was a favorite practice of poets to attach poems to
the trees at her tomb, remembering her beauty and grieving her death.
jin 109/5; mò 32/11.

Original comment: kiou 1/4; zl 41/3.

40.2 The line is nominal place comment to Line 1.

40.6 shiƚu 42/1 is etymologically related to shiĕu; the compound
shiƚu nen "young in years" is a metonym and a noun: "one who is young",
so it is a nominal comment, and the predication is modified by iou.

40.7 bio 130/11; ji and dhei are used to describe skin and hands
in the passage from the Book of songs, No. 57, quoted above at 13.2.

40.8 iou 43/1 forms a compound with miət, which in view of the
following lines had perhaps better be taken literally: "surpassingly
good thing", though it also means "beautiful woman".

40.11-12 Each line is a nominal comment to miət in Line 8.

41. New music bureaus 新樂府 Sin ngak biǒ (Xīn yuè fǔ)--
No. 4 of fifty: The sea is vast 海漫漫 Xǒi man-man (Hǎi mán-mán);
original comment: On refraining from seeking immortalhood 戒求
仙也 Gǎi ghiou siɛn iǎ (Jiè qióu xiān yě)

xǒi man-man   海漫漫

djhiək hà   mio děi   直下無底旁無邊
    bhang mio ben°

iuən dhɑu   qen° làng   雲濤煙浪最深處
    tzuǎi shim chiǔ

njin djhiuɛn   djiung iǒu   人傳中有三神山
    som jhin° shran

5 shran zhiàng   dɑ shræng   山上多生不死藥
    biət sǐ iɑk

bhiuk° ji   iǒ xuǎ   服之羽化為天仙
    ui ten siɛn

dzhin huɑng   xàn miǒ   秦皇漢武信此語
    sǐn tsǐ ngiǔ

biɑng° jrhǐ   nen nen   方士年年采藥去
    tsěi iɑk kiǔ

bhung-ləi   gim gǒ   蓬萊今古但聞名
    dhǎn miən miæng

10 qen shuǐ   mang-mang°   烟水茫茫無覓處
    mio mek chiǔ

xǎi mɑn-mɑn
    biung hǎu-hǎu

海漫漫風浩浩

ngǎn chiuɛn° biət gèn
    bhung-ləi dǎu

眼穿不見蓬萊島

biət gèn bhung-ləi
    biət gǒm giuəi

不見蓬萊不敢歸

dhung nom guǎn niǔ
    jiou djiung lǒu

童男卯女舟中老

15 ziu° biuk miən zhiæng
    dɑ giuǎng dhǎn

徐福文成多誑誕

zhiǎng ngiuæn tǎi qit
    xiu ghiəi dǎu

上元太一虛祈禱

giuən kǎn li shran děng zhiǎng
    mòu liəng dhou

君看驪山頂上茂陵頭

bit° giæng bi biung
    chui miæn tsǎu

畢竟悲風吹蔓草

hɑ xiuǎng huen ngiuæn shiæng tzǒ
    ngǒ tsen ngiæn

何況玄元聖祖五千言

20 biət ngiæn iɑk
    biət ngiæn siɛn

不言藥不言仙

biət ngiæn bhæk njit
    shiəng tseng ten

不言白日昇青天

(Music Bureau poem)

Title: On music bureaus, see Prosodic note 6, p. 51 .
Associated with the revival of poetry with lines of uneven length,
written with didactic or critical purpose, are the names of Iuɑng Giæn
and Bhæk Giu-ł. In a preface to this group of fifty poems, the poet
says that the lines of the poems have no set length, and that the con-
tent determines the number of syllables a line should have, rather than
the other way around.
Each of the fifty poems has a title identical to, or based on,
the words of the first line. After the title comes a brief prose de-
scription of what the poem is moralizing about. gɑ̀i 62/3 is an auxil-
iary; ghiou 85/2. siɛn "immortalhood", becoming an immortal or fairy,
was a goal of a certain sort of practical Taoism. Adepts claimed to
have found the herb or elixir (sometimes containing lethal amounts of
mercury) that would enable whoever partook of it to become an immortal.
Often an Emperor, especially if he was getting old, would be taken in
by these quacks, listen to their stories, and spend vast sums of money
in following them up. Bhæk Giu-ł is more concerned with the human
waste involved, and with the fact that the quest for immortalhood is
not really part of what he would call proper Taoism.

41.2 bhɑng 70/6.

41.3 tzuɑ̀i 73/8 makes a superlative out of a following adjective.

41.4 djiung 2/3. The three divine mountains were supposed to be
in the sea east of China, now known as Bó-hǎi 渤海 (or Po-hai).

41.5 dɑ 36/3 is an adverb here. iɑk is modified by the adverb-
verb expression that precedes it.

41.6 iǒ xuⱥ is an adverb-verb compound: "transform in a feather
manner--undergo the feather transformation", said of the emergence of
a butterfly from a cocoon, but also said of the attainment of immortal-
hood by a Taoist believer: an immortal is said to grow feathers.

41.7 dzhin huɑng stands for dzhin shǐ huɑng dɛi 秦始皇帝
Beginning Emperor of the Dzhin (Qín Shǐ Huáng-dì, reigned 221-209 B.C.).
After uniting China, he made several attempts to find the three divine
mountains, and he sent a boat full of children out to find them, but
all to no avail. xɑ̀n miǒ stands for xɑ̀n miǒ dɛi 漢武帝 Martial
Emperor of the Xɑn (Hàn Wǔ Dì, reigned 140-86 B.C.), whose interest in
Taoist magic is well-known.

41.8 A biɑng jrhǐ (70/0, 33/0) is a scholar versed in the skills
of practical Taoism: divination, alchemy, etc. nen nen: GS 3. tsǝ̌i
165/1. kiǔ 28/3 is in a coordinate relationship with the verb-object
construction that precedes it. When kiǔ is the second of two co-
ordinate verbal expressions, often, as here, the first expression tells
the purpose of kiǔ: "go to gather medicinal plants".

41.9 bhung-lǝi is the name of one of the three divine mountains
mentioned in Line 3.

41.10 mio mek chiù: "there was no place where it could be found".

41.12 dǎu 46/6.

41.14 guàn 2/4.

41.15 ziu biuk is the name of a Taoist adept who claimed to know of the existence of the three divine mountains. The Beginning Emperor of Dzhin ordered him to lead several thousands of boys and girls there to find the medicine of immortality. They sailed for the mountains and never returned. miən zhiæng (67/0, 62/2) is the name bestowed on a Taoist adept by the Martial Emperor of Xàn, after the adept brought back from the dead the spirit of one of the Emperor's favorite concubines.

41.16 zhiàng ngiuæn (1/2, 10/2) is the name of a lady attendant present at the apocryphal feast that the Martial Emperor of Xàn is supposed to have participated in with the mythical Royal Mother of the West. tài qit is, first of all, the great underlying unity of the Taoist universe. But it is also the name of the spirit of the North Star. As a third possibility, it is the name of the supreme god of the universe.

41.17 The Beginning Emperor's tomb is at Li Mountain, east of Djhiang-qan. The Martial Emperor's burial place is called Luxuriant Tomb and is located north of Djhiang-qan.

41.19 xiuàng 7/5; cf. 22.57, where it is written differently. ha, regularly an interrogative pronoun, here increases the rhetorical quality of xiuàng: "How much more telling evidence of the folly of seeking immortalhood is...!" huen 95/0. "Mysterious, Primal, and August Ancestor" is a name for the author of the Taoist Classic of the Way and the Power 道 德 經 (Dhǎu Dək geng 〔Dào Dé jīng or Tao Te ching〕), less honorifically known as Lǎu-tzǐ 老 子 (Lǎo-zǐ or Lao-tzu), who is supposed to have lived around the time of Confucius, in the fifth century B.C. The Classic is about five thousand characters long.

41.20 ngiæn 149/0.

42. The parrot 鸚鵡 Qæng-miǒ (Yīng-wǔ)

liǒng sei   qæng-miǒ
    dǒu gang dung

隴西鸚鵡到江東

iǎng dək° geng nen
    tzuǐ dzhiěm hung°

養得經年觜漸紅

zhiɑng kiǒng si giuəi
    sen tziěn shǐ

常恐思歸先剪翅

mǒi qin qǐ jhiək
    dzhòm kəi lung

每因餧食暫開籠

5 njin len kǎu ngiǔ
    dzhiæng sui djhiòng

人憐巧語情雖重

děu qiək gɑu biəi
    qǐ biət dhung

鳥憶高飛意不同

qiəng zǐ° jio mən
    gɑ miǒ ghǐ

應似朱門歌舞妓

shim dzhɑng° lɑu běi°
    hǒu° bhiɑng djiung

深藏牢閉後房中

(Seven-syllable regulated poem)

42.1 liǒng is the name for China's western territories, roughly
corresponding to the modern province of Gān-sū, and further west.
dung 75/4.

42.2 iǎng 184/6. dək, an auxiliary, is the result of the pre-
ceding verb.

42.4 měi 80/3, adverb; jhiək 184/0.

42.5 djhiɒng 166/2.

42.6 gɑu 189/0; dhung 30/3.

42.7 qiəng 61/13; jio mən refers to the homes of the wealthy.

42.8 lɑu 93/3; hɒu bhiɑng 63/4 refers to the women's quarters of a well-to-do house.

43.   Some years ago, a white horse of mine died at Dense Mulberry
Trees, and I wrote a poem on the wall of the government building there.
I come here now, and it is still there.   I am moved again and write
another quatrain. 往年桐桑曾喪白馬題詩廳壁今來尚存又復感懷更題絕句

Iuǎng° nen Djhiou Sɑng, dzhəng sɑ̀ng bhæk mǎ, dhei shi teng bek. Gim
ləi, zhiɑ̀ng dzhuən. Iɔu bhiuk gɔ̌m huai, gæ̀ng dhei dzhiuɛt° giɔ̀. (Wǎng
nián Chóu Sāng, céng sàng bái mǎ, tí shī tīng bì. Jīn lái, shàng cún.
Yòu fù gǎn huái, gèng tí jué jù.)

lò bhɑng mai guət   路旁埋骨蒿草合

    hɑu tsǎu hop

bek zhiɑ̀ng dhei shi   壁上題詩塵蘇生

    djhin so° shræng

mǎ sǐ tsit nen   馬死七年猶悵望

    iou tjiɑ̀ng miɑ̀ng

dzhǐ dji mio nǒi   自知無乃太多情

    tɑ̀i dɑ dzhiæng

                        (Seven-syllable unregulated quatrain)

    Title: Dense Mulberry Trees is a post station located some 160
km. west of Lɑk-iɑng. sàng 30/9; dhei 181/9; iɔu 29/0; gɔ̌m 61/9 takes
a place object here; gæ̀ng 73/3; giɔ̀ 30/2.

    43.1 bhɑng 70/6 is a place word here. The first four words
constitute a clause that is a place topic, to which the last three
words of the line constitute a subject-verb comment. hop 30/3.

    43.2 Note the string of five syllables with the level tone.

    43.3 tsit 1/1.

    43.4 nǒi 4/1; tɑ̀i 37/1; dɑ 36/3.

44. I ask myself a question   自問   Dzhì miən (Zì wèn)

xək xua mǎn ngǎn
   si mǎn dhou

黑花滿眼絲滿頭

tzǎu° shrui qin bhiàng
   bhiàng qin jrhiou

早衰因病病因愁

huàn dho kiəi miəi
   ǐ qom dzhǐn

宦途氣味已諳盡

ngǒ zhip biət xiou°
   hɑ njit xiou

五十不休何日休

(Seven-syllable unregulated quatrain)

44.1 The first four words refer to dimness of sight.

44.3 kiəi 84/6 and miəi in combination extend their basic mean-
ings to "feeling (of a situation, career, etc.)"--the topicalized
object of qom. dzhǐn is the comment to the rest of the line.

44.4 ngǒ zhip refers to the poet's age.

詞 45. Coffin-pullers' song for Minister Ngiuæn 元相公輓歌
Ngiuæn siàng-gung miæn gɑ zi (Yuán Xiàng-gūng wǎn gē cí)--
second of three.

mò mən ǐ bèi°   暮門已閉笳簫去
    ga seu kiù

ui iǒu bio njin   唯有夫人哭不休
    kuk biət xiou

tsɑng-tsɑng lò° tsǎu   蒼蒼露草咸陽壠
    ham iɑng liǒng

tsǐ zhǐ tsen tsiou   此是千秋第一秋
    dhèi qit tsiou

             (Seven-syllable regulated quatrain)

    Title: siàng-gung (109/4, 12/2) is a title of respect for the
highest officials in the empire. Ngiuæn Jin 元稹 (Yuán Zhēn,
779-831) was such an official when he died suddenly in his fifty-third
year. The literary friendship between Bhæk Giu-ì and Ngiuæn Jin, who
was also a poet, is well known, and their names are often linked in
discussions of Chinese poetry.

    45.2 bio njin is a title of respect for the wife of a man of
high rank.

    45.3 ham 30/6. "Sunny Side of Both" (in the modern district of
the same name, Xián-yáng, in Shǎn-xī, northwest of Cháng-ān) gets its
name from being located on the north bank of the Wèi 渭 River and
on the south slopes of the Zōng 嵕 Mountains. It was the capital
city of the Dzhin state and dynasty. The sites of the capitals of
successive dynasties moved farther east until the Dhɑng, with its
western capital at Djhiɑng-qɑn (Cháng-ān).

    45.4 qit 1/0.

46. Sighing about my hair falling out 歎髮落 Tàn biæt lɑk°
(Tàn fǎ luò)

da bhiæng da jrhiou sim dzhî dji
多病多愁心自知

hæng nen miəi lǎu biæt sen shrui
行年未老髮先衰

zui shriu lɑk kiù hɑ sio siæk
隨梳落去何須惜

biət lɑk jiung° sio biɛn tzɑk si
不落終須變作絲

(Seven-syllable regulated quatrain)

46.2 hæng 144/0 forms a compound with nen: "years of age".
lǎu 125/0.

47. Shining Lady Iuang 王昭君 Iuang Jiɛu Giuən (Wáng
Zhāo Jūn)--First of two.

mǎn miɛn ho shra   滿面胡沙滿鬢風

    mǎn bìn biung

mi suǎ dzhan dhɔi   眉鎖殘黛臉鎖紅

    lǎm suǎ hung°

jrhiou kǒ sin ghiən   愁苦辛勤憔悴盡

    dzhiɛu-dzhuì° dzhǐn°

njiu gim kiɑk zǐ   如今却似畫圖中

    huài dho djiung

(Seven-syllable unregulated quatrain)

Title: iuang 96/0 is the surname and jiɛu giuən 30/4 the title
of a famous beauty. Of low birth, she was one of many chosen to re-
plenish the harem of Emperor Ngiuən 元 (Yuán, reigned 48-32 B.C.) of
the Xɑ̀n Dynasty. The wicked official in charge of the selection and
registration of the harem ladies demanded bribes of them to ensure that
the Emperor would notice them; Shining Lady Iuang, trusting in her own
surpassing beauty, refused to give the bribe. In revenge, the official
disfigured her picture in the Imperial harem catalog with the result
that the Emperor never chose her to attend him.

    The ruler of a foreign tribe to the north paid court to Emperor
Ngiuən and asked for a Chinese bride to take back with him. The Em-
peror presented him with Shining Lady Iuang, whom he had never yet
seen. Only when he presented her to the northern chief did the Emperor
finally see how beautiful she was. He then realized that he had been
deceived, but he felt that he could not back down on his promise to the
northern chief, so he let her go with him, dooming her to a difficult
journey to the cold and inhospitable north.

    47.1 bìn 190/14. shra and biung are the main words of two co-
ordinate place topics.

    47.2 dzhan 78/8.

    47.3 sin ghiən (160/0, 19/11) as a compound generally means "work
hard at one's job under difficult circumstances", but here the context
seems to demand "suffer, grieve".

    47.4 huài 102/7.

48. The red parrot   紅鸚鵡   Hung qææng-miǒ (Hóng yīng-wǔ)

qɑn nom   iuǎn⁰ tzìn⁰
   hung qææng-miǒ
                              安南遠進紅鸚鵡

shriək zǐ   dhɑu xua
   ngiǔ⁰ zǐ njin
                              色似桃花語似人

miən jiɑng   bhiěn huèi
   gai njiu tsǐ
                              文章辯慧皆如此

lung hǎm   hɑ nen
   chuit dək⁰ shin
                              籠檻何年出得身

                              (Seven-syllable regulated quatrain)

48.1 qɑn nom "Annam" roughly corresponds to the present North
Vietnam. The area had been under Chinese rule or protection inter-
mittently since the second century B.C. The name is here a place topic,
telling from what place the action of the comment occurs.

48.2 njin 9/0.

48.3 miən 67/0; jiɑng 117/6; bhiěn 160/14.

48.4 lung hǎm is a synonym compound; it is a topicalized place
object to chuit. shin 158/0.

D. Lǐ Huà 李賀 (Lǐ Hè, 791-817)

Like Mæng Gau, Lǐ Huà belonged to the literary clique that cen-
tered around Han Iǒ. He was not permitted to take the national exam-
ination because of a technicality involving a taboo on his father's
given name. This idiotic ruling was attacked by Han Iǒ in a famous
essay ridiculing undue emphasis on such taboos, but Lǐ Huà was still
refused admission to the examination. The result was that during his
short life, he never attained a high official position.

His most typical poetry is unusual in its emphasis on the macabre
and in the lushness of its imagery.

49. I am moved to make an indirect criticism 感諷 Gǒm biùng
(Gǎn fèng)--third of five.

nom shran ha-ghi bi	南 山 何 其 悲
giuǝi iǒ shrǎ kung° tsǎu	鬼 雨 灑 空 草
djhiang qan ià bàn tsiou	長 安 夜 半 秋
biung dzhen giǝi njin lǎu	風 前 幾 人 老
5 dei-mei huɘn xuǝn gèng	低 迷 黃 昏 徑
nĕu nĕu tseng lek dhǎu	裊 裊 青 櫟 道
ngiuæt ngǒ zhiò mio qiæng	月 午 樹 無 影
qit shran ui bhæk xĕu	一 山 唯 白 曉
tsit ghiǔ ngiæng sin njin	漆 炬 迎 新 人
10 qiou kuàng hueng njiĕu njiĕu	幽 壙 螢 擾 擾

(Five-syllable old-style poem)

Title: gŏm 61/9 is an auxiliary here.

49.1 nom shran refers to the mountains south of Djhiang-qan, where
there are many tombs. ghi 12/6, suffixed to the general content inter-
rogative ha, makes an interrogative with the specific meaning "why?"

49.2 giuŏi 194/0.

49.3 bòn 24/3 is a place noun here.

49.7 ngŏ 24/2.

49.8 The line is a nominal sentence: "The entire mountain is
only white morning"--referring to the brightness of the moonlight.

49.9 tsit ghiŭ anticipates hueng in the next line and perhaps
refers to the spirits of the dead buried long ago. sin njin refers to
the spirits of those recently buried.
   The poet indirectly criticizes the government for (unspecified)
conditions that have caused many recent deaths.

50. The tomb of So the Tiny   蘇小小墓   So Siɛu-siɛu mɔ
(Sū Xiǎo-xiǎo mù)

So the Tiny was a famous singer who lived in the eastern city of
Dzhiɛn-dhɑng   錢塘 (Qián-táng, the modern Háng-zhōu 杭 州 or
Hangchow) around 500 A.D. A Music Bureau poem entitled "Song of So
the Tiny" goes:

> I ride in an oil(cloth) walled carriage;
> my love rides a dark dappled horse.
> At what place shall we bind our hearts that agree
>   (in mutual love)?
> At Western Tombs, below pines and cedars.

The cemetery called Western Tombs is west of Dzhiɛn-dhɑng.

qiou lɑn lɔ	幽 蘭 露
njiu dhei° ngǎn	如 啼 眼
mio miət get° dhung sim	無 物 結 同 心
qen° xua biət kom tziěn	煙 花 不 堪 剪
5 tsǎu njiu qin	草 如 茵
ziong njiu gɑ̀i	松 如 蓋
biung ui zhiɑng	風 爲 裳
shuǐ ui bhɔ̀i	水 爲 珮
iou bek chia	油 壁 車
10 ziæk siɑng dhɛ̌i°	夕 相 待
lɛ̌ng tsuǐ jiok	冷 翠 燭
lɑu guɑng tsɛ̌i	勞 光 彩
sei liəng hǎ	西 陵 下

biung chui iǒ   風 吹 雨

                                    (Music Bureau poem)

50.3   dhung 30/3.

50.11   jiok refers to will-o'-the-wisps.

50.12   lau 19/10; tsǎi 59/8.

50.13-14   For the rhyme here, see above, "Prosodic note 6", p.51.

E. Dhŏ Miuk   杜 牧   (Dù Mù, 803-852)

Dhŏ Miuk's biography includes the usual official career beginning in his mid-twenties, association with one of the two political cliques that were contending for power, interruptions to take care of a younger brother afflicted with an eye disease, and anecdotes attesting his love of singing girls and the gay night life of the southern cities.

His most famous poetry is in the quatrain form, and he is noted for the deftness of his style and for the general cheerfulness of his mood.

51. Returning home   歸 家   Giuəi ga (Guī Jiā)

djhì tzĭ ken qiəi miən   稚 子 牽 衣 問

giuəi ləi hɑ tɑ̀i djhi   歸 來 何 太 遲

ghiòng zhui jræng siuɛ̌i ngiuæt   共 誰 爭 歲 月

iæng dək bǐn ben° si   贏 得 鬢 邊 絲

(Five-syllable regulated quatrain)

51.1 miə̀n 30/8 is intransitive here, unless the rest of the poem, which is the text of the questions, is taken as its object.

51.2 ləi 9/6 is a suffix to the preceding verb, telling the direction of the action of the verb.

51.3 ghiòng 12/4 is a co-verb (cf. iǔ at 21.6). siuɛ̌i ngiuæt are plausibly coordinate time objects to jræng "compete for years and months"—we would say "compete for months and years". But I think they are better considered the direct object of jræng: "compete in years and months", "enter into competition to see who is the older".

51.4 iæng 154/13.

52. Quatrain on passing the Palace of Flowery Purity 過華清
宮絕句   Guà Hua°-tsiæng Giung dzhiuɛt giò (Guò Huá-qīng
Gōng jué jù)--first of three.

djhiɑng qɑn huəi° miàng   長安迴望繡成堆
    siòu zhiæng duəi

shran děng tsen mən   山頂千門次第開
    tsì dhèi° kəi

qit ghì hung djhin   一騎紅塵妃子笑
    piəi tzǐ siɛu

mio njin dji zhǐ   無人知是荔枝來
    lì-ji ləi

                          (Seven-syllable regulated quatrain)

    Title: The Palace of Flowery Purity is an imperial palace in a
mountain hot springs area near Djhiɑng-qɑn.

    52.1 Two peaks in the hot spring area are named siòu because of
the lushness of the trees planted there.

    52.2 tsì 76/2 and dhèi form a synonym compound.

    52'.3 hung djhin is dust stirred up and shining red in sunlight;
a figure for gay life, or for the troublesome distractions of the tran-
sitory world. It is also a name for the litchi, referred to in the
next line. Iɑng Giuòi-piəi (see prefatory note to Poem 22) is said to
have liked litchi nuts, but they had to be fresh. Horsemen bringing
them from the south were required to deliver them to her in the capital
after riding seven days and seven nights straight.

53. The Xàn River 漢江 Xàn Gang (Hàn Jiāng)

iong-iong   iàng iàng   溶 溶 漾 漾 白 鷗 飛
    bhæk qou biəi

liok dzhiæng   chuin shim   綠 淨 春 深 好 染 衣
    xǎu° njiěm qiəi

nom kiù   bək ləi   南 去 北 來 人 自 老
    njin dzhì lǎu

ziæk iang   djhiang sùng   夕 陽 長 送 釣 船 歸
    dèu jhiuεn giuəi

(Seven-syllable regulated quatrain)

Title: The Xàn River is a major tributary of the Yangtze. Its
source is in the modern privince of Shǎn-xī (or Shensi); it flows
east and south, through Siang-iang (see 26.8) and joins the Yangtze
at the modern city of Hàn-yáng.

F. Lỉ Shiɑng-qiẽn 李商隱 (Lỉ Shāng-yỉn, 812(?)-858)

Lỉ Shiɑng-qiẽn pursued the usual career of a civil servant. He
is probably the most admired of late Dhɑng poets, especially for his
poems on the theme of love, unusual in Chinese poetry. His works tend
to be highly allusive and difficult, with lush but somewhat claustro-
phobic imagery.

54. Untitled 無題 Mio dhei (Wú tí)

siɑng gèn   zhi nɑn
    bhiɛt iæk nɑn

相見時難別亦難

dung biung   mio liək
    bæk xuɑ dzhɑn

東風無力百花殘

chuin dzhom   dɑ̀u sỉ
    siᵒ biɑng dzhỉnᵒ

春蠶到死絲方盡

lop ghiǔᵒ   zhiæng xuəi
    luỉ shỉ gɑn

蠟炬成灰淚始乾

5 xĕu giæng   dhɑ̌n jrhiou
    iuən bỉn gĕi

曉鏡但愁雲鬢改

iɑ̀ ngim   qiəng gak
    ngiuæt guɑng hɑn

夜吟應覺月光寒

bhung shran   tsỉ kiù
    mio dɑ lò

蓬山此去無多路

tseng dĕu   qiən ghiənᵒ
    uỉ tɑm kɑn

青鳥殷勤為探看

(Seven-syllable regulated poem)

Title: dhei 181/9. Many of Lǐ Shiɑng-qiěn's love poems are untitled.

54.1 gèn 147/0.

54.2 dzhɑn 78/8.

54.3 sǐ 78/2; biɑng 70/0.

54.4 gɑn 5/10.

54.7 tsǐ 77/2.

54.8 qiən 79/6; uǐ 87/8, like Ǐ at 21.8, is a co-verb, standing alone without an object. tseng děu refers to a supernatural messenger to the world of immortals.

55. The patterned zither 錦瑟 gǐm° shrit (Jǐn sè)

gǐm shrit mio duɑn
     ngǒ zhip hen
                                 錦瑟無端五十絃

qit hen qit djhiǒ°
     sì° hua° nen
                                   一絃一柱思華年

jriɑng° shræng xěu miǔng
     mei° ho-dhep
                                   莊生曉夢迷蝴蝶

miǎng dèi chuin sim
     tɑk dhǒ-guen
                                   望帝春心託杜鵑

5 tsɑng xěi ngiuæt miæng
     jio° iǒu luì
                                   滄海月明珠有淚

lom dhen njit nuǎn
     ngiok shræng qen
                                   藍田日暖玉生烟

tsǐ dzhiæng kǎ dhěi
     zhiæng djui qiək
                                   此情可待成追憶

jǐ zhǐ dɑng zhi
     ǐ miǎng njiɛn
                                   只是當時已惘然

                                  (Seven-syllable regulated poem)

Title: __shrit__ 96/9.

    55.1 __mio duɑn__ "unexpectedly, by chance". The poet refers to an account of Pale Lady, a divinity who was especially good at music. She played a fifty-stringed zither for her ruler, but her playing was so sad that he ordered her to stop. She refused and he broke the zither, so that it had twenty-five strings. In the present poem, the persona plays a zither, and somehow his music is as sad as if it were being played by Pale Lady.

55.3 shræng 100/0; mùng 36/11. The famous story of how Scholar Jriang, the philosopher whose name is attached to the collection of Taoist writings called the Jriang-tzĭ (see 10.7), dreamed he was a butterfly, and how on awaking he was not sure whether it was he that had dreamed that he was a butterfly or whether he now was in a butter-fly's dream, appears at the end of the second chapter of the Jriang-tzĭ: "A discussion on equalizing things 聲 物 論 Dzhei miət luən (Qí wù lùn)".

55.4 miàng 74/7, and see the note to 21.23,pp.   Another version of the story has Emperor Miàng conducting an affair with the minister's wife while the minister is away working on flood control, and it is because of shame for this illicit behavior that Emperor Miàng retires into the mountains. chuin sim refers to thoughts of love.

55.5 This line refers to two myths: pearls are finished when the moon is full, otherwise they are still incomplete. One of the shark people living at the bottom of the sea came and lived in a man's house and after some days produced fine raw silk cloth which she sold. When it came time to leave, she asked the man in whose house she stayed for a container; she then wept pearls into the container and gave them to the man.

55.6 Indigo Fields (see the title of Poem 9) produces fine jade, and the hills there seem to emit a mist when warmed by the sun, but one can see the mist only from a distance. Also, Purple Jade is the name of the daughter of an ancient ruler who fell in love with a slave. When she asked her father's permission to marry the slave, he refused, and she died of grief. One day when her father was combing his hair, a radiance of purple jade filled the room. The father talked with this spirit of his daughter, and her mother heard their conversation. But when she came into the room and tried to embrace her daughter, Purple Jade turned into mist and disappeared.

55.7 djui qiək "pursuing something that has receded into the past and trying to remember it--a hard-won memory".

Note: I have followed the interpretation of A. C. Graham in presenting this poem. See Graham 1965, pp. 169-73.

Introduction

This glossary of all words occurring in the titles and texts of
Fifty-five T'ang Poems is arranged according to a traditional way of
analyzing the shapes of the characters that represent these words.

It has already been pointed out that most Chinese words are one
syllable in length (GS 1). According to the traditional Chinese
orthography, one character represents one syllable. We may go further
and say that in general one character represents one syllable-meaning
intersection. Thus, one syllable-meaning intersection njin "man" is
represented 人 9/0. Another, nearly synonymous syllable-meaning in-
tersection bio "man" is represented differently: 夫 37/1. A third
word, homophonous with bio "man" is bio "skin", and it too is repre-
sented differently: 膚 130/11. Corollaries to this general rule
are: (1) if two words are synonymous but pronounced differently, they
are represented by different characters; (2) if two words are homoph-
onous but have different meanings, they too are represented by differ-
ent characters.

There are many exceptions to these general statements. Sometimes
one character represents two (or more) words that are: (1) homophonous
but not synonymous, like dzhî "from" and dzhî "oneself", both repre-
sented 自 132/0; (2) synonymous but not homophonous, like kan, kàn
"look at, take a look", both represented 看 109/4; neither syn-
onymous nor homophonous, like xău "good" and xàu "be fond of", which
are probably related through some process of word derivation by tone
change no longer operating by the time of MC, and which in MC times
are simply to be counted as separate words; or like ngak "music" and
lak "joy", both written 樂 75/11 . Sometimes a syllable-meaning
intersection has two (or more) written representations, like huəi "re-
turn", which when it occurs alone as a verb is written 回 31/3 or
逈 162/6, and which when it occurs in the descriptive built on
it, bhəi-huəi "(going back and forth)", is written 徊 60/6.

Disyllabic (and polysyllabic) words that cannot be analyzed
reasonably as consisting of two (or more) syllable-meaning intersections
are written with characters that otherwise represent monosyllabic words
that are homophonous with the respective syllables in the disyllabic
(or polysyllabic) words. Thus sin-i "(magnolia)" is written 辛夷 ,
where 辛 160/0 also represents sin "painful, sad", and 夷 37/3
also represents i "(foreign nations east of China)" (though not in
Fifty-five T'ang Poems).

There are three main ways of arranging a dictionary. One is to
group the entries according to meaning. Such semantically arranged
dictionaries, like Roget's Thesaurus, are useful, for example, if you
think you know a word, you cannot quite call it up from your subcon-
scious, and you know other words similar in meaning but not just the
word you are looking for. Another is to group the entries according
to sound. Such phonologically arranged dictionaries are useful if the
standard orthography is at least approximately based on the phonologi-
cal system of the language that is being written, such as English--
most standard lexical works in English are phonologically arranged

working from the beginning of the word to the end: i.e. are alpha-
betically arranged. In Chinese, phonologically arranged dictionaries
typically order their entries working from the end of the word: i.e.,
are rhyming dictionaries. Such works are useful to would-be poets.

As we shall see, the characters of the Chinese orthography have
no reliable correlation between shape and sound. In alphabetic orthog-
raphies, there is more or less such a correlation, hence an arrange-
ment of dictionary listings by shape, more or less corresponds to an
alphabetic listing. Not so in Chinese. Hence for Chinese there is a
third way of arranging entries, namely to group them according to
shape of character. This way is the most useful for those whose knowl-
edge of the Chinese orthography is imperfect and who need to use a dic-
tionary. It is according to the shape of the Chinese characters that
this glossary is arranged.

For the last few centuries, Chinese dictionaries that order their
entries according to the shape of the characters have used a method of
analyzing a character into a meaning indicator, or radical, and a re-
mainder (if any). This glossary is arranged according to this tradi-
tional system, complete with its eccentricities.

What follows is a brief description of how the radical-remainder
system operates in the ordering of the entries of a traditional char-
acter dictionary. First, a character is a radical all by itself, or it
consists of a radical and a remainder. Of the first sort, there are
214; they are listed in Table 5, p. 180. Two characters are conven-
tionally assigned to radicals which have more strokes than they them-
selves have: 扌 is assigned to the 4-stroke "hand" radical 手 ,
number 64, and we give it the code 64/0; 王 is assigned to the 5-
stroke "jade" radical 玉 , number 96, and we give it the code 96/0.

The vast bulk of Chinese characters is of the second sort, con-
sisting of a radical and what remains of the character after the radi-
cal has been accounted for, the remainder. Ideally, the radical indi-
cates the meaning of the word that the character represents and the
remaining strokes give some idea of the sound of the word. The de-
cisions about how to write words in Chinese have always been arbitrary
and conventional, and they have been made in the course of over three
thousand years, during which time the meanings and sounds of the words
have changed, usually quite radically. The result is that at present
observation of the shape of a character really gives no reliable help
as to the meaning or sound of the word that it represents.

Another arbitrary and conventional decision made in the arrange-
ment of a traditionally ordered Chinese character dictionary is which
character constitutes a radical in its entirety, and which is composed
of a radical and a remainder. In the case of the latter, another de-
cision is made as to what part of the character is the radical. The
first major grouping of a body of characters is according to radical:
characters with the same radical are grouped together.

The arrangement of the radical groups within the dictionary and
the arrangement of characters within the radical groups involve a num-
ber of further arbitrary decisions involving the counting of strokes.

It will be observed that a character is composed of a number of lines--
brush- or pen-strokes--whose number and discreteness is arbitrarily
determined and is sometimes obvious, sometimes not. For example it is
fairly obvious that 一 , 丨 , 丶 , 丿 , 亅 each consists of
one stroke only, but it is not so obvious that 乙 is also only one
stoke. Although it is not the province of this introduction to give
detailed instructions on the writing of Chinese characters, Table 6
gives the stroke order and the direction of strokes for each of the
214 radicals. Observation of the way in which the radicals are written
will usually provide the basis for writing other elements appearing in
characters, and also the basis for the following generalizations about
character writing: (1) Left before right. Begin a horizontal stroke
at the left: 二 Write the left-most stroke before the others:
丿 丿丨 丿丨丨 . Write the left-most element (more than one stroke) be-
fore the others: 一 十 才 木 杧 机 枏 相 相 . (2) Top be-
fore bottom. Begin a vertical stroke, with or without a hook or slant,
at the top: 丨 丿 乚 亅 . Write the top-most stroke before the
others: 一 二 . Write the top-most element before the others:
丶 丷 宀 宀 穴 宀 宁 宀 宮 宮 . (3) Horizontal before the
vertical that crosses: 一 十 ; 一 厂 万 百 亙 亞 昌 事 . (4)
Encloser before the enclosed (and close the box last of all): 丨 冂
冂 冃 冃 冃 ; 丶 冂 冂 四 四 . Exception: Radical
162 辵 always comes last: 一 十 才 木 术 术 沭 沭 述 ; cf.
ㄱ 丶 圥 圥 圥 辷 辷 建 建 ; (5)
Upper right-hand dot comes last: 丿 丿 厂 式 戎 戊 戊 . (6)
Center before symmetrical elements left and right: 丨 丿丨 丿丨丶 .

Within the dictionary, radical groups are arranged in a conven-
tional order based on the total number of strokes in the radical when
it stands alone, not as part of another character. In the majority of
cases, a radical appearing in a character has the same number of strokes
there as it does when it stands alone. Thus 樹 has 木 as its
radical (4 strokes), and 騎 has 馬 as its radical (10 strokes).
But many radicals are abbreviated in the characters that they appear in.
Thus 流 has 氵 (3 strokes) as its radical, abbreviated
from 水 (4 strokes); it is therefore grouped as having a four-
stroke radical.

Within each radical group, characters are arranged according to
the number of strokes in the remainder. In <u>Fifty-five</u> T'ang <u>Poems</u>,
characters are referred to by numerical codes consisting of the number
of the radical as it occurs in the traditional order, followed by the
number of strokes in the remainder, separated from the radical number
by a slash. Thus "75/12" means "Radical No. 75, twelve strokes in the
remainder".

In <u>Fifty-five</u> T'ang <u>Poems</u>, beginning with Poem 23, radical-
remainder codes are no longer given for characters with obvious radi-
cals. Radicals considered obvious are listed in Table 7.

Table 5

Radicals

The 214 radicals of traditional Chinese lexicography appear below in their usual order, grouped according to number of strokes. Shortened forms of the radicals are included and are grouped with the radicals that have the same number of stokes as the shortened forms.

1 stroke

一	丨	、	丿	乙	亅
1	2	3	4	5	6

2 strokes

二	亠	人	亻	儿	入	八	冂	冖	冫
7	8	9	(9)	10	11	12	13	14	15
几	凵	刀	刂	力	勹	匕	匚	匸	十
16	17	18	(18)	19	20	21	22	23	24
卜	卩	卪	厂	厶	又				
25	26	(26)	27	28	29				

3 strokes

口	囗	土	士	夂	夊	夕	大	女	子
30	31	32	33	34	35	36	37	38	39
宀	寸	小	尢	尸	屮	山	巛	工	己
40	41	42	43	44	45	46	47	48	49
巾	干	幺	广	廴	廾	弋	弓	彐	彡
50	51	52	53	54	55	56	57	58	59
彳	忄	扌	氵	犭	艹	辶	阝		
60	(61)	(64)	(85)	(94)	(140)	(162)	(on the right: 163)		

阝
(on the left: 170)

4 strokes

心	戈	戶	手	支	攴	攵	文	斗	斤
61	62	63	64	65	66	(66)	67	68	69
方	无	日	曰	月	木	欠	止	歹	殳
70	71	72	73	74	75	76	77	78	79

毋	比	毛	氏	气	水	火	灬	爪	父
80	81	82	83	84	85	86	(86)	87	88

爻	爿	片	牙	牛	牛	犬	王	礻	月
89	90	91	92	93	(93)	94	(96)	(113)	(130)

艹
(140)

5 strokes

玄	玉	瓜	瓦	甘	生	用	田	疋	广
95	96	97	98	99	100	101	102	103	104

疒	白	皮	皿	目	矛	矢	石	示	礻
105	106	107	108	109	110	111	112	113	(113)

肉	禾	穴	立	罒	耒
114	115	116	117	(122)	(145)

6 strokes

竹	⺮	米	糸	缶	网	羊	羽	老	而
118	(118)	119	120	121	122	123	124	125	126

耒	耳	聿	肉	臣	自	至	臼	舌	舛
127	128	129	130	131	132	133	134	135	136

舟	艮	色	艸	虍	虫	血	行	衣	西
137	138	139	140	141	142	143	144	145	146

足
(157)

7 strokes

見	角	言	谷	豆	豕	豸	貝	赤	走
147	148	149	150	151	152	153	154	155	156

走	足	足	身	車	辛	辰	辶	邑	酉
(156)	157	(157)	158	159	160	161	162	163	164

釆	里
165	166

8 strokes

金	長	門	阜	隶	隹	雨	雨	青	非
167	168	169	170	171	172	173	(173)	174	175

食
(184)

9 strokes

面　　革　　韋　　韭　　音　　頁　　風　　飛　　食　　首
176　　177　　178　　179　　180　　181　　182　　183　　184　　185

香
186

10 strokes

馬　　骨　　高　　彡　　鬥　　鬯　　鬲　　鬼
187　　188　　189　　190　　191　　192　　193　　194

11 strokes

魚　　鳥　　鹵　　鹿　　麥　　麻
195　　196　　197　　198　　199　　200

12 strokes

黃　　黍　　黑　　黹
201　　202　　203　　204

13 strokes

黽　　鼎　　鼓　　鼠
205　　206　　207　　208

14 strokes

鼻　　齊
209　　210

15 strokes

齒
211

16 strokes

龍　　龜
212　　213

17 strokes

龠
214

Table 6

Order of strokes of the 214 radicals

N.B. Sometimes a radical occurs as an element in another radical.
When this happens, the stroke order of the smaller radical, having been
given earlier, will not be repeated in the larger radical. Placement
of the stroke-order number indicates the beginning of the stroke.

1 stroke

1 一   2 丨   3 丶   4 丿   5 乙   6 亅

2 strokes

7 二   8 亠   9 人 亻   10 儿   11 入   12 八   13 冂   14 冖

15 冫   16 几   17 凵   18 刀 刂   19 力   20 勹   21 匕   22 匚

23 匸   24 十   25 卜   26 卩 㔾   27 厂   28 厶   29 又

3 strokes

30 口   31 囗   32 土   33 士   34 夂   35 夊   36 夕   37 大   38 女

39 子   40 宀   41 寸   42 小   43 尢   44 尸   45 屮   46 山   47 巛

川 48 工   49 己   50 巾   51 干   52 幺   53 广   54 廴   55 廾

3 strokes--continued

56 弋 57 弓 58 彐, 互 彐 59 彡 60 犭 61 忄 64 扌

85 氵 94 犭 162 辶 163 阝 at right 170 阝 at left

4 strokes

61 忄 62 戋 63 户 64 爿 65 攴 66 皮 攵 67 文 68 斗

69 斤 70 方: 丶 亠 亐 方 71 无 72 日 73 曰 74 月 75 木

76 欠 77 止 78 歹 79 殳 80 毋: 乙 口 毋 毋 81 比:

亅 匕 比 比 82 毛 83 氏 84 气 85 水 86 火 灬

87 爪 88 爻 89 爻 90 爿 91 片 92 牙 93 牛 牛 94 犬

96 玉 113 礻 130 肉 140 艹 艹

5 strokes

95 玄 96 玉 97 瓜 98 瓦: 丆 瓦 瓦 99 甘 100 生

101 用 102 田 103 疋: 丆 疋 疋 疋 104 疒 105 癶 106 白

107 皮: 丿 广 广 皮 皮 108 皿 109 目 110 矛 111 矢

5 strokes--continued

112 右 113 㕚 朮 114 肉 115. 朱 116. 穴 117. 立 122. 曲

145 衤

6 strokes

118 㐬 灬 119. 米 120 糸 糸 121 缶 122. 网 123 羊

124. 羽 125. 老 126 而 127. 耒 128. 耳 129 聿 130 肉 131 臣

132 自 133 至 134 臼 ⺽ 臼 135. 舌 136 舛 夕 舛 137 舟

舟 舟 舟 138 艮 139 龜 140 艸 141 虍 虍 虎 142. 虫 143 血

144 行 145 衣 146 西 西 157 昆

7 strokes

147 見 148 角 149 言 150 谷 151 豆 152 豕 153 豸 154 貝

155. 赤 156 走 寺 赤 走 157 足 𧾷 足 158 身

159 車 160 辛 161 辰 辶 辰 辰 162 辵 辵 辵 辵

163 邑 𠂤 邑 邑 164 酉 165 釆 166 里

8 strokes

167 金： 仝 仝 余 金   168 農   169 門   170 阜： 阝 𨸏 阜

171 隶   172 隹   173 雨： 雨： 雨 雪   174 靑   175 非   184 食：
夲 食 食

9 strokes

176 面： 面 而 面   177 草： 艹 芎 草   178 韋

179 韭   180 音   181 頁   182 風： 凡 凧 風   183 飛： 乀 飞 飛 飛

184 食   185 首   186 香

10 strokes

187 馬： 厂 馬 馬 馬   188 骨： 骨 骨 骨   189 高

190 髟   191 鬥： 丨 鬥 鬥   192 鬯： 乂 鬯 鬯

193 鬲   194 鬼

11 strokes

195 魚　196 鳥: 丫 泊 鳥 鳥　197 鹵　198 鹿: 庐 唐 鹿 鹿

199 麥　200 麻

12 strokes

201 黃: 卅 帯 萬 黃　202 黍　203 黑　204 黹: 业 业 对 黹

13 strokes

205 黽: 宀 龟 黾 黽　206 鼎: 湨 鼎 鼎　207 鼓

208 鼠: 宀 囧 印 鼠 鼠

14 strokes

209 鼻　210 齊: 宀 添 齊

15 strokes

211 齒: 止 燊 齒

16 strokes

212 龍： 育　 龍　龍　龍　　　213 龜： 　 　龜　龜

17 strokes

214 龠： 龠　龠　龠

Table 7

Obvious radicals

Obvious radicals of characters which consist of a radical plus a remainder are listed below according to number of strokes. The position of the remainder is indicated by an "x".

2 strokes

亻x   9   人 : 偷
x刂   18   刀 : 刷
x力   19   力 : 勤

3 strokes

口x   30   口 : 哮
囗   31   囗 : 固
土x   32   土 : 坑
女x   38   女 : 娘
宀   40   宀 : 定
尸x   44   尸 : 居
山x   46   山 : 峽
    : 岸
    : 巒
广   53   广 : 廚
弓x   57   弓 : 強
彳x   60   彳 : 徑
忄x   61   心 : 悵
扌x   64   手 : 掬
氵x   85   水 : 津

犭x   94   犬 : 猛
辶   162   辵 : 進
x阝   163   邑 : 鄰
阝x   170   阜 : 附

4 strokes

忝   61   心 : 怒
挙   64   手 : 攀
攵x   66   攴 : 放
方x   70   方 : 旗
日x   72   日 : 昭
    : 晨
    : 暮
木x   75   木 : 樣
    : 棄
欠x   76   欠 : 歐
水x   85   水 : 泉
火x   86   火 : 烽
灬   : 照
牛x   93   牛 : 物
玉x   96   玉 : 珪

衤x   115   示 : 祖
肝x   130   肉 : 脆
艾   140   艸 : 茂

5 strokes

玉x   96   玉 : 瑩
田x   102   田 : 略
    : 異
    : 留
疒   104   广 : 病
白x   106   白 : 皎
    : 皇
皿   108   皿 : 孟
目x   109   目 : 眼
    : 眉
矢x   111   矢 : 短
石x   112   石 : 碎
    : 碧
禾x   115   禾 : 稍
穴   116   穴 : 穿
立x   117   立 : 端

罒X	122	网	: 羅
衤X	145	衣	: 裙

6 strokes

⺮X	118	竹	: 簡
米X	119	米	: 粧
糹X	120	糸	: 絃
X糸			: 紫
X羽	124	羽	: 翻
羽X			: 翠
X羽			: 翁
耳X	128	耳	: 聒
X耳			: 聲
舟X	137	舟	: 船
虫X	142	虫	: 蠟
X虫			: 螢
X衣	145	衣	: 裳
覀X	146	西	: 覆
𧾷X	157	足	: 踏

7 strokes

X見	147	見	: 視
X見			: 覓
角X	148	角	: 觸
X角			: 觜
言X	149	言	: 訖
豸X	153	豸	: 豺
貝X	154	貝	: 賊
X貝			: 贊
走X	156	走	: 起
車X	159	車	: 輓
X車			: 輩
酉X	164	酉	: 酸

8 strokes

金X	167	金	: 鈴
門X	169	門	: 闌
X隹	172	隹	: 雖
雨X	173	雨	: 露
食X	184	食	: 餘

9 strokes

X頁	181	頁	: 頃
風X	182	風	: 飈
X風			: 飄

11 strokes

魚X	195	魚	: 鯉
X鳥	196	鳥	: 鵬
鳥X			: 鳧
X鳥			: 鷺
鹿X	198	鹿	: 麟
X鹿			: 麗

12 strokes

黑X	203	黑	: 默
X黑			: 黛

1 一

1/0 一 qit one 8.3...; once 4.3, 9.2, 20.10; first 45.4; as soon as 31.7; entire 30.2, 31.1, 49.8; entirely 23.5, 23.6.

1/1 七 tsit seven 43.3.

1/2 三 som three 18.4...; three times 11.8; third 36.1.

丈 djhiǎng husband 39.13.

上 zhiǎng rise, ascend, go up 3.4; send up 37.8; mount, climb, go up 20.14...

zhiàng top, upon 4.3...; above 21.11, 30.12; superior, honored 41.16.

下 hǎ bottom, below 12.2...; under 18.T.

hà descend 5.4, 41.2; proceed down to 20.27...; downwardly 33.10.

1/3 不 biət not 1.4...

1/4 世 shiɛi world, society 39.15, 40.8; way of getting along in the world 22.44.

且 tsiǎ for a time 23.11; and, furthermore 7.4, 22.91.

丘 kiou hill 40.C, 40.2.

2 丨

2/3 中 djiung middle, inside 41.4; in 22.30...; midst, amid 1.1, 5.1, 7.2, 22.75; central 33.6; (people) within (the royal palace) 22.126.

djiùng get, attain 22.13.

2/4 丱 guàn with hair bound in two tufts 41.14.

3 丶

3/3 丹 dɑn cinnabar, red 19.5...

3/4 主 jiǒ master 22.13.

4 丿

4/1 乃 nǒi 無 mio nǒi most likely, no means to cope with 43.4.

4/2 久 giǒu for a long time 16.1, 22.10; last a long time 22.119; get late 23.21.

4/3 之 ji A ji B B qualified by A 9.T...; (3rd-person pronoun, object of preceding verb) 19.C, 41.6; (3rd-person pronoun, preposed object of following verb) 31.9.

4/4 乏 bhiæp lack 22.11.

乎 ho A ho B tzəi 哉 how A B is! 21.1, 21.32.

4/9 乘 jhiəng ride, take advantage of 16.17.

5 乙

5/1 九 giǒu nine 21.16.

5/2 也 iǎ (phrase suffix) 21.31, 40.C.

乙
5
↓
6
二
7
⼁
8
人
9

5/7 乳 njiŏ breast (for feeding infant) 23.14.

5/10 乾 gɑn dry 54.4

  ghiɛn (1st Hexagram, corresponding to heaven) 22.19.

5/12 亂 luàn be in a chaotic state 18.10, 22.90; scattered 22.50.

6 丿

6/7 事 jhrì affair, matter, things that happen 2.2...; circumstance 22.36.

  --- devote oneself to 39.5.

7 二

7/0 二 njì two 23.10...; second 22.1, 39.11; Number Two 8.T.

7/1 于 io at 22.132.

7/2 云 iuən say 21.42.

  互 hò mutually 22.46, 35.9.

  井 tziǎng well 21.17.

  五 ngŏ five 20.11...; fifth 20.17.

7/5 況 xiuàng much more true is it of... 41.19.

  況 85/5.

8 亠

8/1 亡 miɑng destroy 22.117.

8/4 交 gau exchange, mix 18.11.

  亦 iæk also 16.12...; even so 31.20.

8/6 京 giæng capitol 22.110, 26.C.

8/7 亭 dheng pavilion 15.T., 15.2. Cf. 9/9.

9 人

9/0 人 njin mɑn, (other) person 3.1...; man, human being 48.2; a person, one 21.26, 21.41, 31.4; (M: soldiers) 22.101; woman 13.1, 45.2. Cf. 9/2.

9/2 今 gim today, now 19.2...; this (season) 22.33; this (year) 39.12.

  仍 njiəng continuingly, still 32.2.

  仇 ghiou enemy 32.8.

  仁 njin kind, humane 35.8; be kind to 31.6; kindness 32.3, 32.4, 32.5. Cf. 人 9/0.

  仄 jriək slanted 28.9.
  側 9/9.

9/3 伏 djhiàng grasp 122.30.

  令 liæng cause 19.C; 22.55.

  以 Ɩ by means of it 21.8; by means of, with 21.18, 32.3.

(9/3) 仙 siɛn an immortal, fairy 39.15, 41.6; immortal-hood 41.C, 41.20.

代 dhəi era 16.15.

9/4 仰 ngiǎng raise the head to look 21.17, 22.95, 33.9; to a higher authority 30.14.

伊 qi (place) 22.109.

休 xiou excellence, beauty 16.17.

--- stop 22.94...; retire (from public office) 44.4.

9/5 作 tzɑk make 36.2; serve as, become 26.5...; compose 9.T, 16.1.

余 iu my, me 19.C, 26.C.

似 zǐ resemble 47.4, 48.2; be compared with 42.7; be as though 22.86, 33.3.

伴 bhǎn companion 26.6; make...one's companion 18.7.

何 hɑ how...! 16.7...; what? 21.19...; where? 26.3; why? 22.54...

佇 djhiǔ wait 22.107.

但 dhǎn only 3.2...

低 dei lower 14.4, 20.9; dei-mei 迷 (muddled) 49.5.

9/6 來 ləi come 2.1...; (verbal suffix) V ləi V here 51.2; x ləi since x 19.1; 爾 njiě ləi from then coming on toward the present 21.5; 自從 dzhì dzhiong...ləi from the time of... up to now 16.13.

使 shrǐ send on a mission to 8.T; cause 12.11...

佳 gai excellent 17.5; auspicious 22.136.

依 qiəi be set in 9.1.

9/7 便 bhiɛn then 26.8.

信 sìn believe 37.5, 41.7; a trust 20.13.

俗 ziok people 22.100; vulgar 27.9.

9/8 俱 gio all, all at once 22.112.

倒 dàu upside down 21.28, 22.72.

倉 tsɑng storehouse 38.9.

--- tsɑng-tsuət 卒 (hurried, urgent) 24.8.

倚 qǐ be set in 21.28.

候 hòu attend 9.4.

9/9 停 dheng stop (tr.) 19.2; stay (intr.) 30.12. Cf.   8/7.

偷 tou steal 23.11.

側 jriək bend, incline (the body) 21.45.   9/2.

偶 ngǒu by chance 17.3.

9/10 傍 bhɑng neighboring 37.5. 70/6.

備 bhì prepare 23.20.

9/11 傳 djhiuɛn pass on, tell 26.1...

人
9

人
9

儿
10

入
11

八
12

冂
13

冖
(14)

冫
15

9/11 傷 shiɑng hurt, wound 15.1;
         be wounded 22.23.

9/12 僕 bhuk servant 22.48.

10 儿

10/2 元 ngiuæn origin 41.16;
         primal, of the beginning
         16.15, 41.19; (surname)
         8.T, 45.T.
         Cf. 源 85/10.

10/4 光 guɑng light, radiance
         14.1...; radiant 22.79;
         (name) 22.128.

     先 sen first, beforehand
         36.4, 42.3, 46.2;
         previous times 22.122.

10/6 兔 tò rabbit 19.9.

     兒 nji son 22.63, 24.3.

11 入

11/0 入 njip enter (into) 3.3...

11/2 內 nuòi inside 22.43, 36.1.

11/6 兩 liǎng two 20.6...

     --- 㒳 miǎng-liǎng
         (water phantom) 33.3.

12 八

12/0 八 bat eight 21.5; eighth
         20.23, 22.2.

12/2 兮 hei (exclamatory phrase
         suffix), oh! 12.9...

     六 liuk six 20.15, 21.11.

公 gung (title of respect)
     45.T.

12/4 共 ghiòng accompany 22.62;
         accompanying, with 51.3;
         together, with someone
         19.14; make...go to-
         gether, synchronize
         16.18.

12/5 兵 biæng weapon 16.6,
         32.3; soldier 22.101.

12/6 其 ghi its, their 21.31...;
         how...?! 22.119;
         hɑ-ghi why? 49.1

13 冂

13/4 再 tzòi another time,
         again 11.8, 22.127.

15 冫

15/4 冰 biəng ice 28.3...;
         icy 24.5.

15/5 冷 lǎng cold 50.11.

15/8 凋 deu wither 21.26.

     凌 liəng cross over to 4.1.

     凄 tsei cold, desolate
         12.9. 淒 85/8;
         Cf. 悽 61/8.

     凍 dùng freeze 29.3...;
         freezing 31.3;
         freezing (n.) 32.1;
         frozen 9.5, 29.9...;
         frozen thing 35.1.

15/13 凜 lǐm shiver 22.76.

15/14 凝 ngiəng frozen 28.12,
          35.9.

16   几

16/1 几 bhiæm ordinary 39.14.

17   凵

17/3 出 chuit emerge (from), go
          (beyond) 8.4...; proceed
          out (through) 11.9; away
          30.8.

18   刀

18/0 刀 dɑu knife 29.3...

18/1 刃 njìn blade 34.5.

18/2 切 tset keen 22.16; cutting
          33.4.

      分 biən divide, separate
          18.12.

18/4 列 liɛt display 22.78.

18/5 删 shran delete (from a
          literary corpus), edit
          out, make cuts (in a
          literary corpus) 16.21.

      别 bhiɛt part, leave 1.T...;
          different 22.122;
          séparate 9.T.

      初 chriu beginning, time
          when...first begins
          22.121; cause...to start
          22.2; first (adv.) 20.1,
          26.2, 35.12.

18/6 刷 shruat brush 31.13.

      到 dàu arrive 42.1, 54.3.

18/7 前 dzhen front, in front of
          2.3...; forward 22.27;
          that stretches out ahead
          (adj.) 23.23. proceed,
          come forward 22.27.

18/9 剪 tziěn snip, cut 33.7...;
          be snipped, cut off 29.5.

18/10 割 gɑt cut 29.4, 34.5;
          cutting 33.4.

18/11 剗 jiuɛn cut fine 29.4.

18/13 劍 giuæn 2-edged sword
          21.33...

      劇 ghiæk play 20.2.

      劈 pek cut 32.8.

19   力

19/0 力 liək strength 23.17...

19/5 助 jrhiù help 22.99.

19/7 勇 iǒng brave 22.104.

19/9 動 dhǔng move 22.35, 39.10.

19/10 勝 shiəng bear, support
          25.8.

      shiòng exceed 22.64.

      勞 lɑu struggle over, strain
          to produce 50.12;
          troublesome 28.15;
          lɑu-lɑu (sad) 15.T,
          15.2.

19/11 勢 shiɛi circumstances
          22.118.

      勤 ghiən grieve, sad
          47.3; work hard 54.8.

19/18 勸 kiuæn urge 8.3.

20   勹

20/1 勺 zhiɑk ladle 35.8.

20/2 勿 miət do not...! 39.13.

几
16
凵
17
刀
18
力
19
勹
20

(20/2)   ---thorough 22.14.   28.9; make...incline,
                                                        tilt 27.8.

ㄅ
20   21   26/5 却 kiɑk but, now 11.13,
                                                        47.4.   卻 26/7.

ㄈ
21   21/2 化 xuɑ̌ transform 21.37,   26/6 卷 giuě̌n curl 11.3; a
                   41.6.   curl, a roll 30.9; set
                                                        curling 4.4; roll up
匚   21/3 北 bək north 26.T...;   13.3, 26.4.
22   northwardly 22.T, 22.3;
                   from the north 22.97.   26/7 卽 tziək arrive at,
                                                        approach, get to the
匸   point of 22.88; namely
23   22 匚   26.7.

十   22/8 匪 piǎi not be 21.36.   卻 kiɑk nevertheless 19.4;
24   turn (to look at) 26.3.
                     23 匸   却 26/5.
ㅏ
(25)   23/2 匹 pit (M: horses) 22.102.   27 厂

卩   27/8 原 ngiuæn plain, flat ter-
26   24 十   rain 9.6.

厂   24/0 十 zhip ten 20.7...   28 厶
27
        24/1 千 tsen thousand 16.22...;   28/3 去 kiù go 41.8, 53.3;
厶   a thousand times 20.11.   leave, be gone 23.15,
28   45.1, 46.3; be distant
        24/2 午 ngǒ noon, (moon) be at   (from) 21.27, 54.7;
又   zenith 49.7.   of the past, last (year)
29   37.1; send away 37.T
        24/3 半 bàn half 22.55, 38.4;   (or kiǔ).
                   midst 39.3.
                                            28/9 參 shrim 21st Zodiacal
        24/6 卒 tzuət troops 22.94.   Constellation 21.17.

                   tsuət hurried, urgent   29 又
                   22.54, 24.8.
                                            29/0 又 iòu again 43.T; and
        24/7 南 nom south 16.7...;   what is more 21.23.
                   southern 17.9, 49.1.
                                            29/2 反 biǎn rebellion 22.15
                     26 卩   162/4.

        26/4 危 ngui dangerous 21.1,   及 ghip go as far as,

(29/2 及 ghip) until, when 22.58; meet...in time 18.8.

--- and 21.3, 22.71.

29/6 受 zhiǒu receive 22.90.

29/16 叢 dzhung thicket 21.3.

30 口

30/0 口 kǒu mouth, where... begins 9.1.

30/2 可 kǎ can, be able to 11.7...

只 jǐ only 39.16, 55.8.

句 giɔ sentence, line (of poetry) 43.T, 52.T.

古 gǒ ancient times 16.T...; ancient, old 21.21, 31.22.

30/3 吏 lì officer 23.T...

吃 giət stammer 31.5.

吁 xio 噫 qi-xio-xi 戯 whew! wow! 21.1.

合 hop come together 43.1; be with, join 39.16.

向 xiàng head for, toward 19.8...

同 dhung same, similar 42.6; agreeing 50.3; alike, similarly 18.11, 20.5, 22.124; being together, unity 22.133; be together (with you) 20.12.

吉 git become lucky 22.2.

各 gɑk each 18.12.

30/4 名 miæng name 41.9; be named 39.1.

吾 ngo my, we, our 16.2.

含 hom wear (a smile) 17.2; hold (in mouth), endure 22.19.

吟 ngim chant, recite 31.16, 54.6; song 39.T; groan 22.24.

吮 jhuǐn suck 21.40.

吴 ngo (name) 22.71.

吼 xǒu bellow, roar 22.32.

君 giuən lord, gentleman 27.7, 32.6, 34.7; lady 47.T; you (honorific) 2.1...

吹 chui blow 4.1...

30/5 呼 xo call, yell 23.5.

命 miæng mandate, destiny 22.119.

周 jiou (dynasty) 22.127.

味 miəi flavor 44.3.

咏 iuæng sing, chant 30.4.

呷 xap drink...while drawing in breath, gasp out 30.13.

呻 shin groan 22.24.

30/6 品 pǐm personality 39.5.

咽 qet sob 22.62, 23.22.

咸 ham both 45.3.

哉 tzəi (exclamatory phrase suffix) A ho   B tzei How A B is! 21.1, 21.32.

又
29
口
30

(30/6) 咨 tzi sigh 21.45.

口
30

哀 qəi sadness 16.8, 30.3,
       34.10; lament 35.10; be
       sad, mournful 20.18.

口
31

30/7 哭 kuk weep 22.61, 45.2;
         cry about 34.1.

嗥 xau scream 30.13.

唐 dhɑng embankment 20.16.

哲 djiɛt wise 22.128.

員 iuɛn iuɛn-nguɑ̀i
        secretary 9.T.

30/8 啖 dhǒm eat 16.5.

問 miən put questions to
        19.T...; ask about 10.7,
        22.4, 22.87; ask a
        question 51.1.

唯 ui only 10.1...
         61/8.

30/9 喜 xǐ enjoy 22.100; joy
        26.4.

喬 ghiɛu tall 9.2.

喪 sàng lose by death 43.T.

喚 huàn call 20.10.

喧 xiuæn yell 21.29.

啼 dhei weep 22.65...;
        weeping 50.2; cry (of
        birds) 21.23...

喝 xɑt shout 22.88.

喘 chiuěn breathe hard,
          whisper 31.8.

唼 chrap drink, gasp out
         30.13.

30/10 嗟 tzia Alas! 21.32
         sigh 21.45.

嗔 chin angry 22.88.

30/11 嘔 qǒu vomit 22.74.

嘗 zhiɑng taste 36.4;
          experience 20.8.

嘐 gau 嗥 xau-gau scream
        30.13.

嘆 tɑn, tàn sigh 21.18
   歎 76/11.

30/12 嘶 sei sob, cry 28.4,
         29.8.

嘯 sèu to whistle (a tune)
        6.2.

30/13 噫 qi qi-xio 吁 -xì 嚱
          whew! wow! 21.1.

30/15 嚙 ngǎu bite 30.5.

30/16 顰 bhin draw...into a
          frown 13.2.

30/17 嚴 ngiæm strictness 31.9.

嚱 xì 噫 qi-xio 吁
      -xì whew! wow! 21.1.

            31 口

31/2 四 sì four 20.7...

31/3 回 huəi make...turn around,
          turn back 4.3, 20.10,
          21.11; go back 21.12.
          迴 162/6, 徊 60/6.

--- huəi-huət
Uighur 22.98.

因 qin because of 32.1...

31/5 固 gò firm 40.7; surely
         22.14, 22.137.

31/8 國 guək nation, state
         16.4, 25.1(?)...;
         capital city 25.1(?).

31/10 圍 iuæn garden 17.1...;
imperial mausoleum
22.137.

31/11 圖 dho picture 22.69, 47.4.

32 土

32/0 土 tǒ territory 33.6.

32/3 在 dzhěi be located at
11.10...; exist, remain,
be here 25.1, 37.7.

地 dhì earth 11.1, 22.29;
ground 14.2, 21.9;
territory, quarters 39.6.

32/4 坑 kæng moat, gulley 31.4.

坐 dzhuǎ sit 6.1...; without
being able to do anything
about it 20.26(?),
21.18(?); unaccountably,
somehow, deepseatedly,
deeply 20.26(?), 21.18(?).

坂 biǎn slope 24.T, 24.1.

坎 kǒm kǒm-kǒm (drumbeat)
12.1.

32/5 坼 tjæk burst 22.69;
crack 28.3.

坤 kuən (2nd Hexagram,
corresponding to Earth)
22.19.

坡 pɑ pɑ-dha 陀
(hilliness) 22.45.

32/6 垢 gǒu dirty 22.66.

城 zhiæng walled city 8.1,
21.42, 23.8, 25.2.
Cf. 成 62/2, 誠 149/9.

垠 ngin shore, bank 16.10.

32/7 埋 mai bury 43.1.

32/8 堅 gen strong 39.17.

堆 duəi pile 20.16, 52.1.

32/9 報 bàu inform, report to
20.28.

堯 ngeu (name) 31.19.

場 djhiɑng field 22.51.

堪 kom bear to 50.4.

32/10 塞 sèi frontier region
21.6, 40.11.

塢 qǒ wall 7.T.

32/11 墓 mò tomb 40.T...

塵 djhin dust 8.1...

32/12 隉 dhuǎ fall into 22.57.

32/13 壁 bek wall 20.9...; cliff
21.28.

32/14 壑 xɑk gulley 21.30.

壕 hɑu moat, trench 23.T,
23.1.

32/15 壙 kuàng tomb 49.10.

32/16 壠 liǒng tomb 45.3.

33 士

33/0 士 jrhǐ officer, soldier
21.9; scholar 41.8.

33/4 壯 jriàng young and able-
bodied 21.9.

33/5 垂 zhui let...hang 16.16,
22.33; down-streaming
16.22.

33/9 壺 ho wine jar 18.1.

口
31

土
32

士
33

夊
35

夕
36

大
37

女
38

35 夊

35/7 夏 hǎ (legendary dynasty)
22.125.

36 夕

36/0 夕 ziæk evening, night
21.39, 50.10, 53.4.

36/2 外 nguài outside, beyond
9.7...; 員 iuɛn-nguài
secretary 9.T.

36/3 多 dɑ much, many 43.4,
54.7; be (more) frequent
38.6; there are many,
there is much 22.23...;
be overgrown with 16.4;
in great amounts 41.5,
41.15.

36/5 夜 ià night 9.8...; by
night 23.2, 23.18.

36/11 夢 miùng dream 55.3.

37 大

37/0 大 dhài great 16.1...
37/1 夫 bio man 4.2, 21.34,
21.35, 22.73; husband
20.14, 39.14, 45.2.

天 ten sky, heavens 11.1...;
Heaven 28.8, 34.8, 39.15.

太 tài great 21.7...; too,
excessively 43.4, 51.2.

37/2 失 shit lose 17.8, 28.13;
failing 22.12.

37/3 夷 i 辛 sin-i (magnolia)
7.2.

37/6 奔 bən hurrying, fast 38.8.

37/7 奚 hei (non-Chinese nation)
24.3.

37/11 奪 dhuɑt fail, falter
22.108.

37/13 奮 biən rouse 22.130.

38 女

38/0 女 niǔ woman 12.T, 12.5;
girl, daughter 22.67...

38/3 如 njiu resemble, be like
19.5...; resemble...in
being good 21.43;
(descriptive-making
suffix), -ly 33.3;
if 16.23.

--- arrive at 37.6,
47.4.

好 xǎu good 26.6, 39.17;
good enough to 53.2.

xàu be fond of, like
10.1.

妃 piəi member of the
Imperial harem 52.3.

38/4 妖 qiɛu weird, ominous
22.96.

妓 ghǐ female entertainer
42.7.

妝 jriɑng apply make-up
22.82.   119/6.

38/5 妻 tsei wife 22.60...

姑 go husband's mother
36.3; female relative
of husband 36.4.

始 shǐ begin to, beginning
by, only then 11.14...

姐 dɑt (name) 22.126.

(38/5) 委 quǐ be abandoned to 16.3.

姜 tsiɛp secondary wife
(used by married women as
a first person pronoun)
20.1, 20.25.

38/6 姮 həng həng ngɑ 娥 (name)
19.10.

姦 gan vicious 22.123.

姿 tzi beauty 39.9;
disposition 22.11.

38/7 娥 ngɑ 姮 həng ngɑ (name)
19.10.

娘 niɑng lady 36.T...

38/8 婦 bhiǒu wife 20.7...;
son's wife 37.T, 37.1.

38/10 嫌 hem suspicion, loathing
20.6; loathe to 37.7.

嫁 gà take a husband 36.T,
39.12.

38/11 嫗 qiò old woman 23.17.

38/12 嬌 giɛu spoil (with
affection), pamper 22.63.

38/17 孀 shriɑng widow, bird with-
out a mate 28.10, 29.12.

39 子

39/0 子 tzǐ child 22.60...;
master 22.3.

--- tzǐ-gui 規 (cuckoo)
21.23.

39/1 孔 kǔng (surname), Confucius
31.20.

39/3 存 dzhuən remain, survive
23.11, 43.T; cause to
remain, keep, preserve
20.13.

39/5 孤 go solitary, alone
19.10, 31.16.

39/7 孫 suən grandson 1.4...

39/13 學 hak learn how to 39.3;
imitate 22.81.

40 宀

40/3 宇 iǒ space 11.9.

安 qɑn peace 16.13, 49.3,
52.1; (place) 8.T, 48.1.

守 shiǒu guard 21.36.

40/4 完 huɑn complete 23.16.

宏 huæng broad 22.140.

40/5 宜 ngi be suitable to, be
proper to 22.120.

官 guɑn of the government
22.111, 26.T.

宛 qiuæn winding 11.16.

qiuǎn qiuǎn-djiuěn 轉
(turning) 17.7.

宙 djhiòu time 11.9.

定 dhèng secure, firm,
certain 30.11.

宗 tzong ancestor 22.139.

40/6 宣 siuɛn (name) 22.128.

客 kæk traveler 8.2, 15.2.

宦 huàn civil service 44.3.

室 shit house 22.4, 23.13.

40/7 害 hài harm 22.56.

宮 giung palace 52.T.

宵 siɛu night 19.7.

女
38

子
39

宀
40

(40/7) 家 ga family 5.T...; home 21.43...

宀
40

40/8 宿 siuk spend the night 29.5.

寸
41

寂 dzhek quiet 7.3; dzhek-mak 寞 (quiet) 22.134.

小
42

冤 qiuæn wrong 30.13.

密 mit dense 11.6; diligent 22.14.

尢
43

40/9 寒 han winter 2.4; wintry, cold 9.6...; coldness 34.1.

尸
44

40/11 寧 neng settled 30.14.

--- how? 19.8.

屮
(45)

寥 leu void 11.10.

寞 mak 寂 dzhek-mak (quiet) 22.134.

實 'jhit fruit 22.41; bear fruit 17.6.

40/18 寶 bǎu jewelled, precious 28.7.

41 寸

41/3 寺 zì temple, monastery 40.C.

41/8 將 tziɑng take 20.28; together with, and 18.7.

--- about to 22.3, 35.10.

tziɑ̀ng lead...as general 22.129.

41/9 尊 tzuən revered 22.93.

41/11 對 duɓi to face 18.4...

42 小

42/0 小 siɛu small 22.67...; young, youngest 39.1; small people 20.6.

42/1 少 shiɛu few, there are few 22.6...; be seldom 38.6.

shiɛu young 40.6; shiɛu-biɓ 府 Police Chief 10.T.

42/3 尖 tziɛm sharp-pointed 33.1.

42/5 尚 zhiàng still, now as before 22.93, 43.T; still, even so 21.13.

43 尢

43/1 尤 iou surpassingly good 40.8.

44 尸

44/1 尺 chiæk (10 Chinese inches, slightly more than one English foot) 21.27.

44/5 居 giu dwell 20.5; staying at home 38.2; dwelling 9.1.

44/6 屋 quk house 22.59.

44/7 展 djiɛ̌n spread (from a frown) 20.11.

44/11 屢 liɓ frequently 22.28.

--- slippers 12.6.

44/18 屬 zhiok (jiok) belong to, be subsumed under 16.17.

46 山

46/0 山 shran hill, mountain 1.1...

46/5 岸 ngàn high bank 28.1, 28.15.

46/6 島 dǎu island 41.12.

46/7 峯 piong mountain peak 21.27.

峽 hap gorge 26.7.

峨 ngɑ (place), moth(?) 21.8.
Cf. 蛾 142/7.

46/8 崖 ngai cliff 21.30, 22.32; ngai-nguəi (cliff, high and rocky) 21.33.

崩 bəng collapse 21.9.

崢 jrhæng jrhæng-huæng 嶸 (high mountains) 21.33.

46/10 嵬 nguəi 崖 ngai-nguəi (high, rocky) 21.33.

46/14 嶸 huæng 崢 jrhæng-huæng (high mountains) 21.33.

嶽 ngak sacred mountain 11.2.

46/17 嶮 jrham steep and dangerous 21.20.

46/19 巒 luɑn mountain range 21.16.

巔 den (mountain) peak 21.8.

46/20 巖 ngam cliff 21.16...

47 川

47/0 川 chiuɛn river 3.T...

48 工

48/0 工 gung workman 30.1.

48/2 巧 kǎu clever 42.5.

48/4 巫 mio shaman 12.5, 26.7.

49 己

49/0 己 Ɪ finished 22.15, 23.12; already 16.12...

49/1 巴 ba (place) 20.27, 26.7.

50 巾

50/4 希 xiəi hope 16.23.

50/5 帛 bhæk silk cloth 22.75, 38.9.

50/6 帝 dèi supreme ruler, emperor 22.1, 55.4.

50/7 師 shri soldier 22.53.

席 ziæk mat 12.7.

50/8 帶 dài belt 10.5; form a belt around 9.2.

常 zhiɑng forever, always 20.13...

51 干

51/0 干 gɑn pole, bar 34.10; (place) 20.T, 20.5.

51/2 平 bhiæng whole 22.63.

51/3 年 nen year 1.3...

51/5 幸 hằng in a way that bestows good luck (such

干
51

幺
52

广
53

又
54

廾
55

弋
(56)

弓
57

彐
(58)

彡
59

彳
60

(51/5 辛 hæng) as that bestowed by an emperor when he makes an imperial visit), condescend (as an emperor) to 27.3.

52 幺

52/6 幽 qiou secluded 6.1...; of seclusion 22.36; gloom 33.8; stifled 22.62, 23.22.

52/9 幾 giǎi how many? 22.94, 49.4; how much? 19.1, 38.5.

53 广

53/4 床 jrhiang bed 20.4. 90/4.

53/5 府 biǒ bureau, office 41.T; 少 shièu-biǒ Police Chief 10.T.

底 děi bottom 22.29...

53/6 度 dhò cross, traverse 21.14.

53/11 廓 kuαk void 11.10.

53/12 廚 djhio kitchen 36.1.

廢 biæi spoil 37.2; decadence, decline 16.11.

53/22 廳 teng government building, hall 43.T.

54 又

54/6 建 giæn build, establish 16.13.

55 廾

55/4 弄 lùng play with, use... as a toy 20.4.

57 弓

57/0 弓 giung bow (for shooting) 24.4...

57/1 弔 dèu produce (as an elegy) 34.10.

57/8 強 ghiαng surpass 38.4.

張 djiαng (surname) 10.T.

57/12 彈 dhαn draw (a bowstring) 34.6; pluck, play (a plucked stringed musical instrument) 6.2, 10.6.

57/13 彊 giàng have rigor mortis, be stiff 34.6.

57/19 彎 quαn bend 24.4.

59 彡

59/4 形 heng shape, form 34.3.

59/8 彩 tsǎi color 50.12; colored 30.10, 39.18.

59/12 影 qiǎng shadow 18.4... 景 72/8.

60 彳

60/4 役 iuæk draft (into military service) 23.19.

60/5 往 iuǎng go, happen in the past 22.54; of the past 43.T.

征 jiæng journey, make a journey 22.T, 22.3.

60/6 徊 huəi bhəi-huəi (going back and forth) 18.9. 回 31/3, 逈 162/6.

後 hòu time afterward 18.12, 21.10; at the back 42.8.

待 dhǎi wait until 24.8, 55.7; wait for 50.10.

60/7 徐 ziu (place) 22.113; (surname) 41.15.

徑 gèng path 49.5.

徒 dho only 18.6; in vain 31.17.

60/8 從 dzhiong follow 21.22, 23.18; head away from, from 16.13, 19.7; go via 26.7.

得 dək get, obtain 48.4, 51.4; find, encounter 22.28; get to V, V successfully 19.3...

徘 bhəi bhəi-huəi 徊 (going back and forth) 18.9.

60/9 復 bhiuk (bhiòu) return to 16.15; return to (in endless cycles) 19.9; again 3.4...; and more 12.4; and 5.4, 6.2.

60/10 微 miəi tiny 16.9; of low rank 31.20; indistinct 28.12.

--- if not 22.131.

60/12 徹 tjiɛt get through, pierce 30.3.

61 心

61/0 心 sim heart, mind 10.2... 彳 60

61/3 忘 miàng forget 22.86. 心 61

忍 njǐn endure 24.8.

志 jì aim, ambition 16.21.

61/4 忠 djiung loyalty 22.130.

念 nèm be brooding 29.8.

忽 xuət suddenly 11.15...

61/5 怳 xuǎng xuǎng-njiu (vague) 33.3. 恍 61/6.

怨 qiuæn grief 13.T, 16.8.

怒 nǒ angry 23.5.

急 gip quickly 23.19.

怵 tjuit fearful 22.10.

思 si, sì thought 14.T; think of 22.43, 22.89, 38.12, 55.2 (sì); think, have it in mind to 11.9...

性 siàng (eating) habits, taste (in food) 36.3.

61/6 恆 həng (place) 22.114.

恍 xuǎng xuǎng-xuət (muddled, unable to make precise plans) 22.18. 怳 61/5.

恩 qən established by (the Emperor's) favor 22.7.

恐 kiǒng fear 17.6...

息 siək breath 21.17.

恨 hèn grieve about 13.4, 25.4.

心

61

61/7 患 huàn misfortune 11.13.

      悦 iuɛt enjoy 22.36.

      恣 sit 纖 siɛm-sit (tiny
          place) 30.8.

61/8 惡 ɡɑk bad, evil 22.73,
          22.124.

      悴 dzhuì decrepit 27.4;
         憔 dzhiɛu-dzhuì (grief)
          47.3.

      悽 tsei sadness 28.16.
          Cf. 凄 15/8, 淒 85/8.

      惚 xuət 恍 xuǎng-xuət
          (muddled, unable to make
          precise plans) 22.18.

      惜 siæk grieve 46.3.

      惕 tek fearful, alarmed
          22.10.

      惘 miǎng miǎng-njiɛn
          (abstracted, absent
          minded) 55.8.

      悵 tjiàng grieve, regret,
          sadly 43.3.

      惟 ui only 9.7... 唯 30/8.

      情 dzhiæng feelings 13.T...

      悲 bi sad 21.21...; be sad
          39.13, 49.1; grieve
          about 24.T; sadness
          28.16, 30.7.

61/9 感 gǒm be moved 43.T;
          respond emotionally to,
          be moved by 20.25, 25.3;
          be moved to 49.T.

      愁 jrhiou sadness, be sad
          20.26...; be sad about
          21.14, 54.5.

      愀 tsiou tsiou-tsiou (change
          of the color of the face)
          33.2.

      意 qì feeling 22.91, 42.6.

61/10 慄 lìt tremble 22.75.

      態 tòi bearing 39.9.

61/11 慟 dhùng bawl 22.61.

      慘 tsom tsǒm-dhǒm 澹
          (dispirited) 22.98.

      憂 qiou sadness 22.20,
          33.10; be sad about,
          lament 37.3.

      慰 qiuòi comfort 22.91.

      慧 huèi intelligent 48.3.

      慙 dzhom to (my) embar-
          rassment 22.7.

      慮 liù anxiety 27.12,
          31.16.

61/12 憲 xiàn law, pattern
          16.12.

      憔 dzhiɛu dzhiɛu-dzhuì
         悴 (grief) 47.3.

      憐 lɛn be fond of 42.5.

      憤 bhiǎn zealous dissat-
          isfaction 22.16.

61/13 憶 qiǎk remember 22.121,
          42.6; something
          remembered, memory
          55.7.

      應 qiəng should 2.2...
          qiàng answer 23.19.

61/16 懸 huen far, distant 35.6.

      懷 huai bosom, breast
          22.73; heart 27.7,
          43.T; be moved by 33.9.

61/19 戀 liuɛn long for 22.17.

61/21 戇 djàng stupidly 28.14.

62 戈

62/0 戈 <u>gua</u> lance 16.6.

62/2 成 <u>zhiæng</u> complete 11.2,
22.118; make a total of
18.4; completely become,
form 31.21...; (name)
41.15.
Cf. 城 32/6, 誠
149/9.

戍 <u>shiɔ</u> garrison 23.8.

62/3 戒 <u>gài</u> refrain from, stop
41.C.

我 <u>ngǎ</u> I, me, my, we, us,
our 12.11...

62/4 或 <u>huək</u> someone or other
21.36; some 22.39,
22.40.

62/12 戰 <u>jièn</u> battle, contend
16.4; in battle 23.10;
a battle 35.12;
battle(field) 22.51.

62/14 戴 <u>dɔi</u> carry 22.34.

63 户

63/0 户 <u>hǒ</u> one-leafed door,
dwelling 7.3.

63/4 所 <u>shriǔ</u> (verbal prefix),
<u>shriǔ</u> V: where someone
V's 21.36; whom someone
V's 22.23, 22.63, 22.105;
what something V's 22.41;
what is V'd, wherein
something is V'd 22.16.

房 <u>bhiæng</u> building 42.8.

63/8 扉 <u>biɔi</u> door 1.2.

64 手

64/0 手 <u>shiǒu</u> hand 21.18...

才 <u>dzhəi</u> talent, talented
man 16.17.

--- barely 22.68.

64/4 把 <u>bǎ</u> grasp 19.T, 39.3.

折 <u>jièt</u> break 31.7, 40.5;
break off, pick (flowers)
20.2; turn back 21.12,
21.16, 22.70, be broken
30.12.

投 <u>dhou</u> spend the night
23.1.

64/5 拙 <u>jiuєt</u> clumsiness
22.44.

抱 <u>bhǎu</u> wrap the arms
around and hold 20.13.

拜 <u>bài</u> bow 22.9.

抹 <u>mat</u> smear 22.82.

抵 <u>děi</u> pay 25.6.

拔 <u>bhat</u> take by storm
22.110.

抽 <u>tjiou</u> draw, pull out
32.7, 39.4.

64/6 拱 <u>giǒng</u> fold arms or
paws 22.50.

挂 <u>guài</u> be suspended
121.28.

指 <u>jǐ</u> point at 22.109.

64/7 挽 <u>miǎn</u> pull 22.87.
鞔 159/7.

捉 <u>jrak</u> catch, sieze (for
service in the army)
23.2.

戈
62

户
63

手
64

手
64

支
(65)

攴
66

文
67

斗
(68)

斤
69

方
70

64/8 掬 giuk amount that can be scooped up with two hands 27.11.

掩 qiĕm cover 34.9; shut 1.2.

掌 jiǎng palm (of the hand) 22.109.

掃 sǎu sweep 20.21, 22.138.

探 tom spy 54.8.

捫 mən lay hands on, touch 21.17.

64/9 揚 iɑng (surname) 16.9.

援 iuæn drag, pull oneself up, climb 21.14.

揮 xiuəi wipe 22.17.

64/10 搔 sɑu scratch 25.7.

64/11 摧 dzhuəi be crushed 21.9; destroy 40.5.

64/12 撫 piǒ touch gently with hands 21.18.

64/13 擊 gek hit 12.1.

擒 ghim capture 22.118.

64/14 擣 dǎu pound (in a mortar) 19.9.

64/15 擾 njiěu disorderly 49.10.

攀 pan climb (toward) 19.3...; climb (up branches) 28.10.

擺 bǎi shake 35.1.

66   攴

66/2 收 shiou recover, take back 22.109...

66/3 改 gǎi change 22.95, 54.5.

66/4 放 biàng let loose 26.5.

66/5 故 gò old, from an earlier time 2.1...

66/7 救 giòu save 22.76.

66/8 敢 gǒm dare 24.4, 41.13.

散 sàn scatter, separate 18.12...

66/11 敵 dhek enemy 22.106.

數 shriò number 22.138; several 22.74; a few 24.4.

67   文

67/0 文 miən having lines, decorated with patterns 48.3; refinement of (literary) style 16.19; (name) 41.15.

69   斤

69/9 新 sin new 8 2...; newly 22.91...; appear anew, crop up 31.16, 35.10; young (wife) 37.1.

69/15 斷 ngiən argue 31.18.

69/21 斸 djiok hoe, cut 28.15; chopped 34.9.

70   方

70/0 方 biɑng direction 22.104; place, area 33.5.

--- only then 54.3.

(70/0 方 biαng)

    --- way, method, skill
    41.8.

70/4 於 qiu at 16.24; (in
    comparative constructions)
    than 21.2, 21.25, 21.44.

70/5 施 shi give away 22.83.

70/6 旁 bhαng side 41.2; beside
    43.1.
    Cf. 傍 9/10.

70/7 旌 tzi$\mathit{æ}$ng pennon 22.26.

    旋 ziuϵn whirlingly, all
    around 22.114.

70/10 旗 ghi flag 22.26.

71 无

71/7 既 gi∂i from the beginning
    18.5.

72 日

72/0 日 njit sun 11.1...; day
    1.2...; daylight 26.5,
    41.21; day after day
    24.3.

72/2 早 tz$\v{a}$u soon 17.8...; be
    early 20.22; at an early
    age (adv.) 44.2.

72/4 易 i easily 39.18, 40.10.

    昇 shi∂ng go up, ascend
    41.21.

    昊 h$\v{a}$u vast 22.115.
    Cf. 浩 85/7.

    旻 min autumn sky 16.20.

    明 mi$\mathit{æ}$ng bright 6.4...;
    grow bright 22.6; next

(year) 1.3, 24.8, 39.12;
clear vision, enlightened
intelligence 16.17;
having clear vision,
enlightened intelligence
22.128; understand 27.9.

昏 xuϵn evening 49.5.

72/5 昨 dzhαk former times
    22.121.

    昭 jiϵu bright, shining
    31.17...

    春 chuin spring (season)
    1.3...; year 16.22...

    映 qi$\mathit{æ}$ng illuminate, shine
    16.22.

    星 seng star 16.20...

    是 zh$\v{i}$ be 14.2...

72/6 時 zhi time 18.11...;
    events of the present
    time 25.3.

72/7 晚 mi$\v{a}$n late in the day
    22.26; late 10.27; of
    one's old age 10.1.

    晨 zhin morning 23.20.

72/8 景 gi$\v{a}$ng 28.12, 35.2. **scene**

    影 qi$\v{a}$ng (sun)light 3.3.
    59/12.

    晴 dzhi$\mathit{æ}$ng (weather) clear
    up 31.13.

72/9 暇 h∂ have leisure time
    to 37.2; free, for
    leisure 22.6.

    暖 nu$\v{a}$n warm 35.8, 55.6.

    暗 q∂m dark 20.9.

72/11 暫 dzh∂m for the time
    being 18.7; for a
    moment 42.4.

方
70

无
71

日

72

日
72

(72/11) 暮 mò evening, become evening, be at evening 1.2...

72/12 曉 xĕu morning 19.8...

日
73

72/15 曠 kuàng expansive 11.10.

月
74

73 曰

木
75

73/2 曲 kiok a bend, crook 22.70, 28.9, 31.1, 35.5.

--- verse, song 12.T.

73/3 更 gāng to a greater extent, more 8.3, 25.7, 27.6, 31.6; furthermore 22.24, 23.13; again 43.T.

73/6 書 shiu letter 20.28...; document, text 31.21.

73/8 曾 tzəng actually, but 27.8.

dzhəng to experience (adverb indicating completed action of the following verb) 19.12, 43.T.

最 tzuài most 41.3.

74 月

74/0 月 ngiuæt moon 6.4...; month 20.17...

74/2 有 iŏu have, there is 9.7...; a, an 23.2.

74/4 服 bhiuk submit to 22.104; take (medicine) 41.6.

74/6 朔 shrak north 30.3.

74/7 望 miàng gaze 12.4...; view 25.T; hope 38.10; (name) 55.4.

74/8 期 ghi meet 18.14; time 35.6.

朝 djiɛu morning 8.1...

djhiɛu court, audience with emperor 22.6.

75 木

75/0 木 muk tree 9.2...; branch 7.1.

75/1 未 miəi not yet 2.4...

末 mɑt end, tip 22.48.

75/2 朱 jio red 21.26; rouge 22.83.

75/3 杜 dhŏ (surname) 22.3; dhŏ-guen 鵑 (cuckoo) 55.4.

李 lĭ plum tree 39.11, 40.5.

村 tsuən village 9.2...

75/4 杯 bəi cup 8.3, 18.3, 19.2. 盃 108/4.

松 ziong pine tree 10.5...

枝 ji 荔 lì-ji litchi 52.4.

析 sek separate, disperse 22.124.

東 dung east 42.1; eastern 17.1...

林 lim collection of trees, grove, woods, forest 3.3...

枉 qiuǎng to no purpose 9.3.

果 guǎ fruit 22.37; in fact, really 22.128.

75/5 柱 djhiǒ pillar, stanchion, upright wooden support 20.13; tuning peg 55.2.

柳 liǒu willow 8.2...

枯 ko withered 21.28; withered branch 28.10.

染 njiěm dye 53.2.

柀 go slip, note paper 31.5.

75/6 桓 huɑn huɑn-huɑn (martial) 22.129.

桃 dhɑu peach tree 17.1...

桑 sɑng mulberry tree 22.49, 43.T.

柴 jrhai brushwood 1.2; stockade 3.T.

栗 lit chestnut 22.38.

75/7 梳 shriu comb 46.3.

條 dheu twig 15.4.

梯 tei ladder 21.10.

梅 məi plum tree 2.4; plum tree branch 20.4.

75/8 極 ghiək far 4.1, 12.4.

棄 ki be abandoned 29.5.

棲 sei perch, alight, sojourn 19.10, 30.12.

棧 jrhàn reinforced road 21.10.

棘 giək bramble 28.15, 29.13.

75/9 楮 tzen notepaper 31.5.

業 ngiæp task 22.139; villa, estate 9.T.

75/10 榮 iuæng flowering 17.3.

榛 jrin thicket 16.4.

木
75

75/11 樂 ngak music 41.T.

lɑk joy 11.16...; full of joy, fun 21.42.

欠
76

樣 iàng manner 39.7.

標 biɛu marker 21.11.

75/12 樹 zhiǒ to plant, establish 22.140.

zhiò tree 11.6, 49.7.

樽 tzuən goblet 19.16.

機 giəi a loom 37.8.

橡 ziǎng acorn 22.38.

橫 huæng in a cross-wise manner, right across 21.8.

75/14 檻 hǎm cage 48.4.

75/15 櫟 lek oak 49.6.

櫛 jrit comb 22.80.

75/19 欒 luɑn (place) 5.T.

76 欠

76/2 次 tsì order, rank 52.2.

76/7 欲 iok wish to, want to 21.14; be about to 22.86...; be going to 39.12.

76/8 歆 qi (place) 4.T.

76/9 歇 xiæt stop 28.11, 40.10.

76/10 歌 gɑ sing 18.9, 42.7; song 10.8...

欠
76

止
77

歹
78

父
79

毋
80

比
(81)

毛
(82)

氏
83

气
84

水
85

76/11 歎 tàn sigh 22.44, 46.T.
嘆 30/11.

76/18 歡 xuān joy 18.11, 38.5.

77 止

77/1 正 jiàng correct, right 16.7; upright, of justice 22.116; exactly 38.12.

77/2 此 tsǐ this, these 17.4...; at this place, here 31.9; from here 54.7; at that time, then 22.113.

77/3 步 bhò a step, footstep 21.16...

77/4 武 miǒ martial, brave 34.7, 41.7.

77/9 歲 siuèi year 21.5...

77/12 歷 lek pass through 21.17.

77/14 歸 giuəi go home 22.8, 22.58, 22.91, 42.3, 53.4; return 1.4...

78 歹

78/2 死 sǐ die 21.9...; dead body 34.3; death 54.3.

78/6 殊 zhio uncommon 39.9.

78/8 殘 dzhɑn wither 54.2; be nearly used up 37.4; withered 27.4; remaining 47.2; the remains 34.8; harm 22.56.

79 父

79/6 殷 qiən taking pains, careful 54.8; (last part of the Shiɑng Dynasty,

B.C. 1401-1123) 22.125.

79/7 殺 shrat kill 21.41...; killing 31.10, 32.2.

79/9 殿 dhèn hall 22.133.

80 毋

80/1 毋 mǒu mother 22.81...

80/3 每 měi each time 42.4.

83 氏

83/0 氏 zhǐ Mr. (follows a surname) 28.2.

83/1 民 min people 22.55.

84 气

84/4 氛 piən emanations 22.96. Cf. 芬 140/4.

84/6 氣 kièi spirit 22.108...; smell 44.3.

84/10 氳 qiuən misty 31.12.

85 水

85/0 水 shuǐ water 19.13...; stream 22.30, 22.47.

85/1 永 iuěng for a long time, forever, eternally 18.13

85/2 求 ghiou seek 41.C; find 32.6.

85/3 汝 njiǔ you 22.76, 31.19.

江 gang river 11.12, 53.T; Yangtze River 40.12, 42.1.

85/4 沉　djhim　to sink 29.6.

決　guet　decision 22.104.

沙　shra　sand 20.30, 29.6;
47.1.　112/4.

沒　mət　sink, disappear
19.8, 22.46.

85/5 泄　siɛt　have diarrhea 22.74.

況　xiuàng　much more is it
true of... 22.57.
况 7/5.

河　ha　river 24.5, 25.1;
Yellow River 23.19, 26.T.

泗　sì　snivel, tears (in the
nose) 34.2.

泥　nei　mud 21.15...

油　iou　oil 50.9.

泉　dzhiuɛn　spring (of
water) 22.62, 27.13.

波　ba　wave (of water)
5.3...

泣　kip　weep 23.23.

85/6 洗　sěi　wash 27.1...

洛　lɑk　(river) 22.109,
26.8, 28.1.

洞　dhùng　hole 12.3.

津　tzin　ferry, ford 35.6.

--- moist 27.10.

活　huɑt　alive 22.132.

85/7 流　liou　flow 16.10, 22.24;
flowing 19.13; flowing
water, stream 21.29,
33.6.

浩　hǎu　hǎu-hǎu (big wind
blowing waves) 41.11.

Cf. 昊 72/4.

涇　geng　(place) 22.30.

涕　tèi　tears (in the
eyes) 22.17...

海　xěi　sea 11.12...

浦　pǒ　beach 4.1...

消　siɛu　melt away, disperse
27.12...

浪　làng　wave 41.3.

85/8 涼　liɑng　cool 11.16,
22.133.

淳　zhuin　(personal name)
19.C.

淪　luin　engulfed, sunk
16.12.

涯　ngai　horizon 38.10.

涸　hɑk　dry up 11.4.

淒　tsei　cold 22.133.
凄 15/8;
Cf. 懔 65/8.

淺　tsiěn　shallow 5.2...

淚　luì　tears, teardrops
13.3...

深　shim　deep 3.3...;
deeply 22.111, 42.8;
thick, dense 20.21,
25.2; far back 13.2.

淨　dzhiæng　clean, pure
27.11, 53.2.

清　tsiæng　clear 29.2,
35.5; pure 11.16...;
purity 16.16, 52.T.

85/9 渴　kɑt　thirst 22.86.

湯　tɑng　soup 36.2.

水
85

水
85

(85/9) 湛 djham fill to the
brim 12.8.

湍 tuɑn rapids 21.29.

湖 ho lake 4.T, 4.3.

渭 iuəi (place) 8.1.

渾 huən entirely 25.8.

85/10 滄 tsɑng (color of the
sea) 55.5.
Cf.   140/10.

源 ngiuɐn spring (of water)
22.43, 27.14.
Cf.   10/2.

溪 kei mountain stream,
rapids 27.T...

溶 iong iong-iong (amply
flowing water) 53.1.

滅 miɛt go out (like a
fire) 22.26; extinguish,
disperse 19.6.

溜 liəu (water) slip 5.2.

滑 huat slippery 30.11;
slipperiness 27.5.

85/11 滿 mǎn fill 11.1...

滴 dek drip 35.3.

漸 dzhiɛm gradually 42.2.

漫 mɑn mɑn-mɑn (vast water)
41.T...

màn randomly, in a hit
or miss fashion 26.4.

漱 shriəu rinse 27.11.

漆 tsit lacquer 22.40, 49.9.

漾 iàng iàng-iàng (motion
of water) 53.1.

漪 qi ripple 35.10.

漢 xàn (river) 53.T; Milky
Way 18.14; (dynasty)
22.127, 41.7.

漣 liɛn 漪 qi-liɛn
ripple 35.10.
Cf. 連   162/7.

漁 ngiu to fish (as an
occupation) 9.5, 10.8.
Cf. 魚   195/0.

85/12 激 gek incite, urge 16.9.

潛 dzhiɛm sink 30.4;
submerged 27.5.

潏 guet spurt 22.30.

潼 dhung (place) 22.53.

澗 gàn stream in a mountain
ravine 7.3.

85/13 澤 djhæk pond 11.4.

濁 djhak turbidity, dirt
11.12.

澹 dhǒm 憯 tsǒm-dhǒm
(dispirited) 22.96.

濆 iɓ 灩 ièm-iɓ
(place) 20.16.

85/14 濤 dhɑu billow 22.69,
41.3.

濕 ship wetness 13.3.

濯 djhak wash 11.8,
35.6.

濱 bin shore, bank 22.47.

濡 njio moisten 22.41.

85/15 瀉 siǎ (water) slide
5.2.

瀑 bhuk waterfall,
cascading 21.29.

(85/15) 濺 tziɛn make...splash 5.3, 25.3.

85/16 瀨 lài rapids 5.T.

85/17 澰 liɛm overflowing water, waves 30.9.

瀾 lɑn billow 29.3, 32.7.

85/19 灑 shrǎ sprinkle 22.138, 49.2.

85/28 灪 iɛm iɛm-iò 澺 (place) 20.16.

86 火

86/0 火 xuǎ fire 9.6...

86/2 灰 xuəi ash 20.12, 54.4.

86/4 炊 chui steamed food 23.20.

86/5 炳 biǎng bright, shine 16.19.

炬 ghiǔ torch 49.9; candle 54.4.

86/6 烈 liɛt zeal 22.130.

烟 qen smoke (as from a chimney or stove) 21.6; mist, haze 19.6, 55.6. 煙 86/9.

86/7 焉 qiɛn how? 22.92, 24.7.

烽 piong torch, beacon 24.6, 25.5.

86/8 無 mio not have, there is no, without 7.3...; mio-něi 乃 most likely, no means to cope with 43.4.

然 njiɛn it is like that 21.10; (descriptive suffix) 21.4, 55.8; (manner suffix), -ly 11.10, 11.16.

焦 tziɛu scorch 11.3.

86/9 煙 qen smoke (as from a chimney or stove) 22.26; mist 41.3; misty 50.4. 烟 86/6.

煥 xuàn bright, shine 16.19.

照 jiɛu illuminate, shine on 3.4...; reflect 27.4, 28.8; be shining 53.10.

煌 huɑng huɑng-huɑng (radiant) 22.139.

煩 bhiæn trouble 11.12.

86/11 熱 njiɛt hot, heat 11.T.

86/12 燒 shiɛu burn 9.6, 37.4.

86/13 燭 jiok candle 37.4, 50.11.

87 爪

87/4 爭 jræng vie to 31.8; compete in 21.29, 51.3.

87/8 為 ui do 21.32, 22.81, 32.3; make, take the role of, be 11.13, 22.103; do (aux.) 37.5; become 20.7...

ùi on one's behalf 54.8.

89 爻

89/10 爾 njǐ approach (the present time) 21.5.

--- you 21.32, 22.131.

水
85

火
86

爪
87

父
(88)

爻
89

90 爿

90/4 牀 jrhiang   bed 14.1, 22.67.
      床   53/4.

90/13 牆 dzhiang wall 23.3.

91 片

91/11 牕 chrang window 2.3.

92 牙

92/0 牙 nga tooth 21.40.

93 牛

93/3 牢 lau pen up 42.8.

        牢--- stiff, firm 39.17,
             40.7.

93/4 物 miət thing 22.56...

93/7 牽 ken pull 51.1.

93/8 犂 lei plough 29.14.

94 犬

94/4 狀 jrhiàng describe 39.9.

      狂 ghiuang crazy 16.6;
               go crazy 26.4.

94/7 狼 lang wolf 21.37; lang-
             dzhiæk 籍 mess 22.84;
             lang-bài 狽 confusion
             22.121.

      狽 bài 狼 lang-bài
             confusion 22.121.

94/8 猛 mæng ferocious 21.38...

猜 tsəi suspicion, loathing
        20.6.

94/9 猱 nau (gibbon) 21.14.

     猶 iou continuingly,
            as before, still
            22.18.

94/10 猿 iuæn gibbon 9.8...

94/12 獠 lǎu (non-Chinese people
             in the South) 30.4.

94/13 獨 dhuk alone 6.1...

94/14 獲 huæk capture 16.24;
             obtain, get 22.127.

      獵 liɛp hunt 9.6.

94/15 獸 shiòu beast 22.134.

95 玄

95/0 玄 huen mysterious 41.19.

96 玉

96/0 玉 ngiok jade 28.5...

      王 iuang prince 1.4;
             princely, royal 16.3;
             king 22.99; (surname)
             47.T.

96/5 玲 leng leng-lung
             (the sound of ornaments)
             39.7.

      珍 djin prize, esteem
             16.14.

      珊 san san-san (tinkle of
             jade) 34.2.

96/6 珪 guei (fine jade) 28.6.

      珮 bhèi ornament worn at
             belt 50.8.

(96/6) 珠 jio pearl 55.5; deco-
rated with pearls 13.1.

96/7 琉 liou liou-li 璃
porcelain 39.18.

理 lǐ pattern, arrangement
22.92; principle 10.7.

96/8 琴 ghim zither 6.2, 10.6.

96/9 瑞 zhui auspicious 31.13.

瑟 shrit 25-stringed zither
55.T, 55.1.

--- 蕭 seu-shrit
(wind in trees) 17.10;
(desolate) 22.22.
颼瑟 182/13.

96/10 瑣 suǎ tiny 22.37.

瑩 iuæng sparkle 27.6.

瑤 ieu (fine jade) 12.7,
28.4.

96/11 璃 li 琉 liou-li
porcelain 39.18.

96/15 瓊 ghiuæng (fine jade)
34.10.

96/16 瓏 lung 玲 leng-lung
(tinkling of ornaments)
39.7.

99 甘

99/0 甘 gom sweet 11.5, 22.42;
sweetly 22.90.

99/4 甚 zhǐm extreme 34.1;
very 22.140.

100 生

100/0 生 shræng appear 38.1, 43.2;

cause to appear, produce
17.4...; life 22.63,
22.92, 23.11; alive
22.85; raw, green 39.7;
(title for a scholar)
55.3.

玉
96

瓜
(97)

101 用

101/0 用 iòng use 22.105.

101/2 甫 bǐo (name) 22.14.

瓦
(98)

甘
99

102 田

102/0 田 dhen field 9.T...

由 iou cause, reason
33.4.

生
100

102/2 男 nom boy 23.8...

102/4 畏 qiuǎi fearsome,
precipitous 21.20.

用
101

102/5 留 liou detain 9.T; keep
40.8, 40.9.

102/6 異 ì different 22.56;
unusual 39.9; strange
33.5.

田
102

畢 bit be finished, cease
22.20; in the end 41.18.

略 liɑk occupy, invade
22.114.

畤 djhǐ sacrificial
mound 22.45.

102/7 畫 huài to paint 22.84;
painting, picture 47.4.

102/8 當 dɑng right at 37.5,
55.8; right where...
is 21.7, 21.34; be
just in the process of
19.15.

103 疋

足
103

103/7 疎 shriu sparse 9.8.

103/9 疑 ngi think, suspect 14.2; cause one to have doubts about 33.10.

广
104

104 广

疒
105

104/5 病 bhiɑ̀ng illness 44.2, 46.1.

白
106

疾 dzhit quick, fast 22.106.

皮
(107)

104/6 痍 i gaping wound 22.19.

痕 hən a trace 13.3.

皿
108

104/10 瘡 chriɑng a wound 22.19, 35.11.

目
109

瘦 shriəu thin 22.79.

104/14 癡 ṭ ji innocent, silly 22.80; unenlightened 28.13.

105 癶

105/7 發 biɐt emerge 19.6; cause to emerge, bring 29.12; send out 22.112; let loose, produce (flowers) 7.2.

登 dəng climb 22.27; start out 23.23.

106 白

106/0 白 bhɐk white 4.4...; bright (sun) 11.2; broad (daylight) 26.5, 41.21; without reason, vain 39.6.

106/1 百 bɐk hundred 21.16...; a hundred times 22.53.

106/4 皆 gai in all cases 11.4...

皇 huɑng supreme ruler, emperor 22.1, 22.120, 41.7.

106/6 皎 gěu (moon-)white 19.5, 31.11.

108 皿

108/3 盂 mɐ̀ng (surname) 28.2.

108/4 盃 bəi cup 29.1. 75/4.

盈 iɐng fill 21.27; grow full, wax 38.4.

108/5 益 giɐk increasingly 22.44.

108/9 盡 dzhǐn finish 8.3, 44.3; be finished, complete 54.3; be gone, removed 35.11; away 19.6, 27.1, 30.9, 33.7; end up with 22.58; extreme 47.3; exhaustively, in all cases 11.3, 22.131.

108/10 盤 bhɑn writhing, turning 21.15.

109 目

109/3 直 djhiək straight (ahead, down) 28.13, 41.2; extending straight ahead 31.1; only 20.30. 直

109/4 看 kɑn, kɑ̀n look at 19.14, 26.3 (kɑn), 38.4; take a look 23.4 (kɑn), 41.17,

(109/4 看 kan, kàn) 54.8 (kan).

眉 mi eyebrow 13.2, 20.11, 21.8, 22.84, 47.1.

眇 miĕu sparse 22.22.

相 siɑng each other, mutually 5.3...; (emphasizes transitivity) 1.1, 6.4, 17.8, 18.2, 19.4, 31.6, 38.7, 50.9.

siɑ̀ng minister, head of a government bureau 45.T.

109/5 真 jin true 40.T...; truth 16.16. 眞

109/6 眼 ngăn eye 39.2...

109/13 瞿 ghio (place) 20.16.

瞻 jiɛm gaze 22.114.

111 矢

111/2 矣 ĭ (phrase-final particle, marking completion of the action of the verb) 23.12.

111/3 知 dji know 11.14...; know about 2.2, 15.3, 17.9; know about it 6.3, 46.1; know enough to 10.4.

111/7 短 duăn short 25.7.

112 石

112/0 石 zhiæk stone 5.2...

112/4 砂 shra powder 22.39. 沙 85/4.

112/5 硑 pæng make a loud sound 21.30.

破 pà smash 22.106; be smashed 25.1.

112/8 碎 suəi fragments 31.3.

碌 luk luk-luk (rumble, clatter) 38.1.

112/9 碣 ghiæt (place) 22.114.

碧 biæk (green stone) 27.11, 30.9; blue 31.14.

112/10 磓 duəi throw 30.1.

112/11 磨 mɑ grind 21.40, 30.5.

113 示

113/4 祈 ghiəi pray 41.16.

113/5 祖 tzŏ ancestor 41.19.

祠 zi religious 12.T.

神 jhin divinity 12.T...; divine spirit 22.137; divine 41.4.

113/9 禍 huă calamity 22.117.

福 biuk (name) 41.15.

113/14 禱 dău, (dàu) pray 41.16.

115 禾

115/2 私 si private, personal consideration 22.7.

115/4 秋 tsiou autumn 5.1...

115/5 秦 dzhin (dynasty) 16.6...

115/6 移 i shift, move 22.70, 22.83.

目
109

予

(110)

矢
111

石

112

示
113

内

(114)

禾

115

115/7 稍 shràu gradually 22.78,
28.11.

禾
115

115/8 稠 djhiou packed densely
43.T.

穴
116

稚 djhì offspring 22.85,
51.1.

115/11 積 tziæk accumulate 22.115.

立
117

116 穴

竹
118

116/0 穴 huet nest 22.50.

116/3 空 kung empty 27.3;
devoid of any other
visible person 3.1,
21.24; to no purpose
10.4; spent, used up,
dead 49.2.

116/4 穿 chiuen pass through
26.7, 41.12; bore
through 41.12.

突 tuət rush out 22.100,
24.4.

116/8 窟 kuət cave, grotto 22.28,
24.2.

116/10 窮 ghiung exhaust 10.7.

117 立

117/0 立 lip stand 17.10...;
erect, establish 22.140,
31.9; establishing
16.23.

117/6 竟 giæng in the end 16.2,
22.123, 41.18; at last
31.21.

章 jiang pattern 16.12;
decorated with patterns
48.3; ordered section (of
a literary text) 31.21.

117/7 童 dhung boy, child 22.85,
41.14.

117/9 竭 ghiet dry up 11.4.

端 duan reason 55.1.

117/15 競 ghiæng contend 22.87,
35.10.

118 竹

118/0 竹 djiuk bamboo 6.T,
20.3.

118/4 笑 sièu smile 17.2,
52.3.

118/5 笳 ga (foreign wind
instrument, made of a
curled reed leaf) 45.1.

第 dhèi order, rank 52.2;
(prefix changing fol-
lowing number from
cardinal to ordinal)
45.4.

118/6 策 chræk strategy, plan
10.3.

筆 bit writing brush
16.24.

118/8 箕 gi winnowing basket
31.18.

118/9 箭 tzièn arrow 22.106.

篋 kep small trunk 38.9.

篁 huang bamboo thicket
6.1.

118/10 篙 gau boat pole 30.1.

118/11 簇 tsuk bamboo frame tied
with grass which
mature silkworms climb
to make their cocoons
37.2.

118/12 簪 <u>jrim</u> hat fastener 25.8.

籟 <u>seu</u> flute 4.1...

簟 <u>dhěm</u> bamboo mat 11.7.

簡 <u>gǎn</u> simple (or no meaning other than sound) 39.T, 39.1.

118/13 簾 <u>liɛm</u> (window) screen 13.1.

118/14 籍 <u>dzhiæk</u> 狼 <u>lɑng-dzhiæk</u> mess 22.84.

118/16 籠 <u>lung</u> cage 42.4, 48.4.

119 米

119/4 粉 <u>biǎn</u> powder 22.77.

119/6 粧 <u>jriɑng</u> make-up 39.3. 妝 38/4.

粟 <u>siok</u> grain 38.9.

119/8 精 <u>tziæng</u> spirit 35.9.

120 糸

120/3 紈 <u>huɑn</u> white, unbleached silk cloth 11.5.

紇 <u>huət</u> 回 <u>huəi-huət</u> Uighur 22.98.

紅 <u>hung</u> red 7.2...; grow red 42.2; rouge (make-up) 47.2.

120/4 素 <u>sò</u> pale, colorless 28.3.

紛 <u>piən</u> scatter 7.4...; be scattered, flurried 34.4.

120/5 終 <u>jiung</u> in the end, finally 46.4; after all 31.22.

紫 <u>tzǐ</u> purple 22.71.

絃 <u>hen</u> string 31.7...

細 <u>sèi</u> tiny 22.37.

120/6 結 <u>get</u> bind 50.3; mend 22.60; contract to 18.13.

--- bear (fruit) 22.42.

--- freeze 27.10; freeze and become, harden into 28.5.

絲 <u>si</u> (white) silk thread 37.8...; silk thread or thought, love (conventional pun on 思 <u>si</u>) 54.3.

絕 <u>dzhiuɛt</u> · stop 16.24, 22.120; cut off 43.T, 52.T; be stopped, interrupted, broken off 23.21; cut across to 21.8; stopping, blocking, precipitous, impassable 21.28.

120/7 絹 <u>giuɛn</u> raw silk cloth 37.7.

經 <u>geng</u> warp, lengthwise threads in a fabric 22.14; pass through 22.51...; experience 19.12.

絺 <u>djhi</u> fine linen 11.8.

綌 <u>kiæk</u> coarse linen 11.8.

120/8 綺 <u>kǐ</u> patterned silk cloth 2.3; intricately decorated 16.14.

綻 <u>djhàn</u> rip 22.68.

綠 <u>liok</u> green 1.3...

竹
118

米
119

糸
120

糸
120

缶
121

网
122

羊
123

羽
124

(120/8) 綱 gɑng strand, line (of succession) 22.120.

維 ui this 22.5.

120/9 緣 iuɐn because of 38.7.

練 lèn to train 22.94.

緬 miěn longingly 22.43.

緯 iuɐi crosswise threads in a fabric, weft 22.14.

120/10 縈 qiueng wind around 21.16.

縣 huɐn town 22.25.

120/11 縷 liǒ strand, thread 30.10.

縱 tziɒng have...when one pleases 26.5; give oneself over to 37.7.

繁 bhiæn heavy, severe 39.11.

縫 bhiong sew 37.2.

120/12 繞 ngiɛu wind around, gallop around 20.4; fly around 21.22.

織 jiək weave (thread) 37.7.

繡 siɒu embroider 39.4; embroidery 22.70, 52.1.

120/17 纖 siɛm slender, tiny 27.2, 30.8.

121 缶

121/4 缺 kuet lack 22.138; wane 38.4.

122 网

122/3 岡 miǎng miǎng-liǎng 兩 (water phantom) 33.3.

122/10 罷 bhǎi finish, be finished be done 1.1.

122/14 羅 lɑ spread out 22.78; net, spread like a net over 16.20; spreadingly 22.38.

123 羊

123/3 美 mǐ beautiful 13.1.

123/5 羞 siou embarrassed, shy 20.8.

123/7 羣 ghiuən flock, in a flock (pluralizing prefix) 16.17.

義 ngì proper conduct 32.3.

--- interpretation 31.22.

123/13 羹 gæng chowder 36.2.

124 羽

124/0 羽 iǒ feather 29.5, 41.6.

124/4 翁 qung old man 23.3...

翅 shǐ wing 42.3.

124/6 翔 ziɑng soar 22.25.

124/8 翠 tsuì kingfisher (blue-green) 22.135, 50.11.

124/12 翻 piæn returningly, again 22.89.

125 老

125/0 老 lǎu old 22.73...; become old, show signs of old age 20.26, 41.14, 49.4, 53.3; old man 34.1; (years of age) be many 46.2.

125/4 者 jiǎ (suffix changing the preceding word or phrase into a clause meaning "one who [does or undergoes the action of the preceding phrase], the fact of [that action or state]") 22.54, 23.11, 23.12.

126 而

126/0 而 ngi and 21.33.

127 耒

127/4 耕 gæng plow 29.14.

128 耳

128/3 耶 ia daddy 22.65.

128/6 聒 guɑt din 22.90.

128/7 聖 shiæng inspiring respect because of morality developed to the highest degree, august 16.15...

128/8 聞 miən hear 3.2...

128/11 聲 shiæng sound 16.7...; voice, cry 20.18.

128/16 聽 teng listen 28.13...; hear 21.26, 23.7.

129 聿

129/7 肅 siuk severe 22.116.

130 肉

130/3 肝 gɑn liver 34.4.

130/4 肯 kěng be willing to 39.6.

130/5 背 bəi avert 22.65.

胡 ho non-Chinese people in the north 22.15...

--- why? 21.32.

胔 tsi rotten flesh 34.9.

130/6 脅 xiæp hold in (breath) 21.17.

脆 tsiuɛi brittle 39.18.

能 nəng can, be able to 20.21...; can obtain 38.5.

胼 bhen chapped, having calluses 37.1.

脂 ji lard, creamy 40.7.

130/7 脚 giɑk foot 22.6, 31.15.

130/9 腮 səi cheek 39.2.

腥 seng stench (of fish or blood) 32.5 195/9.

130/11 膠 gau be stuck in 9.5.

膚 bio skin 40.7.

130/12 膩 nì greasy 22.66.

130/13 臉 lǎm face 47.2.

老 125
而 126
耒 127
耳 128
聿 129
肉 130

(130/13)膺 qiəng breast 21.18.

肉
130

131 臣

臣
131

131/0 臣 zhin official 22.123;
        I 22.16; subordinate
        official 31.20.

自
132

131/2 臥 nguà lie down 22.74.

131/11 臨 lim look down from
        19.5; approach 27.3.

至
133

132 自

臼
134

132/0 自 dzhì from 2.1, 16.13.

        --- oneself 10.3...;
        by oneself 22.80; of
        oneself, of one's own
        accord 5.3, 22.126,
        53.3; according to one's
        own nature 17.10.

舌
135

舛
136

133 至

舟
137

133/0 至 jì go as far as 20.30;
        reach 22.59; arrive
        23.9; most, extremely
        22.93.

艮
138

133/4 致 djì convey (words),
        make (a statement) 23.7.

色
139

133/8 臺 dhəi watchtower, platform
        (for looking off into
        the distance) 20.14.

134 臼

134/7 與 iǔ accompany, together
        with 21.6; and 20.12,
        21.37, 29.4; (part) from
        23.24; (neighbor) to
        19.10, 27.14; (different)
        from 22.122.

        --- give, for, to 24.7.

134/9 興 xiəng revival, revive
        16.11...

        xiəng happiness 22.35.

134/10 舉 giǔ raise 14.3, 18.3;
        attack 22.113.

134/12 舊 ghiòu old 22.70; from
        an earlier period in
        one's life 10.4.

135 舌

135/0 舌 jhiɛt tongue 31.18.

135/2 舍 shià shelter 8.2.

136 舛

136/8 舞 miǒ dance 12.6, 18.10,
        42.7.

137 舟

137/0 舟 jiou boat 9.5...

137/5 船 jhiuɛn boat 53.4.

138 艮

138/11 艱 gan difficulty 22.5.

139 色

139/0 色 shriək color 22.64...;
        appearance, beauty 17.5.

140 艸

140/4 芬 piən fragrance 28.11.
Cf. 氛 84/4.

花 xua flower 7.1...

芙 bhio bhio-iong 蓉
lotus 7.1, 39.2.

芳 piɑng fragrant 35.6.

140/5 苞 bau parcel 22.77.

若 njiɑk resemble 19.13,
21.31.

苦 kŏ bitter 22.42;
bitterness, suffering
15.3, 47.3; be in pain
12.11, 23.6, 37.6;
suffer from 11.T.

苔 dhəi moss 3.4...

茂 mòu luxuriant 41.17.

茅 mau (grass), thatch
22.59.

140/6 荆 giæng thornwood, bramble
16.4.

荔 lì lì-ji 枝 litchi
52.4.

茵 qin cushion 50.5.

美 dhei sprout 40.7.

荒 xuɑng ruined 9.2.

草 tsǎu grass 1.3...

茫 mɑng 蒼 tsɑng-mɑng
(distant and indistinct)
22.4; 微 miəi-mɑng
(indistinct) 16.7, 28.11;
mɑng-njiɛn 然 (in-
distinct) 21.4; mɑng-
mɑng (indistinct) 41.10.

140/7 莊 jriɑng village 28.2;
(surname) 55.3.

莫 mɑk none 21.35; never
27.14, 29.9, 29.11;
do not! 24.8.

莞 guɑn rush mat 11.7.

140/8 華 hua flowery 52.T;
varicolored 22.135;
flecked (with white)
22.58; of one's youth
55.2.

菜 ləi 蓬 bhung-ləi
(place) 41.9...

菊 giuk chrysanthemum
22.33.

菜 tsəi (edible) vegetable
39.7.

140/9 莿 jriu chop 22.123.

萼 ngɑk calyx, flower
7.2.

著 djiù produce (flowers)
2.4.

葉 iɛp leaf 20.22, 39.2.

落 lɑk fall, drop 7.4,
17.8; fall out 46.T,
46.3, 46.4; fallen
20.22.

萬 miæn ten thousand
21.5...; thousands
of 11.1, 21.30, 22.102;
in thousands of ways
16.11.

140/10 蒼 tsɑng green 22.32, 44.3;
tsɑng-mɑng (dis-
tant and indistinct)
22.4.
Cf. 滄 85/10.

蒙 mung receive 17.3; be
covered by 22.93.

140 艸

艸 140

(140/10) 蓉 iong 芙 bhio-iong lotus 7.1, 39.2.

蓄 xiuk nurture, amass 22.112.

虍 141

蓋 gài cover, canopy 50.6.

蒿 hau (wormwood, sagebrush) 43.1.

虫 142

140/11 蔓 miàn vine, creeper 16.3, 41.18.

蓽 bit bramble 22.8.

蓮 len lotus 40.5.

蓬 bhung tumbleweed 22.8; bhung-ləi 萊 (place) 41.9...; for bhung-ləi 萊 (place) 54.7.

140/12 蕩 dhàng cleanse 11.12.

--- flow 22.30; (water) spread 16.10; disperse 22.124.

140/13 蕭 seu seu-shrit 瑟 (wind in trees) 17.10; seu-shrit 瑟 飋 (desolate) 22.22, 24.5.

蓟 gèi (place) 26.1.

薔 dzhiang dzhiang-miəi 薇 rose 39.8.

薇 miəi 薔 dzhiang-miəi rose 39.8.

薄 bhak thin 11.6.

140/14 藏 dzhang bury 39.6; hide 42.8.

藍 lom indigo, blue 9.T, 55.6.

140/15 藥 iak medicinal plant, medicine 19.9...

140/16 蘇 so (fragrant herb) 43.2; (surname) 9.3...

140/17 蘭 lan (fragrant shore plant) 50.1.

141 虍

141/2 虎 xò tiger 16.5...

141/5 處 chiù place 15.3...

141/6 虛 xiu empty 27.3; in vain 31.18, 41.16; composedly 22.107...

141/7 號 hau call, cry, howl 21.21, 31.3.

虞 ngio sorrow 22.20; cause for anxiety 22.5.

142 虫

142/1 虯 kiou young dragon with two horns 35.4.

142/5 蛇 jhia snake 21.39.

142/7 蛾 nga moth (especially Bombyx mori, the larva of which is the silk-worm) 13.2. Cf.   46/7.

蜀 zhiok (place) 21.T...

142/9 蝶 dhep 蝴 ho-dhep butterfly 20.23, 55.3.

蝴 ho ho-dhep 蝶 butter-fly 20.23, 55.3.

142/10 螢 hueng (firefly) 30.2, 49.10.

142/15 蠟 lop wax 54.4.

142/18 蠶 dzhom silkworm 21.3...

143 血

143/0 血 xuet blood 21.40...

143/6 眾 jiùng crowd, multitude
(pluralizing prefix)
16.20.

144 行

144/0 行 hæng go, travel 20.15...;
move, motion 19.4;
walk 28.14, 39.5; leave,
departure 20.19; make...
happen 18.8; pass through,
live 46.2.

--- words (of a song),
verse 20.T.

144/9 衝 chiong dash against,
pound 21.12.

145 衣

145/0 衣 qiəi upper garment,
clothing 16.16...

145/4 衰 shrui decline 23.17,
44.2; downfall 16.2,
22.125; (hair) fall
out 46.2.

衾 kim quilt 22.78.

145/5 袖 ziòu sleeves 39.8.

被 bhǐ (cover like a)
blanket 22.7; suffer
(marks following verb
as passive) 22.23.

145/6 裂 liɛt split 34.4; be
split 22.32, 35.7.

145/7 裙 ghiuən lower garment,
skirt 23.16.

補 bǒ patch 22.68.

褆 zhiǒ child's short
garment 22.72.

裛 qip moisten 8.1.

裏 lǐ inside, in 6.1,
19.16; at (night)
37.4.   166/0.

裊 něu něu-něu (waving
branches) 49.6.

145/8 綢 djhiou lightweight
blanket 22.78.

裳 zhiɑng lower garment,
clothing 26.2, 39.4,
50.7.

145/9 襃 bɑu (name) 22.126.

褐 hɑt coarse clothing
22.72.

145/11 襄 siɑng (river) 26.8.

145/15 襪 miæt sock, stocking,
have socks on 22.66.

145/17 囊 nɑng satchel 22.75.

146 西

146/0 西 sei west 8.T...;
western 20.24...;
westwardly 8.4...;
from the west 22.97.

146/12 覆 piòu to cover 20.1.

147 見

147/0 見 gèn see 3.1...; meet

虫
142

血
143

行
144

衣
145

西
146

見
147

見
147

角
148

言
149

(147/0 見 gèn) 54.1; (passive prefix) 9.T.

147/4 規 gui   tzǐ-gui (cuckoo) 21.23.

覓 mek find 41.10.

147/5 視 zhì look 28.13.

147/9 親 tsin be friends with 18.2, 21.36.

147/13 覺 gak awake 11.14; feel, perceive 11.5, 22.96, 54.6.

147/18 觀 guɑn see 22.95.

148 角

148/5 觜 tzuǐ mouth 42.2.

148/6 解 gǎi loosen, untie 10.5, 22.77; come apart 35.4; understand 18.5.

148/13 觸 chiok hit 20.17.

149 言

149/0 言 ngiæn word, syllable 41.19; use the word "...", mention 41.20, 41.21.

149/3 託 tɑk entrust to 55.4.

149/4 許 xiǔ permit 22.8.

149/5 詔 jièu decree 22.8.

詞 zi words, statement 23.7; song, lyric 36.T, 45.T.

詎 ghiǔ how...! 17.9.

訴 sò litigate 30.14; explain 33.3.

149/6 誇 kua show off, brag 17.2.

詩 shi (poem) 2.T...

誠 zhiæng truly 22.13. Cf. 成 62/2, 城 32/6.

詣 ngèi head for 22.9.

誅 djio execute, kill 22.126.

149/7 說 shiuɛt speak 33.3; discuss 22.92.

語 ngiǔ speech 48.2; talk, words 3.2...; word 37.5; say 29.7.

誕 dhǎn deceive, tell lies 41.15.

誑 giuɑng deceive, tell lies 41.15.

149/8 調 dheu prepare 39.5.

諍 jræng remonstrate, expostulate 22.11.

誰 zhui who? whom? 9.4...

請 tsiæng request 22.111, 23.18.

149/9 諫 gàn admonish 22.11; admonition 31.21.

諳 qom be familiar with 36.3.

諷 biùng criticize indirectly 49.T.

149/11 謫 djæk banish 39.15.

149/12 識 shiək recognize 40.3.

149/13 議 ngì deliberation 22.108.

149/16 變 biɛ̀n change 16.11, 46.4.

讎 zhiou enemy 32.8.

149/17 讒 jrham slander, one who can detect slander 31.17.

150 谷

150/0 谷 guk valley 9.1...

150/10 豁 xuɑt be open 27.7; disperse 22.96.

151 豆

151/3 豈 kiə̌i how can it be that...! 17.5...

151/21 豔 iɛ̀m radiant 17.4.

152 豕

152/3 豗 xuəi clash 21.29.

153 豸

153/3 豺 jrhai wolf 21.37.

154 貝

154/4 貧 bhin poor 9.1.

154/5 貴 giuə̀i value, esteem 16.16; be valued 22.103.

154/6 賊 dzhək bandit, rebel 22.89.

賈 gǎ (surname) 19.C.

154/7 賓 bin pay a visit 31.8.

154/8 質 jit substance, object, thing 17.4; content (of a literary work) 16.19.

154/13 贏 iæng win 51.4.

155 赤

155/0 赤 chiæk red 11.1.

156 走

156/0 走 tzǒu leave, away 22.3; travel 38.10; walk, one that walks, animal 31.6, 34.3.

156/3 起 kǐ arouse 16.8, 35.12.

157 足

157/0 足 tziok foot 37.1.

--- be worth (doing the action of the following verb) 16.14, 22.110.

157/6 跡 tziæk footprint 20.19.

跳 dheu jump 5.3.

路 lò road 9.3...

157/8 踏 top tread 29.2.

157/9 踰 iu jump over 22.21.

157/10 蹊 hei footpath 28.14.

157/11 蹤 tziong bearing footprints 28.14.

157/14 躍 iɑk leap 16.17.

157/18 躡 niɛp tread 30.11.

言 149
谷 150
豆 151
豕 152
豸 153
貝 154
赤 155
走 156
足 157

158 身

身
158

車
159

辛
160

辰
161

辵
162

158/0 身 <u>shin</u> body 11.13...;
          personal, own 22.44;
          personal success,
          advantage 48.4.

159 車

159/0 車 <u>giu</u> (literary pronun-
          ciation; also <u>chia</u>,
          which is more colloquial)
          chariot, carriage 22.34,
          50.9.

159/2 軍 <u>giuən</u> army 22.111...

159/6 載 <u>tzəi</u> year 22.1.

159/7 輓 <u>miǎn</u> pull (a coffin at
          a funeral ceremony)
          45.T.   64/7.

      輕 <u>kiæng</u> light(weight)
          8.1, 11.5.

159/8 輝 <u>xiuəi</u> brilliance, glory
          16.22, 19.6.

      輞 <u>miǎng</u> (place) 3.T.

      輩 <u>bəi</u> sort 22.103.

159/11 轉 <u>djiuěn</u> make a turn 17.7,
          22.117, 39.10.

       <u>djiuèn</u> cause to turn
          21.30.

159/12 轍 <u>djhiɛt</u> rut 22.34.

160 辛

160/0 辛 <u>sin</u> painful, sad,
          sadness 31.4, 47.3;
          be in pain, be sad
          37.6.

--- <u>sin-i</u> 夷 (magnolia)
          7.2.

160/12 辭 <u>zi</u> take leave 22.9.

160/14 辯 <u>bhiěn</u> clever in speech
          48.3.

161 辰

161/0 辰 <u>zhin</u> heavenly body
          31.14.

162 辵

162/4 迎 <u>ngiæng</u> welcome 12.T,
          20.29, 49.9.

      返 <u>biǎn</u> return 3.3, 10.4.
          Cf. 反 29/2.

      近 <u>ghiən</u> approach 11.7.

162/5 述 <u>jhuit</u> narrate 16.21.

162/6 追 <u>djui</u> pursue 55.7.

      逃 <u>dhɑu</u> escape 30.7.

      迴 <u>huəi</u> return 9.3,
          22.61; make...turn
          around 22.25; turn
          (around) (intr.)
          52.1. 回 31/3,
          徊 60/6.

      送 <u>sùng</u> see (someone) off
          (on a journey) 1.T...;
          send 22.101.

      逆 <u>ngiæk</u> roll back against
          the current 21.12.

      迸 <u>bæng</u> scatter 30.2.

      迷 <u>mei</u> muddled 49.5;
          let...be deluded 39.6;
          be deluded into thinking
          that one is... 55.3.

162/7 途 dho path, road 21.20...

通 tung pervade, get through to 10.7; let...through, exchange 21.6.

連 liɛn connect to 21.10; pass through...in succession 21.27, 25.5; delay, keep 40.8, 40.9. Cf. 85/11.

162/8 逮 dhᵊi arrive at, until 16.6.

進 tzìn approach 12.5; bring 48.1.

162/9 過 guà pass over, cross 21.13; exceed 22.106; pass (by) 9.T, 22.68, 29.2, 52.T.

遊 iou travel, wander, stroll 18.13, 21.19.

道 dhǎu road 21.T...

dhàu say 20.29, 37.6.

遇 ngiò encounter 22.23.

達 dhat thorough, far-reaching 22.140.

遂 zui in the end 22.55.

運 iuᵊn turn of fate 16.17.

162/10 遣 kiěn chase 38.7; send out, produce 15.4; give 36.4.

遠 iuǎn far 20.15...; from afar 48.1.

162/11 遲 djhi late, tardy, delaying 20.19, 37.7, 51.2.

遭 tzɑu encounter 22.5.

162/12 遺 ui left behind, re-

maining 22.12.

162/13 邀 qiɛu invite 18.3.

還 huan return 21.19, 21.43, 22.85, 22.6; and 37.4.

避 bhì avoid 21.38, 21.39.

162/14 邈 mak distant 18.14.

162/15 邊 ben side 41.2; edge 51.4; side, beside 28.1.

辵 162

邑 163

163 邑

163/4 那 nɑ how...?! 22.75.

邠 bin (place) 22.29.

163/6 郊 gau cultivated area outside a town, suburbs 22.29.

163/7 郎 lɑng young man, you (used by wife in addressing husband) 20.3.

163/8 部 bhǒ (government) bureau 9.T.

163/9 都 do capital city 22.135, 39.17.

163/10 鄉 xiɑng home town 2.1...

163/11 鄰 sit knees 22.68.

廓 pio (place) 22.45.

163/12 鄰 lin neighboring 37.8; be neighbors 19.10. 隣 170/12.

163/13 鄴 ngiæp (place) 23.8.

164 酉

酉
164

米
165

里
166

金
167

長
168

164/3 酌 jiɑk serve wine 18.T, 18.2.

酒 tziǒu alcoholic beverage 8.3...

164/5 酤 hǒ day-old liquor 12.8.

164/6 酬 zhiou reply to 9.T, 10.T.

164/7 酸 suɑn sour, sad 30.6; sourly, painedly, with pain 29.8.

164/8 醉 tzuì intoxicated 18.12.

164/9 醒 sěng be sober 18.11.

164/10 醢 xǒi to mince, hash 22.123.

165 米

165/1 采 tsǒi gather 41.8.

166 里

166/0 里 lǐ village 20.5.

--- (linear measure, about one-third of an English mile) 11.11,35.7.

--- inside, in 6.T.
裏 145/7.

166/2 重 djhiong be in layers 28.15; folds 22.27.

djhiòng heavy 11.5; intense 42.5.

166/4 野 iǎ uncultivated area 22.6, 24.5; wild (animal) 22.50.

167 金

167/0 金 gim gold, golden 19.16, 22.136; gold pieces 25.6.

167/2 針 jim needle 29.13, 39.4.

167/3 釣 dèu to fish (with a line) 53.4.

167/5 鈴 leng eaves bell 30.6.

鈎 gou be hooked up 21.10.

鉛 iuɛn lead (the metal), white face powder 22.83.

鉞 iuæt large axe 22.130.

167/6 銜 ham hold (in mouth), hold in, hold back 35.2.

167/7 銳 iuɛi vigor 22.112.

167/8 錦 gǐm brocade 21.42; patterned 55.T, 55.1.

167/10 鎖 suǎ bring...together in a frown, enclose, hide 47.2.

167/11 鏡 giàng mirror 19.5...

167/12 鐘 jiong bell 9.8.

167/13 鐸 dhɑk large eaves bell 30.6.

168 長

168/0 長 djhiɑng long 20.T, 20.5, 49.3; long-range 10.3; long, protractedly 6.2, 19.16, 21.18, 21.39, 21.45; always, forever 23.12, 38.8, 52.1, 53.4; from a great distance 11.11, 20.30.

169 門

169/0 門 mən gate 9.4...

169/3 閉 bèi to block 33.8; close (someone) up 42.8; be closed 45.1.

169/4 開 kəi open 20.8, 21.35, 42.4, 52.2; (flowers) open 7.4, 17.1; display 31.14; begin 16.10; to found 21.4; liberate (territory) 22.113.

閒 gan space between, position at or among 18.1...

閏 njuìn intercalary 22.2.

169/6 閣 gɑk tall building 21.33.

169/9 闌 lɑn railing 34.10.

闊 kuɑt wide 22.84.

169/10 闕 kiuæt tower erected outside city gate, watchtower, gate of a royal palace 19.5, 22.9, 22.136.

169/11 關 guan (mountain) pass 8.4, 21.34, 22.53.

--- concern 10.2.

169/13 闥 tɑt gate 22.134.

170 阜

170/3 阡 tsen (north-south) path between fields 22.21.

170/5 附 bhiò send 23.9, 24.7.

阿 ɡɑ (prefix for human terms) 39.13.

陀 dhɑ 坡 pɑ-dhɑ (hilliness) 22.45.

170/6 陌 mæk (east-west) path between fields 22.21.

170/8 陰 qim shade, shadow 11.6; dark 22.97.

陵 liəng tomb 22.137, 41.17, 50.13.

陳 djhin spread 12.7; be spread out, occur 31.10; make plain 31.22; tell about, narrate 16.2; (surname) 22.129.

陷 hàm make...fall 27.8.

170/9 陽 iɑng sunny, sun 17.4, 53.4; sunny side: north bank, south slope 23.19, 26.8, 28.1, 45.3.

170/12 隣 lin be neighbors 27.14. 鄰 163/12.

170/13 險 xiěm danger 21.31.

隨 zui follow 18.6...; subsequently 22.124.

170/14 隱 qiěn hide 27.5.

170/16 隴 liǒng (place) 42.1.

172 隹

172/4 雄 hiung male bird 21.22.

雅 ngǎ elegant, elegant composition, ode 16.1.

172/5 雌 tsi female bird 21.22.

172/9 雖 sui although 16.11...

172/10 雜 dzhop mixed up 31.3; various 22.38, 22.90; unclassified 2.T.

門 169

阜 170

隶 (171)

隹 172

172
隹

173
雨

174
青

175
非

176
面

(177)
革

(178)
韋

179
韭

180
音

181
頁

(172/10) 雙 shrang in pairs 20.24, 30.10.

172/11 難 nɑn be difficult 21.T...; difficulty 21.2, 21.25, 21.44; with difficulty, hard to, impossible to 29.14...

173 雨

173/0 雨 iǒ rain 5.1...

173/3 雪 siuɛt snow 22.64...; snowy 24.5.

173/4 雲 iuən cloud 4.4...

173/5 零 leng be in bits 18.10; in bits 17.8; fall 30.10.

雷 luəi thunder 21.30.

173/9 霜 shriɑng frost 14.2...

173/12 露 lò dew 11.15...; dewy 45.3.

--- be revealed 27.6.

173/14 霽 tzèi sky clearing 33.9.

174 青

174/0 青 tseng green, blue or gray 4.4, 21.15; green or blue 28.4, 54.8; green or gray 24.6; green 3.4...; blue 19.1...; (place) 22.113.

174/8 靜 dzhiǎng quiet 10.1, 14.T.

175 非

175/0 非 biəi not be 22.131.

175/11 靡 mǐ mǐ-mǐ (slow) 22.21.

176 面

176/0 面 miɛn the face 22.65...

179 韭

179/10 韲 tzei mashing, smashing 31.14.

180 音

180/0 音 qim sound, voice 30.6, 31.4.

180/12 響 xiǎng echo 3.2.

181 頁

181/2 頂 děng top, peak 41.17, 52.2.

181/3 順 jhuìn obey 22.99.

須 sio must 18.8...

181/4 預 iù beforehand 20.28.

181/5 頗 pɑ very 22.107.

181/7 頹 dhuəi collapse 16.9.

頭 dhou head 14.3...; head of hair 22.80...; tip (of knife) 32.5, 32.6; place where... begins, place, at 40.4, 41.17.

181/9 額 ngæk forehead 20.1.

顏 ngan face, expression 20.8...

題 dhei inscribe 43.T, 43.2; title (of a poem) 54.T.

181/10 顠 ngiuɐn want to 19.15...

顛 den overturn 22.72. 顛

181/12 顧 gò regard 11.13; look
after, take care of
10.3.

--- nevertheless, yet
22.7.

182 風

182/0 風 biung (blowing) wind
10.5...; air, song 16.T,
16.3.

182/5 颯 sop sop-sop (blowing
wind) 5.1.

182/10 飆 iɛu 飄 piɛu-iɛu
(fluttering silk) 39.8.

182/11 飄 piɛu flutter 30.10,
39.8.

182/12 飈 biɛu whirlwind 31.3.

182/13 飋 shrit 蕭 seu-shrit
(desolate) 24.5.
瑟 96/9.

183 飛

183/0 飛 biəi fly 17.7...;
flying 19.5...; one
that flies, bird 31.6,
34.3.

184 食

184/0 食 jhiək eat 16.5...;
feed, rear 42.4.

184/2 飢 gi hunger 22.86.

184/4 飲 qǐm drink 18.5, 29.1.

qìm to water (animals),
give...water to drink
22.28, 24.2.

184/6 養 iǎng support, nourish
42.2.

184/7 餘 iu remaining, last
31.8, 35.1.

184/8 館 guàn hut 6.T.

餼 qì feed (animals,
birds) 42.4.

184/17 饞 jrham crave food
30.4.

185 首

185/0 首 shiǒu head 4.3, 22.25.

186 香

186/0 香 xiɑng fragrance 39.8.

187 馬

187/0 馬 mǎ horse 20.3...; for
si-mǎ (surname)
16.9.

187/3 馳 djhi gallop 22.100...

187/5 駕 gà ride (in a
carriage) 9.3.

187/8 騎 ghi ride (astride)
20.3.

ghì rider, man on
horseback 24.4, 52.3.

187/10 騰 dhəng leap 22.105.

騷 sɑu sorrow 16.8.

頁 181
風 182
飛 183
食 184
首 185
香 186
馬 187

馬
187

骨
188

高
189

髟
190

鬥
(191)

𩰋
(192)

鬲
(193)

鬼
194

魚
195

鳥
196

鹵
(197)

187/11 驅 kio chase 38.7; rush,
        urge (a horse) on 22.102.

187/13 驚 giæng to alarm 25.4;
        start up, take flight
        5.4.

187/19 驪 li (place) 41.17.

        188 骨

188/0 骨 quət bone 22.52, 24.6,
        43.1.

188/6 骼 gæk non-human, dried
        bones 34.9.

        189 高

189/0 高 gɑu lofty 22.35; high
        place 21.1; to a great
        height 42.6; situated in
        a high place 21.11,
        31.14.

        190 髟

190/5 髮 biæt hair (on top of
        the human head) 20.1,
        22.58, 46.T, 46.2.

190/6 髻 gèi dressed hair of a
        woman 39.7.

190/12 鬚 sio beard 22.87.

190/14 鬢 bìn hair at sides of
        head 47.1, 51.4, 54.5.

        194 鬼

194/0 鬼 giǔəi ghostly 49.2.

        195 魚

195/0 魚 ngiu a fish 12.T...
        Cf. 漁 85/11.

195/9 鯹 seng stench (of fish or
        blood) 30.4.
        130/9.

195/12 鱗 lin scales (of a fish)
        16.18, 27.2; scaly
        31.2, 35.4.

        196 鳥

196/0 鳥 děu bird 21.21...;
        suitable only for
        birds 21.7.

196/2 鳧 bhio mallard 21.3,
        29.4.

196/3 鳳 bhiùng (fabulous bird)
        22.25, 22.71.

       鳴 miæng (bird)call 22.49.

196/5 鴟 chi (owl) 22.49.

196/7 鵑 guen 杜鵑 dhǒ-guen
        (cuckoo) 55.4.

       鵡 miǒ 鸚鵡 qæng-miǒ
        (parrot) 42.T, 42.1,
        48.T, 48.1.

196/10 鶴 hɑk (crane) 21.13.

196/11 鷗 qou (gull) 53.1.

       鷖 qei (mallard), gull
        29.4.

196/12 鷺 lò egret 5.4.

196/13 鷹 qiəng (eagle) 22.105.

196/17 鸚 qæng qæng-miǒ 鵡
        (parrot) 42.T, 42.1,
        48.T, 48.1.

198 鹿

198/0 鹿 <u>luk</u> deer 3.T.

198/8 麗 <u>lèi</u> pretty 16.14.

198/12 麟 <u>lin</u> for 麒 <u>ghi-lin</u>
fabulous one-horned elk,
unicorn 16.24.

200 麻

200/0 麻 <u>ma</u> hemp 21.41.

201 黃

201/0 黃 <u>huang</u> yellow, brown
21.13, 22.49, 24.3,
49.5.

203 黑

203/0 黑 <u>xək</u> black 22.40, 44.1.

203/4 默 <u>mək</u> quietly 29.8.

203/5 黛 <u>dhèi</u> eye-black 22.77,
47.2.

點 <u>děm</u> dot 22.40; apply
(make-up) 39.3.

207 鼓

207/0 鼓 <u>gǒ</u> drum 12.1.

208 鼠

208/0 鼠 <u>shiǔ</u> rat 22.50.

210 齊

210/0 齊 <u>dzhei</u> be equal,
impartial 28.8; be
undifferentiated 28.12,
29.10; equally 22.42.

211 齒

211/0 齒 <u>chǐ</u> tooth 30.5.

212 龍

212/0 龍 <u>liong</u> dragon 16.5,
17.7, 21.11, 31.2.

鹿
198
麥
(199)
麻
200
黃
201
黍
(202)
黑
203
黹
(204)
黽
(205)
鼎
(206)
鼓
207
鼠
208
鼻
(209)
齊
210
齒
211
龍
212
龜
(213)
龠
(214)

Bibliography

Aoki 1965 Aoki Masaru. Ri Haku. Kan shi tai kei 8. Tokyo, 1965.

Downer and Graham 1963 G. B. Downer and A. C. Graham. Tone patterns in Chinese poetry. Bulletin of the School of Oriental and African Studies, University of London 26 (1963): 145-148.

Graham 1965 A. C. Graham, trans. Poems of the Late T'ang. Harmondsworth, Middlesex: Penguin Books, 1965.

Hawkes 1959 David Hawkes. Ch'u tz'u: The songs of the South: An ancient Chinese anthology. London: Oxford University Press, 1959.

Karlgren 1957 Bernard Karlgren. "Grammata Serica recensa." Bulletin of the Museum of Far Eastern Antiquities 29 (1957): 1-332.

Martin 1953 Samuel E. Martin. The phonemes of Ancient Chinese. Supplement 16 to the Journal of the American Oriental Society, 1953.

Owen 1975 Stephen Owen. The poetry of Meng Chiao and Han Yü. New Haven: 1975.

Stimson 1966 Hugh M. Stimson. The Jongyuan in yunn: A guide to Old Mandarin phonology. New Haven: Far Eastern Publications, 1966.

Stimson, 1973 -----. "The rimes of 'Northward journey,' by Duh-Fuu, 712-770." Journal of the American Oriental Society 93 (1973): 129-35.

Stimson 1976 -----. A T'ang poetic vocabulary. New Haven: Far Eastern Publications, 1976.

Waley 1918 Arthur Waley, trans. A hundred and seventy Chinese poems. London: Constable and Co., Ltd., 1918.

Waley 1919 -----, trans. More translations from the Chinese. London: George Allen and Unwin, Ltd., 1919.

Waley 1949 -----. The life and times of Po Chü-i, 772-846 A.D. London: George Allen and Unwin, Ltd., 1949.

Wilhelm/Baynes 1967 Cary F. Baynes, trans. of the Richard Wilhelm translation (1924). The I ching, or Book of changes. Bolingen series 19. 2 vols. Princeton: Princeton University Press, 1950; 3rd edition, 1 vol., 1967; reprinted with corrections, 1968.

Printed in the USA
CPSIA information can be obtained
at www.ICGtesting.com
LVHW101036240124
769416LV00001B/111